Emerging Market Democracies

A *Journal of Democracy* Book

•

Published under the auspices of
the International Forum for Democratic Studies

Emerging Market Democracies

East Asia and Latin America

Edited by Laurence Whitehead

The Johns Hopkins University Press

Baltimore and London

9 8 7 6 5 4 3 2 1

Chapter 2 of this volume appeared in the April 2000 issue of the *Journal of Democracy*; chapters 1, 5, and 6 appeared in the October 2000 issue. For all reproduction rights, please contact the Johns Hopkins University Press.

The Johns Hopkins University Press
2715 North Charles Street
Baltimore, Maryland 21218-4363
www.press.jhu.edu

Library of Congress Cataloging-in-Publication Data

Emerging market democracies: East Asia and Latin America / edited by Laurence Whitehead.
    p. cm. — (A Journal of Democracy book)
  Includes bibliographical references and index.
  ISBN 0-8018-7219-7 (pbk. : alk. paper)
  1. Democratization--East Asia. 2. East Asia--Economic policy.
  3. Democratization--Latin America. 4. Latin America--Economic policy. I. Whitehead, Laurence. II. Series.

JQ1499.A91 .E44 2002
320.95--dc21

                                              2002069486

A catalog record for this book is available from the British Library.

CONTENTS

ACKNOWLEDGMENTS

This book had its origins in a major conference on "State, Market, and Democracy in East Asia and Latin America" that was held in Santiago, Chile, on November 11–13, 1999. The meeting was cosponsored and jointly organized by three research institutes from three different continents—a feat that would no doubt have been nearly impossible before the advent of e-mail. The Institute for National Policy Research (INPR), one of Taiwan's leading think tanks, was the driving force behind the project and its principal funder. The Washington-based International Forum for Democratic Studies of the National Endowment for Democracy, which had previously collaborated with INPR on a number of other international conferences, played a key role in elaborating the agenda and in making many of the logistical arrangements. And the Santiago-based Centro de Estudios Publicos (CEP), one of Chile's leading think tanks, acted as host, making the needed local arrangements and arranging for Chilean participation. In addition, a critical contribution to the intellectual structure of the conference was made by the editor of this volume, Laurence Whitehead, Official Fellow in Politics at Nuffield College, Oxford. So the planning of this project actually spanned four continents!

In addition to the authors whose essays appear in the pages that follow, many distinguished scholars and public figures participated at the conference. Keynote addresses were presented by two of Latin America's most respected former presidents—Patricio Aylwin (1990–94) of Chile and Gonzalo Sánchez de Losada (1993–97) of Bolivia. Other speakers and commentators included Thomas Biersteker (U.S.), Senator Edgardo Boeninger (Chile), Ricardo Henriques (Brazil), Humberto Belli (Nicaragua), Harald Beyer (Chile), Koh Tai Ann (Singapore), Blanca Heredia (Mexico), Salvador Valdes (Chile), Sebastian Edwards (U.S.), Sang-Woo Nam (Korea), Barbara Stallings (Chile), Juan Andrés Fontaine (Chile), and Albert Fishlow (U.S.). Also participating were the heads of the three cosponsoring institutions—Arturo Fontaine Talavera, director of CEP; Carl Gershman, president of NED; and Hung-mao Tien, president of

INPR. In fact, Hung-mao Tien had been planning to coedit this volume with Laurence Whitehead, but in 2000 he was appointed by newly elected Taiwanese president Chen Shui-bian as his country's foreign minister, making his further involvement with the project impossible.

Putting together a conference of this magnitude was an enormous task, requiring the assistance of a host of aides on three continents. At INPR, Chih-cheng Lo, Bo Tedards, and May Chen all made important contributions. For the International Forum, the logistical chores were handled with aplomb by Amy McKee, Kim Healey (who attended the conference and provided invaluable assistance in Santiago), and Ma'ia Davis. At CEP, Harald Beyer, did a fine job of overseeing the conference preparations. The conference took place during the runup to Chile's hotly contested December 1999 elections, and one of the high points of the meeting was an evening of election analysis, organized by CEP and featuring a fascinating debate between Arturo Fontaine and sociologist Manuel Antonio Garretón.

Preparing this volume was another large-scale undertaking, and we are enormously grateful to Laurence Whitehead for having directed it in such capable fashion. This is the first *Journal of Democracy* book for which neither of the *Journal*'s own editors (Larry Diamond or Marc F. Plattner) had served as a coeditor. Although our many other obligations did not permit either of us to take on the editorial direction of this project, we were extremely pleased that Laurence Whitehead agreed to assume this responsibility. We are profoundly indebted to him for the intellectual structure and vision he provided the project, and for his diligence in working with the authors on their revisions. Anyone who has ever edited a book has a special appreciation for the substantial effort that is required to produce a coherent volume, and we believe that he has done an outstanding job.

Most of the essays included here are based on papers presented at the conference, though in many cases these were considerably revised by the authors. Elizabeth King had accepted an invitation to present a paper at the conference, but then proved unable to participate, and the chapter by her and Ananya Basu was prepared after the conference. Four of the chapters–Laurence Whitehead's introductory essay and the essays by Francis Fukuyama and Sanjay Marwah, Stephan Haggard, and Sylvia Maxfield—were initially published in the *Journal of Democracy*, and benefited from the editorial work of Mark Eckert, Zerxes Spencer, Stephanie Lewis, and Jordan Branch. The remaining essays were edited by Jackie Richards and Rebecca Vickers, with the assistance of Sarah McGuigan. A subsequent round of editing, principally to ensure that these chapters conformed to *Journal of Democracy* style, was performed with great skill and diligence by Jordan Branch. Stephanie Lewis did her usual excellent work in preparing the tables and readying the entire manuscript for publication, and Zerxes Spencer joined Jordan and Stephanie in proofreading the final text. Henry Tom and his colleagues at the Johns Hopkins University Press once again were most helpful and welcome collaborators.

We owe a debt of thanks to Arturo Fontaine and CEP for having been such gracious hosts at the conference and especially to Hung-mao Tien and INPR for having generated the idea for this project and for contributing the lion's share of the necessary funding. We also wish to thank once more the Lynde and Harry Bradley Foundation for its ongoing financial assistance to the *Journal of Democracy*. Finally, we wish to acknowledge the steadfast support of our parent organization, the National Endowment for Democracy. It is a pleasure to express our gratitude once again to the Endowment's longtime president, our good friend Carl Gershman, and to thank the new leaders of the Endowment's Board of Directors, Chairman Vin Weber and Vice-Chairman Tom Donahue.

—Marc F. Plattner and Larry Diamond

Emerging Market Democracies

1

STIRRINGS OF MUTUAL RECOGNITION

Laurence Whitehead

Laurence Whitehead *is an Official Fellow in Politics at Nuffield College, and series editor for Oxford Studies in Democratization.* He is author of Democratization: Theory and Experience *(Oxford University Press, 2002), the most recent volume in that series, and editor of* International Dimensions of Democratization *for the same series (2001 updated edition). He is also coeditor (with Guillermo O'Donnell and Philippe Schmitter) of* Transitions from Authoritarian Rule *(1986), and lead contributor to John Crabtree and Laurence Whitehead (eds.),* Toward Democratic Viability: The Bolivian Experience *(2001).*

The newly industrialized countries (NICs) of East Asia and Latin American liberal democracies have at least this much in common: The end of the Cold War, the "third wave" of democratization, and the consolidation of more uniform rules and institutional procedures concerning international investment and trade have presented them with increasingly convergent international opportunities and constraints. The East Asian financial crisis of 1997–98 and the recent advances of democracy in Indonesia, South Korea, and Taiwan underscore this parallelism and prepare the way for broader comparisons between these two large regions. As opinion-formers on both continents adjust their frames of reference to include the experiences of their counterparts across the Pacific, it becomes possible to detect stirrings of mutual recognition.

Between mid-1997 (the floating of the Thai baht) and early 1999 (the devaluation of the Brazilian real), the new democracies and recently liberalized economies of East Asia and Latin America found themselves cross-referenced and interconnected as never before. At one stage in the crisis, the dominant concern was to reassure the markets that the processes of liberalization and institution-building in Latin America had proceeded to the point where it would be insulated against "contagion" from the Asian financial turmoil. When this effort failed, the door was opened to a more frank and balanced two-way interregional comparison. In addition to the regionwide contrasts discussed below, a series of more specific comparisons also arose. When Malaysia successfully defied prevailing orthodoxy and imposed controls on capital movements, it led to a reevaluation of Chile's milder but similar policy. When Hong Kong's currency peg proved capable of surviving, it reinforced confidence in Argentina's convertibility plan. Indonesia's eventual withdrawal from East Timor conveyed a clear message to any other military establishment contemplating extreme measures to control insurgency in dissident provinces. To some extent, this cross-referencing operated in both directions. Mexican president Ernesto Zedillo had benefited from a fairly democratic electoral mandate, which helped him to maintain political cohesion during the 1995 peso crisis. There was a parallel here to South Korea at the end of 1997, when the currency collapsed on the eve of a highly contested presidential election. Similarly, Chile's success in preserving its dynamic economic model while coping with democratic alternation carried reassuring implications for Taiwan on the brink of its own presidential elections.

Although the mechanisms of interregional transmission and contagion were essentially financial, the linkages that emerged were much broader. Questions of political structure, as well as of economic performance, arose. Long-term development paths were reassessed, not just immediate crisis-management capabilities. The vast implications of the commitment to economic and political liberalization became apparent. In general, the crisis had a sobering effect. It dampened enthusiasm for headlong liberalization, although without generating a clear alternative. Doubts surfaced and half-digested counterproposals were floated, but the underlying assumption of the inevitability of further liberalization was not broken. On the contrary, after the Brazilian devaluation the financial climate cleared. "Emerging" economies regained access to global capital markets, trade prospects improved, and most of the new democracies resumed something approaching their "normal" political routines. The East Asian economies are recovering faster that those of Latin America, but within both regions, national and sectoral divergences are striking. Banking systems have been weakened on both sides of the Pacific. There are also marked tensions and uncertainties over democratization in both regions. Hence the cross-regional comparisons that seemed so urgent at the height of the crisis have begun to fade from view. Yet the logic of global liberalization persists, and the broader linkages, comparisons, and contrasts that commanded attention a couple of years ago are likely to resurface over time, either under the spur of further crises or as the long-term consequences of alternative development paths unfold.

Sequences and Geopolitics

Contrasting sequences of democratization and economic crisis provide one standard way of distinguishing between the two regions. In Latin America, the first democratizations were well underway by the end of the

1970s. By the time the Berlin Wall came down, all of South America had undergone democratic transitions. Mexico and Central America moved more slowly, but they too opted for liberal democracy, leaving Cuba alone outside the regional political consensus. By contrast, in East Asia, the first democratic transition of the third wave did not occur until 1986 in the Philippines. Only three more had occurred by the time of Tiananmen Square. Hong Kong's initial hopes of democracy were dashed, and Malaysia and Singapore continued to display key features of authoritarian rule. During the early 1990s, Thailand dispensed with military intervention in politics, and in the late 1990s, Indonesia followed suit. The regional balance in East Asia has tilted toward democracy, but it is much more precarious than in Latin America.

Yet Latin America also preceded the Asian NICs in experiencing economic crisis. Moreover, the crises that hit Latin America in the 1980s were far more likely to overwhelm preexisting models of state interventionism in the economy. Thus, by the early 1990s, most of the new Latin American democracies were more or less firmly set on a path of liberalizing economic reforms. Most of the NICs of East and Southeast Asia had experienced some cyclical difficulties, but it was not until 1997 that they went through anything at all comparable to the Latin American debt crisis that began in 1982. These differences in timing generated distinctive interactions between the political and the economic components of liberalization in the two regions. Most democratic transitions in Latin America involved competitive elections in which at least some significant contenders for office were identified with a return to the old, exhausted models of economic management. The uncertainty associated with political opening was therefore potentially compounded by a heightened fear of economic instability. This was not generally the case in East and Southeast Asia (except in the Philippines), where, prior to 1997, political opening was mostly premised on the assumption that past economic success had become self-sustaining and secure enough to support pluralist competition without much risk to business confidence. Despite these differences, however, the two regions have enough in common to elicit a degree of mutual recognition. Some in Latin America used East Asia's success to support the view that economic reform required stronger government rather than more democracy. Some in East Asia viewed Latin America's social and economic disorders as correlates of democratization, and therefore as reasons for delaying or foregoing political reform. And the intermediate case of Chile attracted attention in both regions.

It is also possible to interpret these cross-regional differences in the light of geopolitical considerations. Since Latin America was so firmly within the U.S. sphere of influence, its early adoption of Western-style liberal democratic politics might simply have reflected American pressure and the power of the U.S. example. By contrast, East Asia was subject to crosscutting political influences—partly from the United States, of course, but from Japan and from mainland China as well. It is small wonder, then, that East

Asia's choice of political models was more diverse and more uncertain, or that policy makers were reluctant to dismantle economic models that, in addition to delivering sustained growth, had provided defenses against excessive foreign intrusion into domestic economic matters. For a significant number of East Asian NICs, security had to be the paramount objective of public policy.

This is not just a question of economic security. For Taiwan, in particular, survival as a separate political entity is at stake. South Korea may be more secure, but technically the Korean War has never been concluded, and Seoul must always remain on guard in case the truce breaks down. Singapore is also very security-conscious, even though its separation from Malaysia has full international recognition. Hong Kong's "one country, two systems" formula for reincorporation into mainland China is time-limited and subject to reinterpretation. A democratic Indonesia risks disintegration as a state. Each case may be different, but the general picture is clear: National security issues remain urgent and potentially overriding in much of East Asia, but not in Latin America (with the possible exception of Cuba).

By contrast, the pressures arising from the institutions that regulate the international economy push the two regions toward convergence. Oil-exporting Indonesia was brought together with its Latin American counterparts, Mexico and Venezuela, when the Asian crisis precipitated an oil glut on world markets. The annual process by which the U.S. State Department's Bureau for International Narcotics and Law Enforcement Affairs certifies countries according to their compliance with U.S. drug policies applies as much to Thailand as it does to Colombia or Peru. Similar cross-regional convergences arise in relation to money laundering, arms trafficking, the pirating of intellectual property, and the use of child labor. With regard to legitimate trade, the World Trade Organization is elaborating a structure of obligations backed by dispute-settlement procedures that apply to all of its members. Finally, and most crucially—as demonstrated in the recent financial crises—debtor states in both regions are still dependent on the Bretton Woods Institutions for "last-resort" liquidity (and the associated conditionalities) when private capital flows dry up.

Global Economic Position and Domestic Structures

There are also important contrasts in the positions that the two areas occupy in the world division of labor. The East Asian NICs have proven capable of rapidly moving up the hierarchy of specialization, capturing strategic positions in the most dynamic industries. South Korea, for example, has moved from textiles to steel to shipbuilding to semiconductors. Taiwan has perhaps been even more agile. By contrast, most South American economies have tended to slip down the competitive ladder. Frequently, their exports remain natural resources–based. Much of their manufactures are sold in the relatively sheltered markets of regional integration schemes like Mercosur. Despite a great increase in direct foreign investment by multinational corporations, Latin America does not yet display much evidence of technological upgrading. There are some bright spots, notably Chile and the dynamism of Mexican export sales within NAFTA. Telecommunications may be on the verge of a technological leap forward. Overall, however, the East Asian NICs have a far greater capacity for long-term industrial upgrading than the Latin Americans have displayed so far. Any calculation of competitive advantage will thus tend to favor the East Asian side.

Such comparisons, however, must be considered in a global context. As mainland China increases its involvement in the world economy, its East Asian neighbors are coming under mounting pressure to specialize in more advanced industrial niches that can produce higher wages than those prevailing in the People's Republic. To some extent, Latin American exporters face the same kind of competitive pressures, but by clinging to their natural-resource bases and capitalizing on their locational advantages, they may be less exposed. Viewed from this broader perspective, the cross-regional comparison becomes somewhat less lopsided. Nevertheless, it is difficult to escape the conclusion that the East Asian NICs have derived an added competitive spur from their lack of land and mineral wealth, whereas the Latin Americans have tended to be held back by the "natural-resource curse."

Under global liberalism, it is not sufficient to characterize the international economy in exclusively structural terms. One must also consider the dominant ideas and practices that accompany this formula for economic integration. During earlier periods of rapid growth in international trade and investment, the leading economic powers engaged in military coercion and political imperialism. In the post-1989 liberal world system, the prevailing orthodoxy is of a different type. Although coercive diplomacy is still widespread and still awakens fears in peripheral states, the prevailing ethos is more liberal than before. Coercive diplomacy in East Timor was deployed with broad international support and was intended to support human rights and uphold international law, not to seize territory. Even U.S.-Cuban relations may be evolving toward a more mutually respectful balance, and the hardest case of all—reconciliation between North and South Korea—now seems to be making considerable progress.

In both regions, the dominant ideas and practices of global liberalism pose challenges to core features of state organization and underscore the privatized nature of the world market economy. Just as both regions are essentially "rule takers" at the institutional level, they are recipients, rather than transmitters, of prevailing ideas about the international system. Both have had their own distinctive points of view, of course, and both have attempted to contribute to a dialogue on global principles. The Latin Americans were long associated with export pessimism and "dependency theory";

TABLE 1—SAVINGS & EXPORT RATIOS
(PERCENTAGE OF GDP)

	1980	1998
GROSS DOMESTIC SAVINGS		
East Asia & the Pacific	30	37
Latin America & the Caribbean	22	19
EXPORT OF GOODS & SERVICES		
East Asia & the Pacific	22	42
Latin America & the Caribbean	12	15

Source: World Bank, *World Development Indicators 2000* (Washington, D.C., 2000), 216.

more recently, various East Asian governments have espoused the notion of "Asian values." None of these positions, however, has had much lasting impact on the general intellectual climate, and Latin American policy makers and opinion-formers have largely abandoned their old views. Indeed, some of the most enthusiastic endorsements of "neoliberal" ideas (or the "Washington consensus") have come from Latin American elites.[1] Such enthusiasm is less common in East Asia, but in practice (as opposed to public discourse) that region also generates little sustained opposition to the international liberal consensus. Indeed, one effect of the Asian crisis may have been to shake the confidence of the most vociferous defenders of "Asian values." As policy makers in both regions come to share a common understanding of the rationale behind the liberalized global world system, they are likely to develop more common ground across the interregional divide.

If we turn to comparing socioeconomic structures, a convenient point of departure is to contrast the role typically played by domestic savings in each region. In most of Latin America, an insufficiency of domestic savings, perhaps associated with a long history of inflation and related insecurities, helps account for the region's chronic dependence on external capital inflows and its propensity toward repeated cycles of overindebtedness and debt repudiation.

If domestic savings had been greater and more effectively allocated, Latin America need not have been so lastingly damaged by the 1982 debt crisis; the region could have negotiated with the outside world on more favorable terms to preserve those features of the old economic model that were thought to have lasting value. But since the public sector could not finance itself without resorting either to unsustainable sovereign borrowing or to the inflation tax, it was forced to cut back indiscriminately. The failure of state welfare programs (and especially of the region's deficit-plagued and mismanaged social security systems) led to socially regressive forms of state-shrinking and of pension privatization. Even so, public-sector savings remained scarce. To stem capital flight, it was necessary to give investors incentives and reassurances that left little scope for discretionary public policies. Although the allocation of resources through the market is far more prevalent than before, domestic savings rates in most of Latin America remain insufficient to finance high rates of capital accumulation, and the region remains vulnerable to changing fashions in world capital markets.

By contrast, East Asia saves above one-third of its GDP, more than any other developing area (and double the U.S. savings rate), and five or six times the level of its foreign investment. East Asia's export performance is even more remarkable (see Table 1). Unlike in Latin America, domestic welfare programs have imposed little fiscal burden, and caring for the elderly has been considered a family responsibility. Neither endemic inflation nor capital flight has characterized the region's economic life. This made East Asia's 1997 financial implosion all the more remarkable and unexpected, and also explains why the region may emerge from this turmoil while making only limited concessions to its external backers. Unless such structural contrasts are taken into account, attempts to transfer policies appropriate to one region to the other will fail.

Economic Policy Priorities

To compete effectively in a liberalized global market and to underpin democratic institutions through the involvement of an informed citizenry, high and rising standards of universal education are clearly necessary. Educational policies seem to have been surprisingly similar in the two regions. Roughly similar shares of GNP have been devoted to public spending on education, and there is comparable evidence of unequal access (with the spectacular exception of democratic South Korea). Pupil-teacher ratios do not differ significantly across the two regions. Yet the cross-regional differences in educational performance are remarkable. The East Asian NICs have the highest scores for mathematics and science on internationally comparable tests (although Thailand scored below the international average), while Latin America has often performed badly on other cognitive-achievement tests. Venezuela, for example, came in last in a standardized reading test for nine-year-olds; the sample included Indonesia as well as Singapore and Hong Kong.

It is not just the standard of public provision that determines educational outcomes, as can be seen from the contrasting performance of Asian and Hispanic immigrant children in the California school system. Family and cultural backgrounds are always important in explaining student achievement. Yet there are broader factors that help account for the contrasting outcomes in the two regions. Rapid and sustained economic growth in East Asia provides strong incentives for students to acquire skills that will be rewarded in the labor market, whereas in parts of Latin America, efforts to raise educational standards may only increase the supply of qualified new entrants to an employment market that cannot absorb them. Because of the debt crisis, average real expenditure per primary-school pupil actually fell by one-third in Latin America between 1980 and 1989, while it continued to rise in East Asia. There are some preliminary signs of analogous effects in some of the more fragile East Asian educational systems, but it is too soon to judge whether this is really a point of downward convergence. A more positive form of mutual recognition would be for East Asians to learn from Latin America's misfortunes and to shelter their relatively high-quality educational endowments from the harmful effects of a cyclical austerity drive. Similarly, under the pressure of competition from East Asian workers with rising educational standards, the Latin Americans might be induced to upgrade their basic education systems. This will continue to be a fertile area for cross-regional comparisons.

With regard to poverty and inequality, the two large regions are frequently presented as counterposed to each other. In general, income and wealth inequalities are notoriously large in Latin America, whereas some of the most successful East Asian countries show up much better on such measurements as Gini coefficients and poverty counts (see Table 2 above).[2] Here, too, the cross-regional comparison raises similar issues. Internal political co-

TABLE 2—COEFFICIENTS OF INCOME INEQUALITY
(SELECTED COUNTRIES RANKED BY ORDER OF INEQUALITY)

COUNTRY	YEAR	GINI INDEX
Brazil	1996	60.0
Guatemala	1989	59.6
Colombia	1996	57.1
Chile	1994	56.5
Mexico	1995	53.7
Malaysia	1995	48.5
Costa Rica	1996	47.0
Philippines	1997	46.2
Uruguay	1989	42.3
Thailand	1998	41.4
China	1998	40.3
Indonesia	1996	36.5
Korea	1993	31.6

Source: World Bank, World Development Indicators 2000 (Washington, D.C., 2000), 66–68. An index of zero would represent perfect equality (of household income, or in some cases, of consumption). An index of 100 would represent perfect inequality.

hesion, social stability, and international competitiveness all may be damaged by extremes of social and economic inequality. Successful NICs such as Korea and Taiwan demonstrate that it is possible to reduce inequality while pursuing outward-oriented economic strategies and progressing toward full democratization. In general, East Asia's high savings rate reflects a reliance on private provision for hardship and old age, in contrast to the Latin American tendency to rely on government "safety nets" that may be morally admirable but are not usually financially sound, and may not reach the truly poor. So there is room for debate as to whether East Asian achievements could be easily replicated in Latin America. Such issues are at the heart of public-policy debate in the two regions and underscore the practical relevance of well-structured comparisons and the potential pitfalls of superficial or propagandistic reasoning about distant "showcases" or external models. Mutual recognition provides a defense against a danger common on the periphery—the risk of following inappropriate advice from the center in the erroneous belief that there is no alternative.

With limited domestic savings and low, erratic growth rates, Latin American states have found it hard to raise revenue. With severe social inequalities and instabilities and a rhetoric of welfare provision that often exceeds the state's capacity to deliver, they have found it just as hard to control government spending. The result has been a tendency toward chronic fiscal stress, with periodic eruptions of full-scale fiscal crisis. This is the background to the characteristic Latin American record of high and variable inflation, erratic compliance with international financial obligations, and periodic lurches in exchange-rate policy.

Privatization and Foreign Capital

Three areas of economic policy are especially illustrative of the underlying differences between the two regions: privatization, the stance toward inflows of foreign capital, and exchange-rate policy. In each of these three areas, the "neoliberal" policy style prevalent in Latin America today can be contrasted to that of East Asia. At root, this contrast has reflected Latin America's desire and need to overcome a negative reputation in order to become more closely integrated into the global liberal economic and political system and, in particular, to attract foreign capital. In East and Southeast Asia, at least until 1997, states with a better reputation for fiscal control enjoyed more leeway (that is, retained more creditworthiness) to maintain their "developmentalist" economic policies, which rested on a solid partnership between business and the state, along with a strong commitment to growth and broad scope for policy discretion.

Thus it would seem that East Asia enjoys a clear competitive advantage over Latin America. Neoliberals could argue, however, that Latin Americans are closer to the *Zeitgeist* of global liberalism, while East Asians still need to make considerable adjustments to their thinking. Successful integration into a liberal international system certainly requires a capacity to maximize economic advantage, but that alone is not sufficient. Integration also involves both developing the cognitive capacity to understand and to influence the prevailing international system and transmitting its assumptions to domestic constituencies and veto groups. Over the past 20 years of often painful learning experiences, Latin American elites have improved their grasp of how global liberalism works and of how to communicate its logic to internal audiences. Although they may achieve only modestly successful economic results, they are relatively well-placed to legitimize their place in a liberal international order. According to this argument, although East Asia's economic performance was far better in the past and its future economic prospects are also relatively good, neither Asian decision makers nor their larger publics are as well-prepared to absorb the costs, shocks, and tradeoffs associated with liberalization. The orthodox liberal critique of the East Asian model suggests that its legacy of past success could make it harder to accept the need for externally directed reform. Reliance on "performance legitimacy" can pose a threat to policy coherence whenever, for whatever reason, good economic results are no longer immediately available. Such arguments seemed more compelling at the height of the Asian financial crisis; they have gone into rapid retreat in the face of a strong rebound in the East, accompanied by renewed strains over liberalization in the Western hemisphere.

One way that Latin American governments were able to escape the worst pressures of fiscal stress was by selling off to private owners the large stock of productive enterprises and revenue-generating activities that had progressively accumulated in the public sector since the 1930s. This had the immediate effect of raising revenue without taxation and of cutting unproductive subsidies and excess public employment. The private owners of the new enterprises could be expected to charge market prices for their products and to allocate resources with an eye to efficiency. Privatization also reduced the discretionality of public policy, as the new managers would no longer be cross-pressured between political and commercial objectives. Their focus would be clear, and their tenure would be determined by market performance rather than the vagaries of bureaucratic politics. Although this brief summary is an overstylized account,[3] it nonetheless provides a counterpoint to the so-called crony capitalism that prevailed in much of East Asia, where privatization was much rarer until the 1997 financial crisis and still remains so.[4]

The counterpart to Latin America's emphasis on privatization was its desire (and need, after the 1982 debt crisis) to attract direct foreign investment. By contrast, East Asia's record of dynamic growth and successful modernization in the 1980s meant that large volumes of private foreign capital could be attracted into the region without bringing with it the prospect of a change in enterprise ownership. At the peak of the Asian crisis, it was believed in the West that the result might be a wave of international takeovers (as happened earlier in Latin America), but that now seems much more doubtful. Powerful considerations of national economic security tend to deter the Koreans from allowing their commanding heights to be taken over by foreign multinationals—especially if these are Japanese-led. In contrast to Latin America, many East Asian policy makers are not (yet) preoccupied by the deleterious effects of chronic fiscal stress, nor do they accept that their use of discretionary policy instruments is necessarily counterproductive. Some of the East Asian NICs (Malaysia, for example) have rapidly rebuilt their foreign-exchange reserves and restored their export competitiveness in a way that was not possible in Latin America in the 1980s. Many hope to restore their reputations for successful economic management without dismantling too many features of their hitherto effective "developmental state" structures.

Yet even if many aspects of the crisis have been quickly overcome, lasting damage has been done to most of the region's financial systems. Nonperforming loans loom very large—especially in Indonesia and Thailand—and much bank collateral is being warehoused to avoid distress liquidations, so it is not yet clear whether the specter of mass privatizations has been exorcised or merely postponed.

State-Business Relations

Regional differences regarding privatization reflect broader contrasts in the character of state-business relations. In the successful East Asian NICs, it is hardly surprising if leading businessmen assume that the state will normally act as the ally of a competitive private sector. This type of relationship has been referred to by such shorthand phrases as "Korea, Inc."[5] For our purposes, the two key features of this relationship are that it generated a shared approach to long-term development issues and that it rested on the presumption that the state would normally support the expansion of domestic business interests. Although many leading business dynasties in the Western hemisphere also owed part of their early success to collusive relations with government, by the 1980s this type of mutual confidence had become increasingly rare. Few Latin American states seemed capable of implementing any type of long-term development strategy, and in conditions of austerity and fiscal stress the public sector was seen as a source of inefficiency and predation rather than as a trusted partner. Many Latin American businessmen were won over to the neoliberal view that state interventionism was stifling the region's growth prospects, trapping private business in a web of constraints that left it vulnerable to arbitrary taxation, price and credit controls, and generalized insecurity. According to this view, collusion is harmful, and business should seek to establish a more armslength, rule-governed relationship with the public authorities. Moreover, business should welcome support and advice from external sources (above all, from the United States) to counteract destructive populism and economic nationalism within the domestic political system.

Most East Asian governments were skeptical of these neoliberal arguments. Although they might sometimes use their discretionary powers to enforce economic policies that were unwelcome to local businessmen, they did not believe that either the historical record or the dynamics of the policy process indicated that they would systematically thwart private-sector expansion over the long run. The assumption of an underlying harmony of interests between the domestic private sector and the state was seen as an asset not to be cast aside lightly, particularly if the main advocates for doing so (and the potential beneficiaries) were not local businessmen but Western banks and corporations. A major drawback of the neoliberal model was that it would entail a loss of national influence over resource allocation and strategies of industrial promotion and technological upgrading.

Nevertheless, a central question remains about the type of state-business relations that can be maintained in developing countries at the periphery of a liberal global system. One possibility is that over time, perhaps under the pressure of successive crises, both Latin America and East Asia will be constrained to adopt the full panoply of neoliberal prescriptions required to lock in international business confidence. A second possibility is that the Latin Americans, having already incurred most of the costs of dismantling their developmental states, might respond to further crises by completing the process, whereas the East Asians, still enjoying the advantages of a more intact alternative, might manage to adapt without relinquishing state-business collusion. A third possibility is that convergence between the two models may now proceed, but on a more balanced basis than before: East Asian states might retain their distinctive capabilities while undertaking partial liberalizing reforms, while their Latin American counterparts might establish more constructive and forward-looking partnerships between the private and public sectors, promoting developmentalism within the constraints of a liberal order. These are three very broad and imprecise scenarios. The Asian crisis is so recent that the spectrum of possible outcomes remains quite wide. This discussion makes it clear, however, that each region has a substantial interest in monitoring and accurately comparing the responses of the other.

Learning to Live with Globalization

Mutual recognition is both empowering and disturbing. It may harm national pride and deepen the divide between global-minded elites and parochial constituencies, but it also reinforces national capacities for policy evaluation and strategic planning. Peripheral states are being inducted into a learning process, and those who develop an accurate capacity for mutual recognition will be better placed to undertake the behavioral adaptations required both by economic liberalization and by coexistence in a world political system tilted in favor of liberal democracies.

In principle, global liberalism promotes an unsettling shift of perspective for all those it enmeshes. Instead of leaving all free to perceive international affairs from their own national vantage point, it invites an imaginative leap to a more universal and reflexive outlook. "Faraway countries about which we know little" become interlocutors of equal standing, and discordant interpretations of global issues have to be brokered through international fora that are not just façades for the most powerful. *In principle,* the interests and perceptions of rivals and antagonists should peacefully compete for endorsement with one's own, and the competition should take place on level terrain. *In practice,* however, some major powers enjoy advantages that permit them to project their own interests and perceptions outward and to shape international rules and agendas in ways that minimize disturbance to their inner composure. This may require the great majority of states to make disproportionate efforts to adjust.

In general terms, the NICs of East and Southeast Asia find themselves in roughly the same boat as the Latin Americans regarding the demands of global liberalism. As it enmeshes them further, they are all required to make disproportionate efforts to adjust to its logic, for they are all clearly located on the periphery of this system. Indeed, the very vocabulary we use to bracket them together underscores this need to adjust—*peripheral* states, *emerging* markets, *developing* economies, *transitional* policies, *pathways* to liberalization. Their peripheral status limits their scope to pick and choose between the desired components of global liberalism and those elements more likely to disturb their internal equilibrium. This global system is not designed to minimize their adjustment costs; instead, it pressures them to continue on the path of liberalization despite internal resistance.

Economic and political liberalization may empower consumers and enfranchise voters, subjecting business and governments to increased scrutiny from below. At the same time, liberalization increases external scrutiny and international comparisons of performance on such key dimensions as pro-market orientation and democratic commitment. Countries and even subcontinents find themselves grouped and rated alongside other nations or regions about which they know little, but with which they must increasingly compete. However partial or oversimplified these external perceptions may be, in a liberalizing world system it is hardly possible to ignore them. Access to financial markets, trade advantages, technological innovation, political alliances—all are necessary for national well-being, and all are conditioned on the satisfaction of external standards and expectations. The internal and external components of liberalization feed into one another, setting up virtuous circles for those believed to be performing well, but threatening those who fall short with the prospect of a downward spiral.

Not only are East Asia and Latin America subject to converging pressures in favor of economic and political liberalization, they are also proving responsive to the forces—domestic as well as international—that favor democratization. In Latin America, the trend has been clear and sustained since the late 1970s and has just been reinforced by the election of a non-PRI government in Mexico. Among the East Asian NICs, the trend began later (with the fall of Marcos in the Philippines) and is less complete. But the recent and still fragile democratization of Indonesia constitutes a remarkable turning point in East Asia, as does the election of a non-KMT government in Taiwan. As democratic regimes become the standard in both regions, the scope for mutual recognition is reinforced, not merely on the grounds of shared economic realities but also on the basis of common political norms and practices.

There is a striking convergence between the two regions in this respect, but there are also some limitations that should not be underestimated. In contrast to, say Western Europe, neither Latin America nor, still less, East Asia can yet be regarded as a regional community of secure democracies. In addition to Cuba, Latin America still contains a variety of fragile new democracies potentially vulnerable to reversal (Paraguay), illiberalism (Peru), or disintegration (Colombia). In East Asia, the dissensus is greater, with Malaysia and Singapore explicitly espousing "Asian values" as an alternative to "Western" democracy, and with Hong Kong unable to democratize so long as mainland China remains wedded to a different course. Thus although a fairly standard form of political democracy may now be regarded as the prevalent model of desired political organization in both regions, it is by no means the only available model, nor is it a settled reality. There is now increased scope for mutual support and encouragement among aspiring democratic forces both within and between these two regions, but there are also serious countertrends. If democracy were to fail in, say, Indonesia or Venezuela, it would have severe regionwide repercussions.

The NICs of East Asia and Latin America may be converging toward democratic politics, but they are doing so from very different backgrounds and at different speeds. The countertrends with which the two regions must contend are also quite varied. In most of Latin America, the military has been substantially defanged with the ending of the Cold War and the ascendancy of the U.S. security umbrella. Problems of transnational criminality and state weakness are relatively urgent and often compounded by extremes of social and educational inequality. In much of East Asia, however, the potential for international conflict remains considerable, and military establishments are accordingly more influential. State organization is, in some major instances, more effective and self-assured, at least in part because citizen aspirations are closer to attainment, but state-business relations are more collusive and problems of "arms-length" institutionalization more pronounced.

The NICs of East Asia and Latin America may be converging toward democratic politics, but they are doing so from very different backgrounds and at different speeds.

These are very broad generalizations, of course, and they mask considerable variations within each region. But they point to a fundamental long-term question: Is there a basic dynamic of convergence around economic and political liberalization, eventually followed by democratization and the generalization of citizenship rights, within and across the two regions? It may be too early to return a settled verdict on this issue, but many developments in both regions indicate that this is a serious possibility. Mutual recognition entails only the acknowledgment of this common potential, not the claim that it has already been realized.

NOTES

1. Admittedly, this describes only a broad tendency, and the content of "neoliberal" orthodoxy is in any case by no means stable. The Chávez administration in Venezuela—if it survives—constitutes a potentially significant counterexample.

2. In fact, the East Asian pattern (exemplified by South Korea) is different from that of Southeast Asia, and within Latin America there is great variation, from Uruguay at one extreme to Guatemala and Brazil at the other.

3. This is especially true in the case of bank privatizations, where the public sector ended up with massive contingent liabilities, and the private owners never ceased to rely on their connections with the state bureaucracy.

4. Hong Kong, of course, was influenced by the British view of privatization (although not all enthusiasts for its liberal economic model noticed how much its revenue base depended upon skillful management of scarce publicly owned land). The Philippines was also

a special case, in that the fall of the Marcos dictatorship produced a temporary transfer of productive assets to the public sector, which were then gradually transferred back (often to the former owners, notwithstanding their designation as "cronies"). The incestuous relationship between the Korean state and the privately held *chaebol* also requires separate analysis, as does Singapore's powerful state pension fund.

5. In practice, this relationship took various forms, as in Taiwan (where a centralized dominant party in control of many business assets directed a private sector mainly composed of family firms) or in Malaysia (where public policy was directed toward the strengthening of a Malay business class to offset the earlier predominance of Chinese entrepreneurs).

2

THE POLITICS OF THE ASIAN FINANCIAL CRISIS

Stephan Haggard

Stephan Haggard, a professor at the University of California, San Diego's Graduate School of International Relations and Pacific Studies, is the author of The Political Economy of Democratic Transitions *(with Robert Kaufman, 1995) and of* The Political Economy of the Asian Financial Crisis *(2000).*

The Asian financial crisis of 1997–99 came as a shock to both the economics profession and the international policy community. Few inside or outside the region had foreseen the depth of the economic problems that followed, and a rich body of writing quickly emerged to offer competing post-mortems. Much of this analysis, however, was limited to purely economic factors. Beyond some references to moral hazard and cronyism, the political dimensions of the crisis were largely ignored.[1] Yet political factors are crucial to understanding the course of the crisis as well as the ways in which governments responded to it.

Here I want to explore three issues posed by the crisis that are also of broader relevance in assessing how developing countries with open economies cope with the political challenges of increased capital mobility. First, how did different types of government (democracies, dictatorships, and varieties of each) fare in managing the crisis? Second, how did the crisis affect the relationship between business and government? Will East Asian governments, even after enacting reforms in the wake of the crisis, have the political capacity to provide an effective counterweight to private business power? And third, how will these governments manage the social consequences of their countries' integration into the world economy? Answering these questions may also provide some insight into the future of the "Asian model."

When countries exhibit signs of financial vulnerability, the reaction of markets is based in part on expectations of how governments will respond. When crises actually break, an even wider array of actors sit in direct judgment on a country's adjustment efforts, including international financial institutions, ratings agencies, financial analysts, banks, and institutional investors. Their assessments also are influenced by political expectations. They are concerned, above all, with the ability of governments to act decisively, coherently, and predictably.

We can gain some insight into how different types of governments react to severe policy challenges by focusing on six administrations in four East Asian countries. Four of these were in democratic regimes, two in Korea's presidential system (the administrations of Kim Young Sam and Kim Dae Jung) and two in Thailand's parliamentary system (those of Chavalit Yongchaiyudh and Chuan Leekpai); one was in a semidemocratic, dominant-party parliamentary system (that of Mahathir Mohamad in Malaysia); and one was in an authoritarian system (that of Suharto in Indonesia). This sample is clearly too small to say anything definitive about the politics of crisis management, but it is useful for revisiting some longstanding issues about the economic and policy performance of different types of regimes and governments.

Thailand and Korea

There can be little question that certain features of democratic politics in Thailand and Korea diminished the capacity of their governments to respond effectively to warning signals and increased uncertainty, although the reasons were different in each case. In Thailand, the problems were more fundamental.[2] All of Thailand's democratically elected governments prior to the crisis rested on shaky multiparty coalitions. These were composed of internally weak and fragmented parties that allowed private interests to gain access to the policy process and made that process extraordinarily contentious. Party leaders constructed parliamentary majorities from a pool of approximately a dozen parties, and coalitions typically consisted of six or more parties. Cabinet instability was a chronic problem. Prime ministers were vulnerable to policy blackmail by coalition partners (and in some cases, by individual ministers) threatening to defect to another coalition in pursuit of better deals. The parties, in turn, relied heavily on businessmen who had strong personal interests in financial-market and other economic policies.

The Chavalit government (1996–97), a six-party coalition that included some of the parties from the previous government, attracted a highly regarded team of technocrats. The Central Bank succeeded in staving off two speculative attacks on the baht prior to its final collapse in July, but the Chavalit government failed to initiate fiscal-policy adjustments or to change the fixed exchange-rate regime. The problems of coalition politics were most apparent in the government's difficulties in confronting the mounting problems in the financial sector, particularly with respect to the finance companies. The government delayed in devising a plan for addressing their weaknesses and continued to provide a number of them with costly liquidity support.

These events unfolded prior to the baht's collapse and were interpreted by market analysts as telling signals of the government's weaknesses. Yet even the onset of the crisis was not enough to spur the government into a more coherent response. The process of reviewing the finance companies that were ultimately suspended was plagued by accusations of corruption. On October 19, a second finance minister resigned in frustration over the reversal of a small gas tax increase a mere three days after it had been announced as part of the government's International Monetary Fund (IMF)–backed program. With public indignation over the government's ineptitude rising, even among the business community, Chavalit resigned, paving the way for a new government.

Korea would seem to have been much better positioned to respond to the crisis than Thailand. Not only does the country have a presidential system in which the chief executive enjoys a range of legislative powers, but Kim Young Sam (1993–98) also enjoyed a legislative majority when the crisis hit. Beyond the adverse effects of a corruption scandal at the outset of 1997, the government faced a series of constraints associated with the presidential elections scheduled for December. A no-reelection rule and increasing concern about deteriorating economic performance fragmented the ruling party. In the ensuing succession struggle, one faction of the party broke away and chose its own candidate to contest the presidential election, contributing to the ruling party's ultimate defeat at the hands of Kim Dae Jung. Legislative elections were not concurrent with the presidential contest, but neither the ruling party's presidential candidate nor its legislators had strong incentives to cooperate with a lame-duck president.

These political problems affected economic policy making in two areas that proved to be of particular importance prior to the onset of the crisis proper in November—the management of major corporate bankruptcies and the passage of financial-reform legislation. The most damaging corporate failure was that of the Kia group. In the summer of 1997, Kia's management exploited the elections and the government's weakness to mount a major campaign for government support in dealing with its creditors. By late October the Korean banking system had been severely damaged, not just by the bankruptcies themselves but by a highly politicized process that left the ultimate disposition of Kia in limbo for months.

In the meantime, the passage of a package of financial-reform bills had been stalled by disagreements within the ruling party. Once the crisis broke, their passage became an important signal of government commitment, and it was explicitly included as one of the conditions of the first IMF program. Yet neither the ruling party's presidential candidate nor the opposition had any incentive to cooperate with the government in getting this controversial legislation passed.

These problems are hardly novel in democratic systems; the effects of weak coalition governments, weak parties, divided government, and the electoral cycle have all been noted before in other contexts. Yet democracies have one important advantage over autocracies: Incumbents can be voted out of office. In both Thailand and Korea, the crisis generated disaffection with incumbents and led to changes in government. In Thailand, the fall of the Chavalit government led to the formation of a new government led by Chuan Leekpai (1997–present) and the Democrats. While the Democrats also had to include parties from the previous government in their multiparty coalition, the crisis allowed Chuan's party to maintain control over the key economic portfolios. The new government was thus able to take decisive action on several fronts, most notably by swiftly closing down virtually all of the suspended finance companies and strengthening the agency responsible for managing the disposition of their assets.

The new government was not altogether immune from the constraints that had plagued its predecessor. The legislative process required that all legislation be reviewed by a Senate filled with businessmen with a direct stake in important reform legislation, which they sought to modify and delay. Divisions both within the coalition and among the Democrats in the cabinet slowed the introduction of a number of important reform measures, including new laws governing foreign investment and bankruptcy, for more than a year.

In Korea, by contrast, Kim Dae Jung (with support from his predecessor Kim Young Sam, whose party still controlled the National Assembly) was able to exploit the important legislative window between his election and inauguration. During this period the legislature passed the same package of financial bills that had languished prior to the elections, as well as a range of corporate-governance reforms.[3]

Both countries thus enjoyed the benefits of new governments coming into office. These governments did not simply take advantage of the circumstances of the crisis (something that their predecessors had been unable to do); rather, they exploited disaffection with incumbents to gain electoral and legislative mandates for reform.

Malaysia and Indonesia

How did the nondemocratic governments fare? Malaysia's was clearly the more institutionalized and pluralistic of the two, and its dominant party, the United Malays National Organization (UMNO), was subject to some electoral and other political constraints. Yet when the crisis struck in mid-1997, UMNO did not face substantial challenges from its coalition partners, from the opposition (who were weak), or from elections, which were not due until 2000. Mahathir did face challenges from within UMNO, however, and these had some influence on the course of policy.

From the outset of the crisis, Mahathir's heterodox views, implicit threats to impose capital controls, and attacks on "speculators" and hedge funds created profound uncertainties and contributed to the rapid decline of the ringgit in the second half of the 1997. Efforts to bail out politically favored companies added to the uncertainty. In December, Mahathir reversed course, delegating authority to Deputy Prime Minister Anwar Ibrahim, who introduced an "IMF program without the IMF." At the same time, however, Mahathir established a parallel decision-making structure, the National Economic Action Council, which served to undermine Anwar's authority. For the next six months, policy see-sawed between Anwar's more orthodox views and those of his reflationist opponents.

These disagreements were related to the question of succession. Anwar's position as deputy prime minister suggested that he would ultimately take over leadership of the party and, with it, the prime ministership. Following the fall of Suharto in May 1998, Anwar appeared to issue a more direct challenge to Mahathir, but Mahathir was able to rally the party at the UMNO General Assembly, to sideline Anwar, and ultimately to have him arrested and convicted on corruption charges. As this political drama was unfolding, Mahathir also dismissed the governor of the Central Bank, took over the finance portfolio, and moved economic policy in a more expansionary direction. The imposition of capital controls on 1 September 1998 was the final act in a set of policy and political conflicts that had been unfolding for over a year.

In Indonesia, by contrast, Suharto cleaved closely to economic orthodoxy and was initially seen as enjoying some of the purported advantages of dictatorship. As in the past, he responded quickly to the crisis by freeing the rupiah rather than subjecting the country to a costly defense of its currency, and he initiated a number of reforms, some of which appeared to cut against the interests of his cronies and his family. Within months, however, Suharto began to take a number of rearguard actions that undercut these initiatives, launching several costly investment projects and extending liquidity support to a number of crony banks following a mismanaged bank closing in November 1997.

In December, Suharto failed to participate in an important international meeting, and rumors circulated that he was in poor health. (It was later revealed that he had had a stroke.) Although such rumors can also be unsettling in democracies, in a highly centralized system like Indonesia's with uncertain succession procedures, they threatened the regime itself and the entire set of property rights that went with it. Even before Suharto's controversial budget was read in January 1998, it was clear that Indonesia was experiencing much greater difficulties than other countries in the region. Suharto's imposition of B.J. Habibie as his vice-president and anointed successor alarmed investors, as did the growing opposition to his regime, which crested in the violence of mid-May that ultimately resulted in his ouster.

It is clear that Indonesia fared worse than other countries in the region. Less attention is paid to the fact that Malaysia's economic decline was much worse than might have been predicted, given that it had a less fragile banking system and a more favorable external position than either Korea or Thailand. Obviously, the outcomes in each country were the result of a number of factors, and Mahathir (along with many American economists) placed particular emphasis on the external ones.

Yet politics mattered as well. The purported advantages of decisive leadership hinge critically on what leaders actually do. In both Indonesia and Malaysia, leaders exploited their powers to isolate technocratic advisors and pursue erratic policies that increased market uncertainty. Indonesia suffered from the more profound uncertainty, due to the absence of channels for managing opposition and the problem of succession. Although the democracies also had difficulties in making timely adjustments, they, at least, provided legitimate procedures for replacing failing incumbents.

Business and Government before the Crash

Although the account of the crisis given above necessarily focuses on the role of government institutions, it also touches on the influence of business on the policy process—as seen in the Kia bankruptcy in Korea, the policy toward the finance companies in Thailand, and the favored treatment of politically connected firms in both Malaysia and Indonesia. Close ties between business and government have long been a distinctive feature of many of the rapidly growing Asian economies, but it was generally believed that these countries had structured business-government relations to minimize the political risks. Some even argued that the costs of rent-seeking and corruption were outweighed by such benefits as increased information flow, trust, and the signaling of government commitment. As Sylvia Maxfield and Ben Ross Schneider put it, "trust between business and government elites can reduce transaction and monitoring costs, diminish uncertainty, lengthen time horizons and . . . increase investment."[4] Even the World Bank became a cautious advocate for consultative institutions linking the public and private sectors.[5]

How did Asian countries manage to maintain relatively close business-government relations without the risks? Chalmers Johnson's analysis of Japan outlined a theme central to all subsequent analyses of the region's political economy: that a "strong," "developmental" state guaranteed a commitment to overall economic growth, while developing a pattern of cooperation with the private sector that "avoided an emphasis either on private profit or the state's socialization of wealth."[6] The aspect of Johnson's thesis that attracted most attention—and ire— was its emphasis on the benefits of industrial policy. But Johnson's account also had a second political dimension: He argued that "strong" governments (in some cases, authoritarian ones) enjoyed an independence or autonomy from private actors that allowed governments to control the policy agenda and granted them the capacity to discipline the private sector by conditioning various kinds of government support on performance. Thus they were able to guarantee that industrial-policy tools did not result in the misallocation of resources so common elsewhere in the developing world.

This picture also featured competent, meritocratic bureaucracies and the concentration of decision-making power in lead economic agencies. By socializing government officials toward common goals, meritocratic bureaucracies limited the opportunities for rent-seeking. Centralizing bureaucratic authority and granting discretion to bureaucrats made policy more decisive and coherent.

Finally, the governments of the region were able to limit rent-seeking by controlling the way business was organized and how it interacted with government. In some cases, as in Korea, the government directly established and effectively ran sectoral business associations. In others, "deliberation councils" made up of representatives of government, business, and other sectors guaranteed broad representation and a certain degree of transparency that limited the opportunities for private dealing.

Over time, this careful historical analysis hardened into an "Asian model" of business-government relations that was generalized across widely disparate cases. As Andrew MacIntyre and his colleagues showed, the Southeast Asian countries differed quite substantially from Japan, Korea, and Taiwan, in that the former lacked not only the industrial policies of the first generation of newly industrializing countries but also the political conditions required to conduct such policies efficiently.[7]

This rosy picture of close business-government relations also downplayed a number of risks and costs. The first of these risks was structural—the high and sometimes growing concentration of private economic power. In some cases this concentration was a direct result of government supports for certain large firms, as in the case of the Korean *chaebol* (large, family-run industrial conglomerates), the expansion of the Indonesian-Chinese conglomerates or Suharto-linked firms, and the ethnically motivated privatizations in Malaysia under the Mahathir government. In other cases, it was a result of government inaction, as in Thailand's *laissez-faire* stance toward the high degree of concentration and collusive behavior in the banking sector. Size did not always translate into proportional political influence; in Indonesia, the ethnic vulnerability of the Indonesian-Chinese conglomerates actually made size a liability. Yet there can be little question that "big business" did wield political influence in all four countries.

A second problem was the way in which government support for the private sector generated moral hazard. Moral hazard has been invoked indiscriminately to explain the crisis; everything from IMF lending to deposit insurance has been held accountable for this particular sin. Some purported sources of moral hazard, such as the existence of industrial policies, either had been reduced (in Korea) or were too small to be consequential (Thailand). Nonetheless, the government's deep involvement in the financial sector in Korea, Malaysia, and particularly Indonesia created the danger that banks and firms would either be protected against excessive risk-taking or (much the same thing) would be allowed to walk away from bad debts.

Corruption and cronyism are an additional source of moral hazard that has received substantial attention in popular Western accounts of the crisis. The Hanbo case of direct bribery of government and bank officials in Korea appears to be a relatively isolated incident in that country. Corruption was more widespread in Thailand and Indonesia, and in the 1990s there was clearly an increase in nepotism in Indonesia. The corruption problem, however, is often misunderstood; the issue is not simply its role in generating moral hazard, but also its effect on governments' management of the crisis. In Korea, the Hanbo scandal further weakened a lame-duck president. In Malaysia, the government's efforts to support politically connected firms at great public expense raised questions about the integrity of the corporate restructuring process. In Thailand, the government exhibited costly forbearance toward ailing financial companies with close ties to the government. In Indonesia, the Suharto government's responsiveness to cronies and close family members raised serious doubts about the government's commitment to reform in the crucial months of October and November 1997.

One objection to the focus on moral hazard and corruption is that these problems had existed for some time and had not impaired the region's spectacular growth in the past. This objection, however, is a bit too facile. First, the history of East Asia's growth is far from crisis-free. Korea, for example, has seen government-led investment booms followed by crises in the past, most recently in the wake of the chemicals and heavy industry drive of the late 1970s. Second, it is not necessarily the case that corruption has been a constant. Although measurements of corruption are always difficult, the case could be made that corruption in Indonesia, Malaysia, and Thailand actually increased during the 1990s.

More importantly, the opening of the economy to capital movements makes it more vulnerable to problems of moral hazard, corruption, and the lack of transparency in business-government relations. When growth is high, foreign investors are perfectly willing to tolerate (and even to contribute to) these problems. But when growth slows, the nontransparent nature of business-government relations can generate substantial uncertainties. Will some firms enjoy special treatment? Will contracts be honored? What financial condition are banks and firms actually in?

This brings me to the final, and perhaps most important, point. Not all of the region's problems stemmed from rent-seeking as traditionally conceived; a final source of risk was the mismanagement of liberalization, particularly in the financial sector. The dangers of opening the capital account while maintaining a fixed exchange rate have attracted the most scrutiny in accounts of the crisis, but the failure of prudential regulation of the banking system was an equally important problem. These failures stemmed not only from the weakness of regulatory statutes but also from politically generated laxity toward the government's financial and corporate oversight role and outright corruption of regulators. These problems were visible in the licensing of Korea's merchant banks and in a variety of weaknesses in Korean corporate governance, in the expansion of the finance companies in Thailand, and most egregiously, in the liberalization of the banking sector in Indonesia, where industrial groups acquired banks, with all of the attendant problems of related-party lending that ensued.

In sum, the region's vulnerability stemmed not simply from discrete policy failures but from a deeper political problem: Business-government relations were often structured in ways that did not allow for effective oversight by outsiders, whether these outsiders were parties, legislatures, regulatory agencies, public-interest groups, financial analysts, stockholders, or voters. The result was policies and practices that increased vulnerability.

Business and Government after the Crisis

The Asian financial crisis is forcing important changes in business-government relations. To understand the politics of this process, it is useful to distinguish policy responses along two dimensions: the decisiveness of governments in addressing the crisis and the ability of governments to assert regulatory authority over banks and firms.

Banks and firms experiencing severe distress have a strong interest in delaying the recognition of losses, since the timing of such decisions can affect their very survival. Delay, however, can also compound losses and increase uncertainty. A second and closely related issue is the extent to which governments support or show forbearance toward distressed banks and firms. Of course, there is no virtue in bankrupting potentially viable firms. In periods of distress, however, all companies have an interest in claiming that they are viable. To limit the public costs of such crises, governments require the political as well as administrative capability to distinguish among the competing claims for financial support and forbearance and to impose regulatory conditions on banks and firms that will limit future risks.

These issues are visible in the problems surrounding financial and corporate restructuring. The crisis initially focused attention on problems in the financial sector. The immediate task was twofold: to decide which financial institutions were nonviable and to close them, and to develop a rehabilitation plan for the remainder. Once these basic decisions were taken, the government confronted the task of disposing of nonperforming loans (NPLs) and recapitalizing the banks.

Comparing strategies across countries is always difficult because initial conditions and the magnitude of their problems vary. Nonetheless, some interesting patterns are visible across the six administrations in the four most seriously affected countries. In Korea, the Kim Young Sam government supported the banking system following the corporate failures of 1997, nationalizing two major banks, but it had no clear strategy for rehabilitating the sector. Following Kim Dae Jung's election, the government quickly established a powerful new regulatory agency to manage the crisis and set aside funds to buy up nonperforming loans (NPLs) and recapitalize the banking system. All banks were subject to thorough review, on the basis of which five were shut down and merged with others under government direction. A large number of nonbank financial institutions were also shut down, although many weak ones were left open. Korea's record in disposing of acquired assets remains weak, but it has moved more aggressively than Indonesia, Malaysia, or Thailand, where governments took a relatively hands-off posture with respect to the banking sector until late 1998. One result of the nationalizations and capital infusions was that governments came to occupy a commanding position in the financial sector; although this was true to some extent in all countries, the change was most pronounced in Korea.

Under Chavalit, the Thai government also initially continued to support weak institutions, particularly finance companies. Although some were suspended and the government created a resolution agency (the Financial Restructuring Agency), the government lacked a clear strategy for managing these distressed companies. After taking over in November 1997, the Chuan government moved quickly to close a number of finance companies and to dispose of their core assets over the next 18 months. It did not recapitalize the banks or purchase NPLs from them directly; rather, it sought to induce banks to recapitalize by enforcing capital-adequacy and loan-loss provisions. This strategy failed because a number of major banks proved unwilling or unable to raise new capital, and in August 1998 the government was finally forced to announce a plan that committed substantial resources to bank recapitalization. The conditions for participation were tough, but precisely for that reason few banks participated, and the government has been forced to manage the crisis through regulatory forbearance and acceptance of a continuing high level of NPLs in the system.

Malaysia's banking problems were less serious, but the government responded to them fairly aggressively, through a combination of recapitalization and a comprehensive merger plan. The Malaysian response was influenced by longstanding issues of ethnicity; the bailout of state banks used to finance investments made by ethnic Malays, and a controversy arose over whether the merger plan would weaken the Chinese presence in the banking sector.

Indonesia responded more decisively to its banking crisis than Korea or Thailand, but the initial closing of 16 banks was badly handled and actually exacerbated the crisis. The government continued to support a number of politically connected banks, with disastrous consequences, and reform efforts were undermined by the deepening political uncertainty about the regime's survival. The Habibie government initiated a strategy for recapitalizing the banking sector and sought to recover debts to the government, but implementation was subject to delay and charges of political interference. By the end of 1999, the government had clearly made the least progress of the four countries in addressing the problems in its banking sector.

A second set of issues surrounds the corporate-restructuring process. Like banks, corporations may have an interest in delaying financial and operational restructuring and may even collude with banks to do so at public expense. The government can solve this problem in one of two ways, each of which requires some political capacity. First, it can enforce capital-adequacy and loan-loss provisions rigorously, while providing incentives for banks to engage in out-of-court settlements. This so-called London Rules approach depends heavily on the credibility of the government's commitment to its regulatory stance. An alternative strategy is for the government to play a more active role. This may include coordinating intracreditor and creditor-debtor relations, monitoring and enforcing agreements, or using various instruments to enforce financial and operational restructuring objectives.

The incentives to corporate restructuring are powerfully affected by foreclosure and bankruptcy laws. If foreclosure and bankruptcy laws are weak or poorly enforced, firms have an incentive to delay debt and operational restructuring and even repayment. Reform of the bankruptcy process and clear enforcement of bankruptcy and foreclosure laws are important not only for managing actual firm failures but also for providing incentives to creditors and debtors to reach out-of-court settlements.

Bankruptcy procedures were strongest in Korea and Malaysia when the crisis hit. In Thailand, bankruptcy reform was delayed; in Indonesia, despite reforms, bankruptcy processes remain weak. In all four cases, out-of-court settlement predominated, but major differences separate Korea from the other cases. Despite nominally embracing London Rules, Kim Dae Jung has negotiated directly with the five largest *chaebol* over their restructuring plans, and the Financial Supervisory Commission has successfully pushed corporate debt restructuring. Moreover, "corporate restructuring" in Korea has included wide-ranging corporate-governance reforms, ultimately enforced through the government's control of the banking system. In Thailand and Indonesia, debt restructuring has been much slower, with much weaker links, if any, to corporate-governance reform. Malaysia lies between these two poles; the government has established a restructuring agency with ambitious goals for the operational restructuring of enterprises, but as of this writing, it remains unclear whether those objectives are being fulfilled.

What accounts for these differences? One hypothesis is that a government's ability to assert its authority depends on the nature of the political links between it and the corporate and financial sectors. In Korea, the government already exercised strong control over the banking sector, and Kim Dae Jung was a relative outsider to the networks of business-government relations that had built up under his predecessors. He was therefore much less indebted to the business sector than his counterparts in Thailand, Malaysia, and Indonesia, where business support was a crucial element of the political formula. In sum, the success of reform requires a new politics, with politicians and parties less beholden to the status quo.

A New Social Contract?

The social fallout from the crisis, manifest in rising unemployment, falling real wages, and a sharp decline in asset values, has naturally forced an immediate response from governments in the region. Whether the crisis will affect the nature of the social contract and the provision of social insurance over the longer run, however, remains to be seen.

Discussions of the political economy of the welfare state have not given much attention to the nature of social bargains in the developing world. For new democracies, the possibilities for welfare policy depend heavily on the implicit social contract and the development strategies inherited from prior authoritarian periods. For example, while welfare reform in Eastern Europe involves some inevitable shrinkage of public commitments and an expansion of private insurance and service provision, East Asia's smaller governments, stronger fiscal position, and limited social contract provide the space to move in the opposite direction.

Prior to the economic crisis, countries in East and Southeast Asia did have an implicit strategy of social protection. It had the following components: 1) healthy per-capita–GDP growth rates, rapid employment growth, increasing participation in the work force (especially of women before marriage), and increasing returns on capital to small businesses and farmers; 2) high levels of private and public investment in education and basic health care; 3) balanced growth strategies that emphasized labor-intensive manufacturing and addressed rural poverty through land reform (Korea and Taiwan) or investment in rural infrastructure and agricultural technologies (Indonesia and Thailand), which made it possible for the countryside to absorb displaced workers during downturns in the urban manufacturing sector; 4) strong traditions of family support, with high levels of private transfers between generations and from urban workers to rural households; and 5) an emerging tradition in some segments of the economy (and most notably in Korea) that made the firm the provider of social insurance.

Notably absent from this picture were extensive government commitments to social insurance. This might be attributed in part to these countries' level of development, but comparisons with other middle-income countries suggest that politics also mattered. Social-democratic and populist parties and movements had little room to operate under authoritarian rule. Labor movements have historically been weak, repressed, or both; even with the transition to democratic rule, labor movements have not been influential political actors, except in Korea. Other features of Asian societies noted above, including traditions of private social assistance, extended family networks, and flexible labor markets linking the urban and rural sector, have all reduced the demand for an extensive state role in providing social insurance.

As a result of this history, the countries hurt most by the crisis had neither social-insurance mechanisms that could serve as automatic stabilizers during a recession nor the capacity to monitor and target those most seriously affected by the crisis. Nonetheless, governments in the region quickly acknowledged the need to deal with the potential social costs. Encouraged by the international financial institutions, Asian governments launched a mix of "social safety-net" programs.

Whatever the successes and failures of these programs in the short run, the more interesting question is what the longer-term future of the social contract might be. One can imagine several possibilities. In Korea, where the labor movement is strongest, there could be movement in the direction of a European-style welfare state. Kim Dae Jung used his credentials with labor to convene a tripartite committee in early 1998, and in the process he extended unemployment insurance to a broader group of workers and raised benefits. The Korean exercise was relatively modest, however, and was aimed in no small part at extracting concessions from labor on issues of labor-market flexibility. Labor fully understood the downside of this bargain, and the more progressive of the two union confederations ended up boycotting subsequent meetings of the committee. This episode casts doubt on the viability of the welfare-state option in the absence of strong unified labor movements and social-democratic parties.

A second possibility would be a conservative reaction. During the crisis, governments in both Malaysia and Thailand outlined a conservative critique of the European welfare experience, citing Asia's traditional reliance on family and community and their own countries' past success in harnessing work, discipline, and responsibility at the individual level to produce high growth. The idea of "social-welfare" programs involving entitlements to government transfers, they argued, contradicted the lessons of past success stemming from productivity-enhancing investments in health, education, and performance-based small credit programs. Business groups also expressed skepticism about any further extension of the safety net, cautioning that it would adversely affect recovery in the short run and competitiveness in the long run.

The large real devaluations that have occurred and the corresponding fall in unit labor costs might indeed tempt governments into reverting to a growth strategy relying on low-cost labor. Yet relying on real-wage adjustments seems self-defeating in the long run, particularly given the presence in the region of China's massive labor-abundant economy. Moreover, such a strategy would overlook the fact that, in some cases (especially in Thailand), the tight labor markets caused by economic booms have masked weaknesses in the quality of the work force that need to be addressed.

A third option is some sort of middle way that builds on the strengths of East Asia's history of equitable growth while addressing the new requirements of those vulnerable to external shocks. This might emphasize a continuing commitment to education, including guarantees of state support for keeping children in school in the event of future shocks (as in the existing Indonesian and Thai programs along these lines), and an expansion of incentives for training, both public and private, in return for labor's commitment to labor-market flexibility.

Yet more than an emphasis on education and labor-market flexibility is probably needed to deal with the insecurities associated with slower and more erratic growth and the likelihood of greater exposure to external shocks. The model that is most likely to fit East Asia's history is something like Singapore's Central Provident Fund, which bundles together pensions with emergency medical and unemployment insurance, rests on employer and employee contributions mandated by the government, is not redistributive in nature, and emphasizes personal control. Such programs offer security against economy-wide shocks, provide benefits that are valued by the emerging middle class, and (except for some transitional costs) do not necessarily have adverse fiscal consequences. Instituting such programs in new democracies would require pressure from middle-class parties and interest groups, including labor, and would have to overcome resistance from cost-conscious employers. Yet even this modest middle way may prove too difficult, leaving incremental expansion of existing efforts as the only remaining option.

Democratic progress in East Asia was already creating pressures for greater attention to social policy as well as greater transparency in business-government relations, and the economic crisis of 1997–99 has accelerated these trends. It has contributed to a change of regime in

Indonesia, to a strengthening of political oppositions elsewhere, and to growing pressures for changes in regulatory regimes and in the social contract. It is still too soon to tell, however, what the legacy of the crisis will be. Ironically, the very resilience of the Asian economies and the speed of their recovery may serve to limit the long-run impact of the crisis (except in Indonesia), allowing a reversion to political habits and institutions that bear a closer resemblance to the past than most observers had initially anticipated.

NOTES

1. See, however, Lawrence Krause, *The Economics and Politics of the Asian Financial Crisis of 1997–98* (New York: The Council on Foreign Relations, 1998); K.S. Jomo, *Tigers in Trouble: Financial Governance, Liberalization and Crises in East Asia* (London: Zed Books, 1998); T.J. Pempel, ed., *The Politics of the Asian Economic Crisis* (Ithaca, N.Y.: Cornell University Press, 1999); and Stephan Haggard, *The Politics of the Asian Financial Crisis* (Washington, D.C.: Institute for International Economics, forthcoming).

2. See Suchit Bunbongkarn, "Thailand's Successful Reforms," *Journal of Democracy* 10 (October 1999): 54–68.

3. See Jongryn Mo and Chung-in Moon, "Korea After the Crisis," *Journal of Democracy* 10 (July 1999): 150–64.

4. Sylvia Maxfield and Ben Ross Schneider, eds., *Business and the State in Developing Countries* (Ithaca, N.Y.: Cornell University Press, 1997), 13.

5. The World Bank, *The East Asian Miracle* (New York: Oxford University Press, 1993).

6. Chalmers Johnson, *MITI and the Japanese Miracle: The Growth of Industrial Policy 1925–1975* (Stanford, Calif.: Stanford University Press, 1982), 57–58.

7. Andrew MacIntyre, ed., *Business and Government in Industrializing Asia* (Ithaca, N.Y.: Cornell University Press, 1994).

3

STATE-BUSINESS RELATIONS IN SOUTH KOREA AND TAIWAN

Tun-jen Cheng and Yun-han Chu

Tun-jen Cheng, professor of government at the College of William and Mary, has written extensively on the political economy of East Asia. His most recent publication is The Security Environment in the Asia-Pacific, *a volume co-edited with Hung-mao Tien. He is also editor-in-chief of the* American Asian Review. *Yun-han Chu is professor of political science at National Taiwan University and president of the Chiang Ching-kuo Foundation for International Scholarly Exchange. He specializes in the politics of Greater China, East Asian political economy, and democratization. He currently serves on the editorial boards of* China Perspective, China Review, *the* Journal of Contemporary China, *the* Journal of East Asian Studies, *and the* Journal of Democracy. *He is the author, co-author, editor, or co-editor of ten books. Among his recent English publications are* Crafting Democracy in Taiwan *(1992),* Consolidating the Third Wave Democracies *(1997), and* China Under Jiang Zemin *(2000).*

The capitalist system is one in which, no matter how competent policy-makers may be, economic performance still depends upon the response of the private sector. The business sector is endowed with a privileged status in a capitalist democracy, owing to its influence over the national economy. The state-business relationship is a particularly important dimension in studies of economic development in the developing world where, for good or bad, state planners play a crucial economic role. In the past decade, institutionalist analyses of development have emphasized that relations between business and government are responsible for a large part of the divergent patterns of industrial transformation.[1] Some have argued that strong collaboration between a meritocratic and resourceful state and a well-organized business sector—one embedded within state-sanctioned policy networks, allowing for continual negotiation and renegotiation of goals and policies—has contributed to the remarkable industrial transformation that characterizes East Asia's newly industrialized countries (NICs).[2]

This chapter analyzes the creation and evolution of the state-business relationship in South Korea and Taiwan, two of the most-often-cited East Asian NICs. We want to make two points at the outset. First, the state-business relationship differs significantly in these two NICs. Studying this difference allows us to disaggregate the East Asian model. South Korea and Taiwan share the same colonial legacies and economic preconditions, much cultural background, and a common developmental trajectory. Yet they employ different policy incentives to foster businesses and to promote industrial development, leading to divergent socioeconomic outcomes. South Korea and Taiwan thus provide an excellent opportunity to demonstrate the path-dependent nature of institutional evolution. Second, the state-business relationship in these two NICs is not static. Forged in the long process of economic development, the state-business relationship in South Korea and Taiwan was transformed upon the advent of democracy and also amid rapid economic globalization. Democratic transition—which began in 1986 for both NICs—has drastically altered the domestic parameters within which state and business elites formerly interacted in a stable and predictable way. Globalization again accelerated after the Plaza Accord of 1985, which has presented a new international setting within which state and business have reshaped their linkages.

The analysis proceeds as follows: First we will trace the origin of state-business relations in the two NICs, uncovering the historical roots of these relationships, the critical junctures during which they were molded, and the resulting modes of interaction. Then we will show how democratization has upset the preexisting patterns of interaction between the state and business, affecting state policies toward business and requiring both sides to seek new rules of engagement. Finally, we will examine how globalization compounds the redefinition of the state-business relationship. The concluding section draws theoretical and policy lessons from the experiences of the two East Asian NICs in coping with the twin challenges of democratization and globalization.

The Genesis and Evolution of State-Business Relations

Although the lineage of some Korean firms can be traced to the colonial era, most Korean enterprises emerged in the wake of decolonization and the ensuing war.[3] Acquiring state-owned enterprises and banks and riding the postwar recovery, leading business firms quickly became the agent of the Synman Rhee government in the pursuit of import-substitution industrialization on the one hand, and in financing often unconstitutional reelections on the other. Essentially a rent-seeking business sector colluded with a rent-granting state in the use of foreign aid, which was the principal capital source for South Korea in the 1950s. Business accumulated illicit wealth while Rhee's government perpetuated itself via election rigging and constitutional maneuvering. By controlling market entry and allocating foreign aid, the government seemed to be able to dictate terms to business. Yet by corrupting itself for the sake of power and facing never-ending social protests, the Rhee regime was effectively captured by the business sector.

The military coup of 1961 transformed the collusive state-business nexus into a mechanism for implementing government-orchestrated development programs. Under the leadership of Park Chung Hee, a reformist military government initially planned to purge preexisting businesses, but quickly chose to co-opt business as an instrument of economic development. Although private banks were nationalized, no businessmen went to jail. South Korea's military rulers did not nurture a new crop of business leaders to contain the old as in Malaysia, or rely on the state sector to shoulder the task of development as in Communist China, or invite foreign capital to become the mainstay of industry as in Singapore. Instead, they formed a sword-won alliance with preexisting businesses.[4]

The alliance was an asymmetric one, as business was essentially given the chance to redeem its sins by performing tasks assigned by the state. Moreover, in addition to the control of market entry and foreign aid, the state now established two new business-controlling policy tools—the nationalized banks and foreign borrowing, which came to replace dwindling foreign aid as the main source of capital.[5] Not only did the state have extensive policy instruments and resources, it also centralized the political leadership structure and overhauled economic bureaucracy by meritocratic recruitment into the civil service.[6] State capacity increased. It was clear now that the state was leading while business was following, with the state defining the terms of engagement between the two sides. Business, however, was a willing junior partner of the alliance. There was a unity of purpose and a harmony of interests between state and business, leading many to describe them as the two wheels of "South Korea, Inc." Both sides embraced twin goals—catching up with earlier industrializers and enhancing national security. What mattered to them was not their strength relative to each other, but South Korea's ranking in the world. Driven by economic nationalism, the South Korean government mobilized domestic savings, borrowed capital from abroad, and used credit allocation as the primary policy tool to support industrial expansion and to promote exports. Preferential loans were tied to export performance. Foreign direct investment was discouraged, while market entry was carefully controlled. Policy incentives for export promotion benefited all firms, new and old, large and small, as long as they performed. The implicit contract between state and business was unbelievably simple: Firms proved themselves in export markets, and the government automatically advanced them loans.

After the launch of heavy and chemical industrialization in 1973, the

state-business cooperation reached a high plateau and underwent a qualitative transformation. The government not only selected industrial sectors
for development but also specified product items and handpicked leading firms for specific tasks in return for bank loans, now heavily
subsidized and allocated in a discretionary manner. Often, preselected
leading firms were rewarded with monopoly privileges and soft credit
the moment a national task was assigned to them. Moreover, facing an
oil-crisis-induced worldwide recession and a mounting oil import bill,
the government encouraged leading firms to go for overseas construction markets and to form general trading companies. It is little wonder
that the metamorphosis of South Korean business took place in the 1970s,
a decade of big industrial push and grand overseas expansion. In 1970,
the top 30 business groups had 126 subsidiaries, but by 1979 the number had increased more than threefold to 429. This massive expansion
required either government encouragement or permission to diversify
or government-sponsored mergers and acquisitions.[7] Leading business
firms evolved into the *chaebol* that we know of today—that is, family-
owned, controlled, and managed conglomerates, whose subsidiaries are
highly diversified but under one single control, with cross-shareholding
and mutual loan guarantees.[8]

Close ties linking business leaders, political leaders, and technocratic
advisers were crucial to policy credibility, as well as to policy effectiveness. To grow, business needed state credit lines and reliable policy;
the state needed a trustworthy and responsive business sector for information and policy implementation.[9] Business-government relations in
South Korea as such were akin to a "quasi-internal organization" in which
a chief executive officer adjudicated, coordinated, monitored, and enforced, thereby reducing information, communication, and transactions
costs for the collectivity.[10] For two decades these intimate ties were not
a recipe for rampant corruption and a predatory state, but rather a device that drove the South Korean economy forward at high speed (with
only one brief interruption in 1971 due to balance of payment problems). First, the essence of the state-business relationship in South Korea
under Park Chung Hee was reciprocity and exchange, not giveaway as
under Rhee.[11] The state did not sign explicit letters of intent with business leaders, but the conditionality was well understood. Second, as
foreign aid dwindled, exports became the only way to earn foreign exchange, and both sides really had to devote themselves to the task, or
else their failure would show up in the export figures. Third, and most
importantly, not only was the reforming military elite—mostly from the
countryside—socially distant from the business elite, the state leadership was also self-disciplined and self-policed. South Korea was lucky
to have an untainted leader, Park Chung Hee, who exercised internal
control over state economic managers, an advantage that was not replicated in subsequent decades under Park's two successors.

Such a state-led and *chaebol*-centered model has built-in defects, however. First, as is nowadays well known, there exists a vicious circle consisting of *chaebol*'s excessive and duplicative investment, an underdeveloped financial sector, and government bailouts. The incentive structure is one of co-insurance and symbiosis, which socializes the risk of investment and aggravates the moral hazard problem. As credit is subsidized and its availability is expected to continue, the *chaebol* have every reason to expand their size beyond the point of financial unsustainability. The state hesitates to withdraw its support from *chaebol* as any subsequent bankruptcies will result in massive layoffs, thereby violating its implicit social contract with the people, under which political acquiescence is exchanged for employment and higher incomes. The larger the *chaebol*, the more likely it is to be rescued, leading it to grow even bigger and become more leveraged. The financial sector, for its part, becomes underdeveloped as the state dictates and micromanages, thereby depriving bankers of any motivation or ability to assess projects and monitor their performance. As bailout cases accumulate, banks' nonperforming loans swell. Second, as Yoo points out, when discretion overrides rules, regulations multiply.[12] And in the absence of legal injunction and political oversight, the *amakudari* phenomenon—bureaucrats dispensing favors in expectation of postretirement appointments—is bound to appear. As the government exercises discretionary power, the private sector has every incentive to engage in rent-seeking activities. And when state-controlled resources are overstretched, collusive ties to the state become crucial to the growth or survival of firms. Third, as a device for rapid economic growth and capital accumulation, the sword-won alliance isolates the regime from all other social sectors: consumers, workers, small and medium enterprises, and so on. As long as the alliance delivers high growth rates and employment expansion without too many side effects, such as inflation and labor suppression, its *raison d'être* can be tacitly accepted, the collusive ties between state and business tolerated, and its accoutrements, such as labor control, foreign borrowing, and preferential loans may go unchallenged. But when an economic crisis erupts, then the nature of the tie becomes the target of social criticism and the rationale of the sword-won alliance is thrown into doubt.

In Taiwan, by contrast, the possibility of developing South Korean–styled conglomerates had been precluded from the very beginning of the post–World War II economic reconstruction. First, the mainlander elite—the émigré group that fled to the island after having been defeated in 1949 by the Chinese communists—discouraged wealth concentration for both political and ideological reasons. Over-concentration of industrial power, as well as wealth, in the hand of a few native Taiwanese was considered a potential political threat to the mainlander elite. Instead, between 1948 and 1951 the Kuomintang (KMT) government implemented a comprehensive land reform, that is, a redistribution of a major form of wealth. This was done to strengthen its legitimacy and to prevent communist insurgence in the rural areas. In addition, over-concentration of industrial power in private hands ran counter to the KMT's official ideology, Sun Yat-sen's eclectic "Three Principles of the People," which advocated the need for regulating private capital and the advancement of state capital. Thus, by default, the KMT government converted all industrial assets assembled under the Japanese colonial administration and *Zaibatsu* into state-owned enterprises. The monopoly, or near-monopoly, of these state-owned enterprises pre-empted private participation in the financial sector, public utilities, and most of the capital-intensive industries.

Unlike Rhee's regime in South Korea, which was in a sense captured by private business interests, there were formidable institutional cleavages erected between the KMT party's national leadership and Taiwan's private business community. The mainlander state elite and the native business elite shared very little in the way of lineage bonds, marital ties, or common social background. The state apparatus was thus initially relatively free of the infiltration of social forces through interpersonal ties. Formal channels linking government officials and private-sector business leaders were confined to the state-sponsored industrial associations. This hierarchical system of business associations was designed clearly along corporatist lines. Each constituent industrial association is a compulsory, noncompetitive, state-sponsored organization enjoying exclusive representation and endowed with certain regulatory authority.[13] At the apex of the hierarchy are three national peak organizations—the Federation of Industry and the Federation of Commerce, representing the entire manufacturing and service sector, respectively, and the blue-ribbon National Council of Industry and Commerce, whose membership includes virtually all elite business groups.

These industrial associations were designed to function as private-sector instruments of the state economic bureaucracy and the authoritarian party. The economic bureaucrats used the constituent industrial associations to conduct industrial surveys, collect and disseminate business information, solicit policy inputs, and implement sectoral policy. The party used these associations to penetrate, organize, and demobilize various sectors of civic society.[14] Association leadership was elected under the guidance of the Social Affairs Department of the ruling party. Officers of the secretariat were appointed on the recommendation of the party, and the leaderships of the national peak organizations were hand-picked by the paramount leader. In short, state-directed corporatist arrangements were backed up by a complex web of clientelist networks that infiltrated the hierarchy of the interest intermediary institutions and provided the party-state elite with a mechanism of intimate control and selected cooptation.

Over the years, the private sector utilized many of these state-sanctioned business associations as an institutional base for organizing cooperative activities. Through regular association meetings, business representatives made policy suggestions to the party and the government. Economic officials then negotiated certain items with association representatives. Continuous policy input from the organized business community strengthened the state's steering capacity as the economic bureaucracy acquired an improved grasp of the dynamics of industrial change. Yet business was not able to assert itself as an autonomous political actor since the party-state exercised control over both interest intermediation and the creation of institutional structures. Within the larger institutional framework, the business elite remained on the fringe of the KMT structure because the political support of the business community was not decisive in order to sustain the political security of the regime. The KMT regime based its legitimacy essentially on international recognition, its irreplaceable function in protecting the island from communist aggression, and its effectiveness in bringing about economic prosperity. None of these required the full-fledged political recognition of the business sector.

The relative autonomy of the economic technocrats derived from the fact that they were answerable only to the party's top leadership, and responsible mainly for the overall performance of the economy and the success of the targeted sectors. Economic technocrats approached business-government liaisons with caution and seldom operated outside prescribed institutional channels. The conduct of economic officials was also subject to the surveillance and scrutiny of security personnel and party bureaucrats. Leniency toward private economic actors could be mistaken for undue favoritism in disguise. Also, economic officials were not entrusted with the power to dispense economic privileges. They had to consult with the party leadership over politically sensitive economic decisions.

The autonomy of the economic technocrats was further buttressed by the existence of an economic base independent of the private sector. Under direct technocratic control were the entire banking sector and a vast array of state-owned enterprises, ranging from energy, public utilities, fertilizer, sugar-refining, tobacco and wine, steel, ship-building, heavy machinery, and construction to defense-related industries.[15] State ownership was also extended to many service-based sectors, including public transportation, shipping, insurance, and financial services. State-owned enterprises provided the technocratic elite with an independent power base and the economic resources for building an array of satellite suppliers and subservient down-stream firms. They also provided a self-sufficient training base for the state economic bureaucracy to accumulate managerial and planning expertise. Numerous elite planning technocrats emerged from the managerial stratum of state-owned enterprises and subsequently retired to the boardrooms of the same enterprises.

Also, in direct contrast to the South Korean experience, Taiwan's economic technocrats relied on state-owned enterprises, not big business, as the primary agent of import-substituting industrialization. Throughout the 1960s and 1970s, state-owned enterprises were important vehicles for the promotion of industrial upgrading and the implementation of anti-cyclical policies and supply-side management.[16] Although the relative importance of state-owned enterprises fell steadily during the 1960s and 1970s as the private sector grew at a much faster rate, they still constituted a preponderant economic power. Throughout the 1970s the total investment in the state-enterprise sector accounted for more than a third of gross domestic fixed capital formation in most years.[17]

Taiwan also differed from South Korea on another important score—the use of discretionary credit policy as an instrument of industrial targeting. In Taiwan, the state also employed a panoply of policy incentives for promoting industrial change and export-oriented manufacturing in the private sector.[18] Many measures were product- or industry-specific, not firm-specific. More importantly, the state's industrial policies did not discriminate against the small- and medium-sized enterprises (SMEs). The expansionist tendency of the planning technocrats was always checked by an overarching principle of fiscal and financial conservatism. The Central Bank of China (CBC), which set limits on the use of credit policy in industrial targeting, has long occupied the commanding heights of the state economic bureaucracy.[19] Under the guidance of the CBC, a conservative ethos permeated the entire banking sector. The CBC customarily insisted that targeted lending to the private sector be backed up by government-financed specialized funds, so that the ceiling of policy loans was subject to "hard budgetary constraints." As a result, the CBC and the Finance Ministry were able to keep the nonperforming-loan ratio of the overall banking system at a very low level, most of the time below 2.0 percent of loans outstanding, and most private firms have been moderately leveraged, with debt-equity ratios averaging around 160 percent.

Also, in contrast to Park's regime, which never succeeded in creating a robust institutional base for its rule, the KMT developed a proven formula for maintaining the entrenched political dominance of the mainlander elite at the national level, and for controlling a limited popular electoral process implemented at the local level.[20] The KMT maintained a stable political order through an elaborate ideology akin to socialism, a cohesive and highly penetrating party apparatus organized along Leninist democratic-centralist lines, and a powerful, pervasive, but less visible security apparatus reinforced by martial law. The institutionalization of the paramount leader in the party power structure laid the foundation for the autonomy and coherence of the party-state.

The party apparatus consisted of crosscutting functional units organized along both regional and sectorial lines. At the grassroots level throughout the island, the KMT utilized existing patron-client networks to establish complex local political machines within the party structure.[21] Above the local level, the KMT controlled and demobilized all modern social sectors through the preemptive incorporation of business and professional associations, labor unions, state employees, journalists, intellectuals, women, students, and other targeted groups. The party cautiously distributed the privileges of participation in state-harbored domestic oligopolies to cement the allegiance of selected groups. The party apparatus filled up all the political space in the society, with party membership reaching almost 20 percent of the entire adult male population.[22]

For almost three decades of its rule, the KMT faced a very unorganized and weak political opposition, consisting primarily of defiant local factions that had no national political aims and posed little threat to the ruling party's dominant position. Thus, for an extended period of time, the ruling elite saw no pressing need for a limited electoral opening at the national level. Only in the beginning of the 1970s when a series of diplomatic setbacks—the loss of the UN seat to the People's Republic of China and derecognition by major allies—severely undermined KMT's claim to be the sole legitimate government of the whole of China did the KMT elite begin to feel the need to strengthen the legitimating function of elective institutions.[23]

On the eve of the democratic opening of the mid-1980s, societal support for the KMT-sponsored development program was more broadly based than that of South Korea's authoritarian rulers. A myriad of SMEs that had grown around the state-sponsored export-oriented industrialization strategy enabled the KMT to broaden its social base, since the emerging industrial structure addressed both growth and equity issues with a high degree of effectiveness. The highly decentralized private sector also generated a large number of owner-operators, as well as a sizable working class that experienced vertical social mobility, that is, class mobility. The development program relied more on SMEs than on big business as agents of industrial upgrading and technological innovation in the export-oriented sector. It was intrinsically difficult for the opposition to win over any major social groups by proposing a distinctive socio-economic program. At the same time, the political opposition lacked the leverage to impose political reforms on the incumbent elite. By and large it lacked the option of organizing crippling strikes or large-scale mass rallies. This condition was bound to strengthen the hand of the incumbent elite in setting limits on the scope and speed of democratic reform.

The Advent of Democracy

The breakup of the sword-won alliance in South Korea. When the state-led and *chaebol*-based industrialization strategy was brought to its knees, the structural defects of the state-business alliance were fully exposed. Excessive investment, overwhelming foreign debts, and high inflation triggered a severe recession and sparked an internal leadership conflict that ended the Park regime in 1979. Initially the new authoritarian regime under Chun Doo Whan (1980–86) blamed the external environment—high oil prices, rising interest rates, and the spread of protectionism—and cyclical factors for the setback. Yet reformers in the Economic Planning Agency and the Blue House, mostly economists trained in the United States, urged a shift away from the old paradigm of state *dirigisme*.[24] Neoliberal ideas were also transmitted into Korea from the United States and the United Kingdom under Reagan and Thatcher, and via the International Monetary Fund, to which South Korea turned for assistance in 1980. But it was the new authoritarian ruler who really counted. Chun's second diagnosis was that inflation was to blame for alienating farmers and workers and generating the social unrest of 1979 and 1980.[25] The weak political legitimacy of the new president— who came to power via a coup and in the wake of the suppression of the Kwangju uprising—gave him every incentive to reform the economy so as to solidify his political control.

But aside from pursuing liberalizing reforms—including the standard stabilization package—Chun also pioneered *chaebol* reform. While Chun did not purge the *chaebol* as he had contemplated initially, he did enact a Fair Trade and Anti-Monopoly Law, ordered the *chaebol* to trim their subsidiaries, attempted to limit preferential access to financial resources, and tied credit access to ownership deconcentration and improvements of corporate financial structure. Despite strong opposition from his own party, Chun also had his assembly pass a law requiring the use of real names in financial transactions. Under the cover of anonymity, *chaebol* had been able to evade taxes, hide corruption, and make political contributions. Moreover, given his embrace of the noble cause of distributive justice (notice the name of his party, the Democratic Justice Party), he was constitutionally enshrining the promotion of small and medium enterprises as a policy objective to redress the previous pro-*chaebol* bias.

The sword-won alliance thus suffered its first fissure. The new authoritarian regime under Chun saw the *chaebol* not merely as a source of economic crisis but as an inherited political liability as well. Attacking the *chaebol* became a safety valve against explosive anti-government sentiment after Chun blocked the possibility of any democratic opening. Distancing himself from the *chaebol* also helped to de-link Chun from his authoritarian predecessor. Reversing Park's "growth at the expense of stability" policy would presumably benefit the middle class. While the size of the middle class had grown, income distribution had worsened and inflation had gone up, leading many to feel insecure. In Chung-in Moon's view, Chun hoped to tap tacit support from the silent majority.[26]

While economic stabilization was successfully executed, the *chaebol* reform turned out to be more apparent than real. The Chun regime did not really carry out any policy to protect and promote SMEs. The real-name transaction law was not enforced. Rhetoric aside, Chun was more interested in goading rather than reforming the *chaebol*. As soon as the economy stabilized, his regime was again endorsing and financing the *chaebol*'s expansion and soon they once more became the agent for another long investment boom from 1983 to 1991. The *chaebol* were able to weather the economic crisis and political turbulence of 1979 much better than the 1961 military coup. As the main foreign-exchange earners, rather than as rent-seekers in a protected domestic market, the *chaebol* had gained some legitimacy. Moreover, given their weight in production and employment, they were crucial to economic growth and social peace. The state-business relationship had mutated from one of dominance (a hierarchy of dependence and patronage) to one of symbiosis.[27] In addition, liberalizing reforms and *chaebol* reform were often in conflict, motivating the *chaebol* to disregard the new authoritarian ruler's decree. For example, the authoritarian ruler ordered each *chaebol* to specialize in a few industries in order to retain access to preferential loans. Yet the essence of liberalizing reform was financial decontrol and the lessening of government interventions in shaping industrial structure.

As shown above, authoritarian rule injected *chaebol* reform into the policy agenda during a severe economic crisis. After the democratic transition of 1987, however, *chaebol* reform came to the center of political discourse for democratic change, and emerged as a political imperative for the government. Democratization opened up political space for new actors, such as workers, farmers, environmentalists, consumers, and other non-business social groups, all of whom had been excluded for so long. Not only did business cease to be the only client group for the government, it quickly turned into the most prominent target for reform as the seamy side of the state-business alliance was exposed. The *chaebol* became nearly synonymous with wealth and political influence, insider information, and regulatory manipulation for private gain, as vividly illustrated by the zoning law governing real estate speculation.[28] The *chaebol* also embodied unfair competition, relentless predation, the crowding out of SMEs, and the squeezing out of even small vendors. Whatever the diligence, intelligence, and accomplishments of the *chaebol,* they were marred by their association with special favors and privileges received from the authoritarian government and with the resulting social injustices.[29]

Upon assuming office, President Roh Tae Woo presided over a sudden and large-scale appreciation of the exchange rate in 1987. There were also double-digit wage increases each year from 1987 through 1989. Both were to the dismay of the *chaebol*.[30] In 1990, Roh turned directly to the *chaebol,* ordering the 49 leading groups to sell their idle land and buildings in six months. Land not sold would be transferred to the state at a discounted price, and access to loans would be denied while outstanding loans were called in. Tax auditing could also be used as a reinforcement. In 1991, the top 30 groups were required to designate three core businesses and urged to specialize in them, with the sweetener that more loans would be available for those lines. They were told to expect no more loans for non-core business. In addition, the state also tightened the legal and tax systems to monitor and prevent cross-investment. Roh even contemplated abolishing chairmanships and multidivisional planning offices, so as to deprive the *chaebol* of their nerve centers for corporate control and expansion.

During his presidency (1992–97), Kim Young Sam (hereafter Y.S. Kim) continued to implement anti-trust law, tax audits, and credit directions, and announced his intention to reject any political contributions from big businesses.[31] Y.S. Kim also used his presidential decree powers to implement the real-name transaction policy. In comparison with Chun's reform proposals in the early 1980s, the reform policies undertaken by both Roh and Y.S. Kim were more drastic and specific, were targeted at all leading *chaebol,* were armed with deadlines, and were backed up by punitive measures for noncompliance. In addition, in newly democratized South Korea the government also enacted affirmative-action programs to assist SMEs, such as setting lending quotas for SMEs and establishing loan guarantee funds to assist them. Meanwhile, the government began to initiate redistributive schemes, including universal welfare programs and specific programs targeted at particular sectors, such as farmers.[32]

Yet all this *chaebol* reform produced only checkered results. Attempts to limit idle land ownership failed; so did credit management. Policies to force *chaebol* to specialize had little success. *Chaebol* subsidiaries increased and these conglomerates were as homogeneous, clumsy, and leveraged as ever. Eventually, in January 1995, the government decided to narrow its goal to just one aspect of the problem, namely to reduce ownership concentration and to separate ownership and management, without attempting to limit *chaebol* size and borrowings.[33] The failure of *chaebol* reform suggests the decreasing ability of the state to impose terms on its developmental agents, the *chaebol.*[34] The democratic transition made the state elite less cohesive and more risk-averse than it used to be, as seen in the proliferation of the advisory councils, where outside experts are included to share the blame and deflect societal pressures. Democratic transition may increase the political vulnerability of big business, yet it may also permit them to be active and manipulative in the political arena, choosing their agents, representing themselves, and defending their interests in the national assembly. For example, while political contributions quickly became a big campaign issue directed against the *chaebol,* public hearings also gave the *chaebol* an opportunity to expose the political extortions of the past, shifting blame onto the shoulders of the politicians. One should also notice that the structural power of business does not hinge on collective action and organization and that, while presidents come and go, *chaebol* stay forever.[35]

Fundamentally, *chaebol* reform failed because the reform strategy was faulty. As Yoo Seong Min trenchantly points out, *chaebol* reform mainly took the form of administrative decrees rather than market liberalization.[36] At least until the 1997 economic crisis, the Korean state continued to regulate the investments, financial structure, corporate structure, and management of the *chaebol,* rather than accelerating financial liberalization and letting market forces (notably the threat of competition and bankruptcy) discipline them. Indeed, the *chaebol* policy of the 1980s and 1990s was similar to that of the 1960s and 1970s, in that the *chaebol* were rewarded or penalized depending on whether or not they complied with government instructions. Previously, the *chaebol* would export and expand. New "codes of conduct" did not damp down the *chaebol*'s reckless expansion, reduce their debt-equity ratios, or disperse their ownership, primarily because the government continued to act as an insurer. As long as the *chaebol* did not violate the informal rules of the game by going against the ruling party, and as long as they were big enough (among the top 30, for example), the bailout policy remained in place if they needed rescuing. The vicious circle of investment, boom, bailout, and stalled financial liberalization thus continued.

This reveals that the government continued to see the *chaebol* more as an agent for development than as a source of economic problems. The ill-fated reform also suggests that the *chaebol* were an essential part of a conservative political coalition grouped around a ruling party. Indeed, both sides were coordinating an overhaul of their alliance. As mentioned above, upon assuming power, President Roh Tae Woo immediately embraced a series of measures aimed at promoting small and medium enterprises. The Federation of Korean Industry, the bastion of the *chaebol,* promptly endorsed SME policy, hoping to cement a mutually supportive subcontracting relationship with SMEs. Under Roh, the government also attempted to recruit farmers via redistributive programs and an extremely cautious approach to agricultural import liberalization, to which export-oriented *chaebol* had no objections. Such a farmer-SME-*chaebol* coalition was akin to the social basis of conservative rule in post-1955 Japan.[37] Indeed, in 1990, Roh succeeded in forging a dominant conservative party, the Democratic Liberal Party (DLP), by merging his Democratic Justice Party with a minor conservative party under Kim Joung-pil (Park Chung Hee's deputy) and a moderate opposition party under Y.S. Kim, in much the same way that two major Japanese parties on the right combined to form the Liberal Democratic

Party (LDP) in 1955. While big business had been instrumental in the funding of the LDP in Japan, however, the formation of the DLP in Korea was primarily based on the action of political power contenders.[38] Yet the creation of a grand conservative party with a comfortable majority in the legislative branch certainly met the expectations of the *chaebol*. In 1991, this conservative coalition backed the presidency of Y.S. Kim, the lesser radical of the two most well-known democracy activists in postwar Korea.

Labor was not necessarily left out of this "political big deal." The *chaebol* resented the government's policy of benign neglect toward militant unions—which mushroomed after political decontrol in 1987 and were instrumental in pushing through double-digit wage increases and sparking the high frequency of industrial conflicts for the first three years of the South Korean democratic transition.[39] Yet rising wages were in part a compensation for the erosion of labor's share of national income in earlier times, and were in part a result of an economic boom following large-scale currency appreciation. When major strikes broke out in 1990, the government stepped in to restore industrial peace and began to revise labor laws to ameliorate industrial relations.[40] Aside from promoting collective bargaining over wages settlements, an implicit tripartite social contract seemed to have emerged, to the effect that the labor unions would ensure industrial peace, the *chaebol* would not lay off workers, and the government would rescue firms in financial distress. During the economic takeoff, unemployment was not a problem. But when the South Korean economy began to mature, liberalize, and face structural adjustment, unemployment and job security became an issue, especially when such an economic process was accompanied by political democratization and while social-welfare policy remained primitive.[41]

This conservative coalition was not easy to maintain, however. The DLP, a marriage of convenience among three factions, had neither an integrated party organization nor established rules for solving the problem of leadership succession. Under the winner-takes-all presidential system, these factions did not really co-rule—a vivid contrast with LDP factions co-governing Japan under a parliamentary system.[42] From the very beginning, the DLP was headed for the rocks, and it disintegrated after Y.S. Kim failed to smooth out the nomination battle for the 1997 presidential race. Moreover, as T.J. Pempel argues in the Japanese case, globalization has been subverting such conservative coalitions.[43] Agricultural protectionism—to which the *chaebol* acquiesced—and SME policy—which the *chaebol* supported—ran counter to economic liberalization. Rigidity in the labor market also prevented South Korean industry from facing the challenge of globalization. The implicit social contract underlying the conservative coalition was difficult to uphold as the pace of globalization accelerated.

Reconsolidating a conservative alliance in Taiwan. While democratization precipitated a rupture in the conservative coalition underlying state-business relations in South Korea, the partnership between the KMT and the business elite in Taiwan moved in a rather different direction. Since the late 1980s, we have witnessed a movement toward a consolidation of a conservative alliance among the KMT, big business, and local factions.

Toward the late 1980s, as a succession crisis developed, a power realignment between the KMT and the business elite started to take shape. The death of the strongman, Chiang Ching-kuo, in February 1988 triggered a split in the party's central leadership and quickened the pace of democratization. The succession crisis and the introduction of democratic institutions provided the business community with a strategic opening.

First, the old institutional insulation between the party-state central leadership and the business sector began to dissolve. The power struggle over political succession compelled competing power blocs within the party's central leadership to bring in new allies from the outside. The business community as a whole began to enjoy more prominence in the KMT's power structure, and the selective incorporation practiced in the past was replaced by a more inclusive approach. More seats in the KMT Central Committee and the Central Standing Committee were reserved for business leaders. The KMT also introduced a more systematic approach to the incorporation of the second-generation business leaders, in particular the heirs to the leading diversified business groups. Also, with the trend toward the indigenization of the party-state power structure came a revival of the infiltration of social forces through interpersonal connections.

Next, an expanded electoral arena and an increasingly assertive parliament provided the business elite with new opportunities to exert influence. The diversified business groups became the most sought-after patrons of elected politicians and local factions. Locally elected members of the Legislative Yuan quickly took control of the legislative process from the aged lifelong members, who were forced to retire at the end of 1991. Business-backed and faction-affiliated lawmakers competed vigorously for the more lucrative committee postings, namely Budget, Finance, and Economics. The Legislative Yuan became an arena of horse-trading among economic officials, party officials, and lawmakers. They often acted as surrogates for special business interests. An immediate consequence of the politicization of economic decision making was that the cabinet could no longer impose its will on the Legislative Yuan.

As parliament rapidly evolved into a junior partner of the KMT and the cabinet in policy making (while striving to become an equal partner), a new policy-coordination mechanism was created within the KMT.

Major disputes were resolved through an ad hoc coordination committee typically composed of the vice-premier, the secretary-general of the Executive Yuan, the chairman of the KMT Policy Coordination Committee, the speaker of the Legislative Yuan, and the party whip. While the party leadership was still able to impose discipline on KMT lawmakers concerning politically sensitive legislative proposals, it evaded such instructions concerning economic and financial matters.

The enhanced political weight of the parliament and the business elite necessarily eroded the authority of the state economic bureaucracy.[44] Economic officials began to embrace liberal economic thinking and a pro-business outlook. Between 1988 and 1993 the state economic bureaucracy introduced more deregulatory measures than it had done during the previous two decades. The government lifted barriers protecting a series of state-owned enterprises and parastatal-dominated sectors, such as commercial banking, investment banking, construction, mass transportation, airlines, and mid-stream petrochemicals. A number of state-sheltered oligopolies, such as security brokerage, newspapers, and insurance, were also opened for new entrants, and many state-owned enterprises were earmarked for stepwise privatization.

Yet the political rise of the legislative branch was not unlimited. The cabinet still had the upper hand over the national legislature because most KMT lawmakers sought extralegal economic prerogatives, such as exclusive rights to fill government procurement orders, obtain public work contracts, participate in joint ventures with state enterprises, receive concessionary loans from state-owned banks, and purchase public land at below-market prices. All these required under-the-table relationships with the responsible state agencies. KMT government officials could also count on the allegiance of a sizable number of lawmakers who depended upon controlled electoral support from state employees and military personnel. The government usually prevailed over key economic proposals. After all, the KMT top leadership still had a final say over nomination decisions and no individual legislator was politically indispensable or electorally invincible. Lastly, both the popular base and the constitutional power of the president—the pinnacle of state power—were further buttressed with the introduction of direct election to the presidency in 1996. Thus, despite the fact that many new channels of political access became available to the business elite, economic officials still enjoyed a decisive say over the timetable of deregulation and liberalization and the design of the new regulatory schemes and mechanisms.

Furthermore, despite its rising political clout, the political influence of the business community was still significantly circumscribed during the KMT's tenure. Throughout the 1990s, the KMT was able to lock in the political allegiance of the business community as there was no alternative power bloc in sight. The KMT achieved a string of electoral victories after the first founding elections of 1992. The Democratic Progressive Party (DPP), the major opposition, found itself steadily losing electoral momentum as its political reform agenda ran out of steam. Thus, until the KMT lost the presidential election in March 2000, the party leadership was able to use its unabated staying power and incontestable ability to make long-term policy commitments and to construct an unequal partnership with the business elite, in which the party-state elite set the limits on influence-buying and policy contestation.

Throughout the 1990s the KMT, being an oversized, richly endowed, and autocratically governed political machine, provided the institutional foundation for the dominance of its national leadership over both local factions and big business. Political democratization did little to transform the KMT's core power structure. The party remained a hierarchically structured constellation of entrenched state and party elites. Emerging out of the 1998 intraparty power struggle over political succession and political reform, Lee Teng-hui successfully marginalized the KMT old-timers and recentralized power in the hand of the party chairman. Also, unlike the LDP in Japan or the ruling parties in South Korea, the KMT does not rely on political donations made by the business community, since the party itself owns a huge array of business interests. In 1998, the Central Finance Company (CFC) invested in 216 companies and increased it total asset to NT$147 billion and its annual after-tax profit to NT$12.1 billion (approximately US$370 million), making the KMT business empire the fifth or sixth largest diversified business group in Taiwan.[45] Through the exercise of monetary incentives, business interests can capture individual lawmakers, or even an entire local faction, but not the ruling party.

Yet the state still controlled the organizational bases of interest intermediation. Only the state-sponsored and party-guided business organizations were granted recognition in processes of policy consultation. Only they were eligible for government grants or delegated regulatory authority. The state regulated the representative function, membership, bylaws, and finance of these associations, while the party exercised considerable influence over their leadership selection and policy agenda. At the same time, most business leaders, especially executives of inward-looking, family-owned business groups, still craved particularistic ties and resisted building the permanent organizational base and impersonal links necessary for broad-based collective actions. As a result, the business community was far from a cohesive entity in either organizational or ideological terms. It also lacked independent think tanks that could scrutinize government proposals, initiate new policy proposals, or counter proposals on behalf of the private sector.

Within this asymmetrical partnership, there were many policy objectives shared by the KMT leadership and the business elite. Both saw the need for the involvement of an active state in the process of industrial upgrading. Both put economic growth before the environment. Both favored a slow growth in social-welfare spending. And, most significantly, both supported a state-orchestrated exclusion of organized labor from economic policy making. On the other hand, sources of old antagonism had been removed one by one through a series of liberalization, deregulation, and privatization programs.[46] This institutional bias helped the KMT retain the partisan loyalty of a large segment of the business elite and perpetuated a perception that the vested interests of the business community were tied to the continued political dominance of the KMT.

The steady consolidation during the 1990s of a conservative alliance linking the KMT, big business, and local factions posed a serious challenge to the economic managers—how to prevent the spread of "money politics" and "crony capitalism" from suffocating the vitality of the economy. Five mechanisms accounted for their limited success. First, the KMT was able to maintain a system of "competitive clientelism."[47] At the local level, the KMT customarily cultivated at least two competing factions in any given county. Therefore, no local faction was able to enjoy a political monopoly over the distribution of economic rents. Within the parliament, the KMT top leadership always manipulated competition between the legislative factions formed by its own lawmakers. This built-in rivalry provided the necessary countervailing mechanism to block collusion among rent-seeking agents.

Second, democratization gave rise to a number of formidable counterweights to big business and local factions. Since 1992, the DPP has started to make "money politics" and "Mafia politics" the most salient issue. The muckraking efforts of the opposition lawmakers were assisted by a growing number of independent-minded young prosecutors and the market-oriented mass media.

Third, there remained a "hard budget constraint" on the demands of rent-seeking actors.[48] For reasons of national security, the top KMT leadership was resolved to protect the autonomy of the Central Bank of China and the Finance Ministry. Fiscal discipline was reinforced by the Public Debt Law, which put a ceiling on the size of new issues of government bonds (no more than 15 percent of the annual budget for any given year). Also, the CBC and the Finance Ministry managed to maintain tight regulatory supervision of all financial institutions. They always moved swiftly to close down insolvent local financial institutions, through forced mergers if necessary.

Fourth, economic managers strengthened their bargaining position versus the rent-seeking actors by broadening their own constituent cases of support. From the early 1980s, the policy-consultation functions of the established industrial associations were upgraded and reinvigorated. In addition, a new array of institutionalized channels of policy consultation were created. Two notable cases were the National Science and Technology Conference, under the auspices of the Executive Yuan, and the Industrial Development Consultation Committee, under the auspices of the Ministry of Economic Affairs (MOEA).

Lastly, the state continued to provide an effective enabling environment for SMEs, especially for start-up companies, to help them compete with big business. Over the years, the economic planners continued to rely more on SMEs and start-ups than on big business as an agent of industrial upgrading and technological innovation. The state economic bureaucracy is keen to address the deficiencies of SMEs through publicly funded research and development (R&D) support and technological transfer, the provision of venture capital, and lending guidelines that require all medium business banks to extend a fixed percentage of their outstanding loans to SMEs. Thus Taiwan's economic structure has been long characterized by a duality—between inward-looking diversified business groups and export-oriented SMEs and high-tech start-ups. The former typically enjoy better political access, but it is the latter that drive Taiwan's economic dynamism.

The Challenge of Globalization

The road to financial crisis in Korea. In South Korea globalization started on the trade front, then extended to the area of foreign direct investment, and culminated in the financial sector. Fueled by ideological persuasion and information technology, the drive for financial liberalization has been the most dramatic dimension. While the first two dimensions were, in the eyes of economic historians, largely *déjà vu,* it is in the area of finance that the impacts of globalization have been particularly novel, shocking, and controversial. It is also in this dimension of globalization that state-business relations in South Korea have been particularly affected.

The principal impetus for trade liberalization came from outside. As soon as South Korea rebounded from its recession in 1981, it started accumulating a trade surplus, thus prodding major trade partners (especially the United States) to demand import liberalization. Except for a few sectors, notably agriculture, import liberalization proceeded steadily. While SMEs and farmers were opposed to import liberalization, export-oriented *chaebol* did not come out against it.[49] Although some *chaebol* had vested interests in the domestic market in some sectors—such as automobiles—the *chaebol* as a whole were not particularly concerned with trade liberalization, as they could at least share the domestic market with foreign suppliers. Here we see a vivid contrast with Taiwan, where business groups are not as diversified as the South Korean *chaebol.* Being in so many lines of business, both import-competitive ones and export-competitive ones, the *chaebol* would not form the core of an entrenched protectionist force. Trade policy did not really impact the state-business alliance.

While import barriers were steadily dismantled, the liberalization of foreign direct investment (FDI) in South Korea has been laggard. Initially the main impetus for FDI liberalization came from foreign economic partners. As South Korea's own overseas investment increased, thanks to currency appreciation, the search for markets and technology and for financial liberalization grew, and restrictions on FDI in South Korea became indefensible.[50] Therefore, in 1993 the government presented a five-year plan to liberalize FDI in the sectors previously closed to foreigners. Despite this liberalization, the pace of FDI inflow was slow, the total amount was insignificant, and until 1998, foreign acquisitions were unheard-of. FDI as a share of GDP and the growth rate of FDI in South Korea were the second lowest in Asia (only those of Japan were lower).[51] The *chaebol*'s attitude toward FDI was negative, the bureaucrats' positions inconsistent, and the public's view ambivalent. As Alford's attitudinal study vividly shows, behind South Korea's apparent embrace of globalization lies a deep fear of losing what they have gained.[52] While the public might perceive the *chaebol* as predators of small and medium enterprises and a source of corruption, they were also a national pride, a testament to South Korean economic prowess, and a hedge against foreign penetration. Democratization further underscored the fact that foreign ownership of corporate South Korea is an emotional and easily politicized issue.

Liberalizing the financial sector has been more consequential than decontrolling FDI in South Korea. Initially the pace was slow, the government was not persistent, and major steps only involved privatizing commercial banks and opening up non-banking financial institutions, both of which gave *chaebol* footholds in the commanding heights of the economy.[53] The process of financial liberalization accelerated in the 1990s, following first the appreciation of the won and then South Korea's successful bid for membership in the Organization for Economic Cooperation and Development. Interest rates were being deregulated, restrictions on capital flow were drastically relaxed, foreign financial institutions increased their presence in South Korea, and lending to South Korean firms mounted.[54] Yet the government's discretionary powers to set interest rates and policy loans did not lessen. Given the high debt-equity ratio of major South Korean corporations, the ceiling on interest rates was not easily removed. In the early 1990s, attempts to phase out policy loans—lending at preferential rates—failed as they resurfaced during the investment boom. Despite the privatization of commercial banks and the establishment of new banks, the government continued to appoint bank management teams and board members to scrutinize major operational decisions and to act as bank caretakers.[55] Credit allocation was still influenced by the Ministry. Despite incessant debates over the role of the Bank of Korea (the central bank in South Korea) in maintaining a credible anti-inflationary policy and curbing rent-seeking activities in the financial sector, it was only in December 1997 that this bank was given more formal independence. Serious efforts to make the banking sector competitive, transparent, more prudentially supervised, and accountable were not made until South Korea was engulfed in the Asian financial crisis.[56]

While the preferences of state and *chaebol* converged regarding trade and FDI liberalization, the two sides diverged in their attitudes toward financial liberalization. Businessmen were concerned by the prospect of interest-rate increases after financial liberalization, but they also abhorred the government's discretion and lending decisions as well as its intervention in their investment decisions. It was the *chaebol*'s non-banking financial institutions that took advantage of reform and became aggressive. Banks were also for liberalization, as it would increase their autonomy vis-à-vis the government, even though their oligopoly would be broken. The government for its part wanted to phase out its credit support and other privileges to the *chaebol* and make banks responsible for their lending decisions, but it was afraid of losing its control over the banks, the most powerful lever controlling the *chaebol*. Indeed, after the onset of democratization, farmers, SMEs, and even the middle class—which had benefited most from government's housing loans—have become new vested interest groups in the state's governance over the banking sector.[57]

Hesitancy and unevenness in South Korea's financial liberalization revealed the tension between economic globalization and political democratization, which led to inconsistent policies. Democracy diluted the old-boy networks and tended to restore transparency and accountability. Yet globalization requires some degree of policy coordination to prevent the denationalization of South Korean business, a scenario that is politically risky for any South Korean government. Democracy tightened regulations on fair trade and anti-monopoly practices, as well as on public goods and consumer protection. Globalization also means deregulation, including in the area of market entry. Indeed, liberalization can actually lead to more concentration. Democracy gave the state an edge and impelled it to discipline the *chaebol*, but globalization gave them leeway. Democracy made industrial restructuring a political project, but economic liberalization gave the *chaebol* an excuse to dodge the assigned task. Domestic financial liberalization gave them a foothold in the commanding heights. It also included trade and investment decontrol, which gave the *chaebol* new opportunities for expansion. The influence of the *chaebol* continued to grow, in part due to the privatization of banks, in part due to intermarriage, and in part due to the ideology of globalization. Moreover, globalization undercut the construction of a conservative coalition that the government party had been trying to forge to meet the challenge of democratization. As we have illustrated, the old formula of economic growth based on a state-business alliance has become more rigid and frequently counterproductive. The imperative of building and maintaining a viable political coalition under democracy further compounds the difficulties of structural reform, a necessary move in making the economy flexible enough to prosper in an age of globalization.[58] Thus, under a democratic regime and with an underdeveloped party system, the state could no longer act effectively as the risk partner of the *chaebol*. In a nutshell, the twin challenges of democratization and globalization have eroded the institutional foundation for the South Korean high-debt model of development.

It took the Asian financial crisis and a leader from outside the conservative coalition, namely President Kim Dae Jung (1997–present), to undertake serious corporate reform and to restructure state-business relations. Heavy corporate debts were a proximate reason why South Korea was engulfed in the regional financial crisis. Debt crisis in turn was attributable to antiquated corporate governance—family control and a lack of accountability and transparency—and an entrapped financial sector that over-lent to, yet was unable to monitor, the *chaebol*. These firms incurred huge foreign debts via their foreign subsidiaries.[59] While the reform package begins with familiar items, such as swapping enterprises to enhance specialization (dubbed "big deals") and selling assets to improve balance sheets, it also includes improvement of corporate governance, the enforcement of bankruptcy law, and active introduction of FDI.

Corporate reform in the midst of the Asian financial crisis quickly degenerated into a test of will between state and business. The government created the Financial Supervisory Commission, Financial Supervisory Service, and Corporate Governance Reform Committee, while invigorating the Fair Trade Commission. Instead of bailouts, forced restructuring and liquidation were in order. The dates for industrial restructuring and asset sales were set. The government also actively courted FDI so that the country could rebuild foreign-exchange reserves, assist with corporate restructuring, and enhance management.[60] Acquisition by foreign enterprises was now seen as acceptable; a number of South Korea's crown jewels are now foreign-owned. As the debt-equity ratio gradually came down, the government moved to improve corporate governance. It also fashioned a loose reform alliance among "minority shareholders, institutional investors, civic groups, information technology start-up companies, foreign creditors, and foreign fund managers."[61]

Business hoped to weather the reform government. Indeed, Kim lost his majority in the Assembly after the 2000 mid-term elections. Few big deals went through. While the *chaebol*'s debt equity level generally dropped, that of the top *chaebol* still exceeded 300 percent. Only two out of ten leading *chaebol* sold substantial assets. Debts are still more often rescheduled than liquidated. Financial vulnerability is still high, as operating profit just about equals interest payments (compared to a multiple of six in the case of Taiwan). The top five *chaebol* only saw modest debt reductions, little effort to induce FDI, but some effort at issuing new stock and bonds, and much effort in turning to non-bank financial institutions. Debt equity with the banks was not welcomed as the *chaebol* did not want to dilute control, and the banks remain inexperienced. The *chaebol* continue to dominate credit allocation, and banks continue to pump in money as a result of reversed leverage.[62] Yet the reformist government has irrevocably introduced new rules of engagement between state and business. While state and business see the corporate debt problem as a national problem and work together to alleviate it, no *chaebol* is now too big to fall, as the case of Daewoo vividly illustrates. Foreign capital is now welcomed as an agent for development. In addition, the *chaebol* are no longer the only interlocutor, as vigilant citizen groups, notably small shareholders, are also challenging corporate power. Moreover, the bargaining arena between state and business is no longer limited to the administration or legislature, but has extended to the judiciary, as the government uses this avenue to enforce inheritance tax laws and shareholder rights. Ironically, family feuds over inheritance are also helping the government to break down and rationalize the *chaebol*. The *chaebol*'s reverse leverage over the banks remains the most potent bargaining chip, as the government cannot let banks fall as it does the *chaebol*.

The emergence of a more polymorphous state-business relationship in Taiwan. Confronted with an identical shift in the global production, trade, and finance regimes since the late 1980s, the Taiwanese economy has exhibited a higher degree of adaptability. The economic restructuring of the past decade also gave rise to a more polymorphous state-business relationship. In South Korea, the *chaebol* remained the key players in both the trend of overseas business expansion and the rush to go high-tech. In Taiwan, it was the export-oriented SMEs that took the lead in building up new transnational production networks throughout the region and the start-ups that laid the foundation for the island's high-tech sector. The established diversified business groups have been laggard on both scores.[63] Both the internationalized SMEs, the so-called mini-multinationals, and high-tech start-ups expanded at a stunning speed during the 1990s. By the end of the 1990s, some of Taiwan's fastest-growing high-tech firms had rivaled or even surpassed the established diversified business groups. Both the mini-multinationals and the high-tech start-ups grew largely outside the official state-sponsored, KMT-directed, corporatist framework. They presented challenges to the state's economic steering capability, but also opportunities for developing new forms of state-business relationships.

The overseas expansion of Taiwanese firms was prompted by rising

labor costs and land prices, the tightening-up of environmental regulation, and, most decisively, by the rapid appreciation of the New Taiwan
dollar since 1987. Initially, most Taiwanese investment capital flowed
into Thailand, Malaysia, and the Philippines. Subsequently, with the
acceleration of economic reform in mainland China, the coastal area
across the Taiwan Straits became more attractive than Southeast Asia to
Taiwanese firms, due to both its geographic proximity and its cultural
affinity. The coastal provinces were especially attractive to Taiwan's
SMEs because most such enterprises lacked the financial resources and
managerial skills for a fully fledged internationalization strategy. In less
than a decade, Taiwan became the largest source of foreign direct investment in the region after Japan.

While encouraging and facilitating a "southward strategy" (that is,
investing in ASEAN), the government imposed stringent restrictions on
the private sector's "westward strategy" (investing in mainland China)
on national security grounds. The top leadership worried that a rising
level of economic dependence on mainland China would eventually
undermine Taiwan's political independence.[64] Thus, since the early
1990s, prohibitions on cross-Strait economic exchange, in particular an
official ban on direct trade and shipping links, have become a new source
of antagonism between the state and a growing number of Taiwanese
mini-multinationals. Lacking the institutional foundation for collective
action, the SMEs engaged the state through mutual adjustment, in lieu
of direct bargaining. The highly adaptable SMEs often found ways to
circumvent existing official regulations. In the end, they simply disregarded the official investment ban. Despite official discouragement,
between 1987 and 1997 Taiwanese firms invested a total of US$35 bil-
lion in mainland China, far more than the US$25 billion invested in the
ASEAN countries. By 1998, Taiwanese investors, mostly SMEs, had
initiated more than 45,000 projects in mainland China.

During the second half of the 1990s some diversified business groups
and high-tech firms also joined in this "China fever." They were increasingly attracted by the growing purchasing power of China's urban
residents, and by the abundant supply of cheap and well-trained techni-
cians and engineers. Large business groups and elite business
associations began to voice their concern that restrictive measures put
them at a clear disadvantage in competition with the American, Japanese, and European transnational firms.

To ameliorate the conflict, planners have tried to foster a rational
division of labor between the two economies. They relaxed restrictions
on small-scale investment but vigorously exercised their discretionary
power over large-scale investment projects in the mainland. The service
sector, state-designated "strategic industries," defense-related industries,
and high-tech sectors that have received R&D subsidies or assistance
from the government were generally barred from making investments

in mainland China. The planners also cajoled a number of large business groups to postpone or scale down their ambitious investment projects. At the same time, to offset the lure of the mainland business opportunities, the government has taken decisive steps to curb the price of industrial land, relax pollution regulations, sweeten tax incentives, and open up more restricted sectors—such as power generation, telecommunications, and railroad and urban rapid transit systems—to private investment.

More significantly, the exodus of export-oriented manufacturing firms has prompted planning officials to devise and implement new strategies to prevent a "hollowing-out' of local industry. They were especially keen to promote high-tech industries to replace the traditional export-oriented industries, such as textiles and consumer electronics. Taiwan's more decentralized industrial structure has compelled the state to play a strong role in the development and diffusion of new technologies. The government has vastly expanded public-sector budget allocations for research and development. Large amounts of government funds are channeled into state research labs, universities, or R&D consortia, or are used to subsidize the R&D activities undertaken by private firms. These research organizations have transferred developed technologies to new semipublic joint ventures or qualified private firms. Virtually all the most complex and expensive research projects, such as the submicron microelectronics technology and high-definition television, were carried out by state-sponsored R&D consortia, which were typically organized around state research organizations such as Industrial Technology and Research Institute. State research organizations and state-owned financial institutions were also intimately involved in the commercialization of newly acquired technologies. In the 1980s and early 1990s a series of semi-public firms were established to commercialize prototype product technologies developed in state research labs. Initially, government-owned investment funds provided venture capital and filled the void created by the unwillingness of the island's conservative banks to invest in risky start-ups. Subsequently, riding on their demonstrated success, private venture-capital funds mushroomed. By mid-1998, 108 venture-capital funds were licensed, with total funds available of NT$60 billion, making Taiwan the only place in Asia that has successfully followed the U.S. lead in promoting venture capital.

By the mid-1990s, high-tech industries emerged as the new backbone of Taiwan's export sector.[65] In 1997 technology-intensive industries[66] accounted for 39 percent of total manufacturing output and 49 percent of total exports. Since 1995, Taiwan has surpassed Germany and become the world's third-largest exporter of "informatic products" (semiconductors, computers, telecommunication equipment, and so on), after the United States and Japan. Taiwan tops the list in the design and production of such products as monitors, motherboards, keyboards, and scanners.[67]

The rapid expansion of high-tech industries in the 1980s and 1990s fostered a new type of state-business partnership. An array of sunrise sectors has grown around the strategic nodes of public universities, public R&D organizations, and state-run science parks. Also, by the early 1990s, a new high-tech policy network began to take shape. The policy network lined up industrial planning agencies, state-owned industrial banks and investment funds, private venture capital, high-tech start-ups, semi-public research organizations, university research centers, foreign consultant firms, and the Chinese-American science and engineering community. This new partnership found its institutional embodiment in a series of specialized policy review groups created under the Science and Technology Office of the MOEA. These advisory panels brought in representatives of industrial associations and civilian scientists to review government-sponsored research projects and appraise new policy proposals.[68]

This new partnership differed from the old corporatist arrangements in several important ways. First, it was an alliance between two equally strong partners. It was best characterized as a complex interdependence between a highly innovative and globalized private sector and a resourceful and purposeful state bureaucracy. What bound them together was their shared stake in success at the technological catching-up game. Second, all high-tech sectors were self-governed. Most of the participants in the high-tech sector had a sharper business focus than the diversified business groups. They had a higher stake in building up a robust industrial governance structure, which facilitates sector-level cooperation and reduces the incentive for making particularistic demands. Third, unlike traditional family-owned firms, most of the high-tech start-ups operated with a more transparent corporate governance structure from the very beginning. This was because most of them were created by returned Silicon Valley professionals. Also, a transparent corporate governance structure was deemed necessary to attract the best professional employees and to convince institutional investors. Thus their internal regulations often banned them from making under-the-table political donations. Last, they flourished in an increasingly liberal and pluralistic political environment. In fact they could afford to avoid partisan politics altogether. Thus both the planning technocracy and the high-tech start-ups were able to work from a clean slate in establishing a new type of state-business partnership characterized by a high degree of transparency and institutionalized coordination and consultation.

Most notably, the new partnership between the high-tech sectors and the state survived the electoral alternation of power when the old KMT-directed corporatist arrangements crumbled under the new DPP-controlled government, which was inaugurated on 20 May 2000. All three peak business organizations may stand to lose their governmental subsidies, coveted status, and privileged access to the policy-making process if they

remain tied to the KMT. The split over the reelection of the chairmanship of the Chinese National Federation of Industry after Chen Shui-bian's
electoral victory[69] suggests that the KMT's days of enjoying a monopoly
over interest intermediation are numbered.

Theoretical and Policy Implications

It is not easy to generalize theoretical and policy implications from
these two East Asian experiences, as the state-business relationships in
South Korea and Taiwan have followed substantially different trajectories. Nevertheless, we would like to make a few concluding points. First,
during the authoritarian years, in these two NICs the state was neither
predatory nor captured. Instead, it was able to structure ties to business
in ways that were conducive to economic transformation. The state provided a powerful locus for coordinating industrial change and helped
the private sector to absorb and socialize risks associated with market
entry and industry creation.

Second, democratization tends to empower the business elite. The
business sector in both countries began to emerge from a relatively dependent and subordinate relationship to the state because the latter could
no longer unilaterally shape the institutional bases for collective action
among private economic actors. Democracy also complicates the insulation of the state bureaucracy from special interests while maintaining
close links to organized business, that is, "being embedded, but not captured." Democracy makes this more difficult, if not impossible. Under a
democratic regime a robust state-business partnership requires both a
competent, resourceful, and relatively autonomous state economic bureaucracy and a well-organized private sector. If the business sector
cannot constitute itself in the form of various broad-based self-govern-
ing entities, the policy concerns of the business elite inevitably become
narrow in scope and short-term. A more encompassing set of policy
networks, including institutionalized state-business coordination and
policy consultation, provides the most effective mechanism to sustain a
robust state-business partnership and to reduce rent-seeking activities.
A robust state-business partnership not only ensures a country's meaningful participation in the global economy, but also enhances the capacity
of a democratically elected government to respond to the socioeconomic
demands of their domestic constituents.

Lastly, globalization compels an adjustment in state-business relations because it redistributes bargaining power between the state and
private-sector actors and redefines the elements of international competitiveness. As long as the nation-state remains the most important locus
for economic accumulation, however, globalization does not necessarily entail a curtailment of the state's involvement in economic
development. It may prompt the state to reinvigorate its developmental

capacities and define new tasks for state-business collaboration directed toward more equitable participation in the global economy.[70] Globalization rewards countries where the state can serve as a strong catalyst for technological diffusion and innovation and can support the internationalization strategies of corporate actors.

Of course, the answer to the question of how the state-business relationship should be best instituted changes over time, over different stages of economic development, and across different national settings. National conditions constrain institutional arrangements and governance structures. The evolution of institutions is necessarily a path-dependent process.[71] While the lessons of the East Asian NICs may not be readily transferable to other countries, we believe that relevance of the East Asian model is gaining importance each day as more developing economies pursue an outward-looking development strategy and wrestle with an increasingly similar task of harnessing the forces of globalization.

NOTES

1. Peter Evans, "Predatory, Developmental and Other Apparatuses: A Comparative Political Economy Perspective on the Third World State," *Sociological Forum* 4 (Fall 1989): 561–87; Peter Evans, *Embedded Autonomy: State and Industrial Transformation* (Princeton: Princeton University Press, 1995); Tun-jen Cheng, "Political Regimes and Development Strategies," in Gary Gereffi and Don Wyman, eds., *Manufacturing Miracles* (Princeton: Princeton University Press, 1990); Tun-jen Cheng, "Industrial Policies in Korea and Taiwan," in Gunnar K. Sletmo and Gavin Boyd, eds., *Industrial Policies in the Pacific* (Boulder, Colo.: Westview, 1994); Stephan Haggard, *Pathways from the Periphery* (Ithaca, N.Y.: Cornell University Press, 1990); Karl Fields, *Enterprise and State in Korea and Taiwan* (Ithaca, N.Y.: Cornell University Press, 1997); Sylvia Maxfield and Ben Ross Schneider, eds., *Business and the State in Developing Countries* (Ithaca, N.Y.: Cornell University Press, 1996); and T.J. Pempel, "The Developmental Regime in a Changing World Economy," in Meredith Woo-Cumings, ed., *The Developmental State* (Ithaca, N.Y.: Cornell University Press, 1999).

2. Chalmers Johnson, "Political Institutions and Economic Performance: The Government-Business Relationship in Japan, South Korea, and Taiwan," in Frederic C. Deyo, ed., *The Political Economy of the New Asian Industrialism* (Ithaca, N.Y.: Cornell University Press, 1987); Alice Amsden, *Asia's New Giant* (Oxford: Oxford University Press, 1989); Robert Wade, *Governing the Market: Economic Theory and the Role of Government in East Asian Industrialization* (Princeton: Princeton University Press, 1990); and Yun-han Chu, "The East Asian NICs: A State-led Path to the Developed World," in Barbara Stallings, ed., *Global Change, Regional Response* (New York: Cambridge University Press, 1995).

3. Carter J. Eckert, *Offspring of Empire* (Seattle: University of Washington Press, 1991); and Dennis L. McNamara, *The Colonial Origins of Korean Enterprise, 1910–1945* (New York: Cambridge University Press, 1990).

4. The won is South Korea's currency. Tun-jen Cheng, "Political Regimes and Development Strategies," 159.

5. June-en Woo (Meredith Woo-Cumings), *Race to the Swift: State and Finance in Korean Industrialization* (New York: Columbia University Press, 1991).

6. Tun-jen Cheng, Stephan Haggard, and Dave Kang, "Institutions and Economic Policies in Korea and Taiwan," *Journal of Developing Studies* (August 1998): 87–111.

7. Seong Min Yoo, "Corporate Restructuring in Korea," *Joint U.S.-Korea Academic Studies* 9 (1999).

8. Ibid., 140.

9. Sylvia Maxfield and Ben Ross Schneider, eds., *Business and the State in Developing Countries*, 6–15.

10. Chung Lee and Seiji Naya, "Trade in East Asian Development with Comparative Reference to Southeast Asian Experiences," *Economic Development and Cultural Change* 36 (April 1988): 123–52.

11. Alice Amsden, *Asia's New Giant*, 15; cf. David Kang, *Crony Capitalism* (Cambridge: Cambridge University Press, 2002).

12. Seong Min Yoo, "Corporate Restructuring in Korea," 141–42.

13. Robert Wade, *Governing the Market*.

14. Tun-jen Cheng, Stephan Haggard, and Dave Kang, "Institutions, Economic Policy and Growth in Korea and Taiwan," a report to the United Nations Conference on Trade and Development, November 1995.

15. Robert Wade, *Governing the Market*; Shi-mong Chen, et al., *Jiegou Dangguo Zibenzhuyi* (Deconstructing the party-state capitalism) (Taipei: Taipei Society [Chengshe], 1991).

16. Tun-jen Cheng and Stephan Haggard, *Newly Industrializing Asia in Transition* (Berkeley: Institute of International Studies, University of California, 1987); and Yunhan Chu, "The East Asian NICs."

17. Shi-mong Chen et al., *Jiegou Dangguo Zibenzhuyi*.

18. Robert Wade, *Governing the Market*.

19. Tun-jen Cheng, "Guarding the Commanding Heights: The State as Banker in Taiwan," in Stephan Haggard and Chung Lee, eds., *Politics of Finance in Developing Rim Countries* (Ithaca, N.Y.: Cornell University Press, 1993): 55–92.

20. Yun-han Chu, "The Realignment of Business-Government Relations and Regime Transition in Taiwan," in Andrew MacIntyre, ed. *Business and Government in Industrializing Asia* (Ithaca, N.Y.: Cornell University Press, 1994).

21. Edwin A. Winckler, "Institutionalization and Participation on Taiwan: From Hard to Soft Authoritarianism?" *China Quarterly* 99 (September 1984): 481–99; Ming-tong Chen and Yun-han Chu, "Quyu lianhe duzhan, difang paixi, yu shengyihui xuanju" (Regional oligopoly, local factions, and provincial assembly elections), *National Science Council Proceedings-C: Social Sciences and Humanity* 3 (December 1992).

22. Edwin A. Winckler, "Institutionalization and Participation on Taiwan," 481–99; Ping-lung Jiang and Wen-cheng Wu, "The Changing Role of the KMT in Taiwan's Political System," in Tun-jen Cheng and Stephan Haggard, eds., *Political Change in Taiwan* (Boulder, Colo.: Lynne Rienner, 1992).

23. Fu Hu and Yun-han Chu, "Electoral Competition and Political Democratization," in Tun-jen Cheng and Stephan Haggard, eds., *Political Change in Taiwan*, 178–81.

24. Alice Amsden, "The South Korean Economy: Is Business-Led Growth Working?" in Donald N. Clark, ed., *Korea Briefing* (Boulder, Colo.: Westview, 1992), 84.

25. Stephan Haggard and Susan Collins, "The Political Economy of Adjustment in the 1980s," in Stephan Haggard et al., *Macroeconomic Policy and Adjustment in Korea 1970–1990* (Cambridge: Harvard Institute for International Development, 1994): 79.

26. Chung-in Moon, "Changing Patterns of Business-Government Relations in South Korea," in Andrew MacIntyre, ed., *Business and Government in Industrializing Asia* (Ithaca, N.Y.: Cornell University Press, 1994).

27. Eun Mee Kim, *Big Business, Strong State: Collusion and Conflict in South Korean Development, 1960–1990* (New York: State University of New York Press, 1997).

28. Eun Mee Kim, "Chaebol: Victor and Villain of Korean Development?" *Academic Studies Series* 1 (1991): 135–53.

29. Carter J. Eckert, "The South Korean Bourgeoisie: A Class in Search of Hegemony," in Hagen Koo, ed., *State and Society in Contemporary Korea* (Ithaca, N.Y.: Cornell University Press, 1993).

30. Tun-jen Cheng, "Democratic Transitions and Economic Policymaking in South Korea and Taiwan," *Journal of International Political Economy* (March 1997): 41–60.

31. Chung-in Moon and Jongryn Mo, "Introduction," in Chung-in Moon and Jongryn Mo, eds., *Democratization and Globalization in Korea* (Seoul: Yonsei University Press, 1999); and Seong Min Yoo, "Corporate Restructuring in Korea."

32. Chung-in Moon, "Changing Patterns of Business-Government Relations in South Korea"; and Chung-in Moon and Jongryn Mo, "The Kim Young Sam Government," in Chung-in Moon and Jongryn Mo, eds., *Democratization and Globalization in Korea.*

33. Jongryn Mo and Chung-in Moon, "Introduction," in Chung-in Moon and Jongryn Mo, eds., *Democracy and the Korean Economy* (Stanford: Hoover Institution Press, 1998).

34. Jongryn Mo and Chung-in Moon, "Democracy and the Origins of the 1997 Korean Economic Crisis," in Chung-in Moon and Jongryn Mo, eds., *Democracy and the Korean Economy.*

35. Charles Lindblom, *Politics and Markets* (New York: Basic Books, 1977).

36. Seong Min Yoo, "Corporate Restructuring in Korea," 143–44.

37. Kent E. Calder, *Crisis and Compensation* (Princeton: Princeton University Press, 1988).

38. HeeMin Kim, "The Formation of the Grand Conservative Coalition," in HeeMin Kim and Woosang Kim, eds., *Rationality and Politics in the Korean Peninsula* (Osaka: International Society for Korean Studies, 1995).

39. Tun-jen Cheng, "Democratic Transitions and Economic Policymaking in South Korea and Taiwan."

40. Fun-koo Park, "Industrial Relations in Transition: Recent Development and Prospects," in Lawrence Krause and Fun-koo Park, eds., *Social Issues in Korea* (Seoul: KDI Press, 1993): 44–55.

41. Se-il Park, "Labor Reform," *Joint U.S.-Korea Academic Studies* 9 (1999).

42. Tun-jen Cheng and Brantly Womack, "General Reflections on Informal Politics in East Asia," *Asian Survey* 36 (March 1996): 320–37.

43. T.J. Pempel, *Paradigm Shift* (Ithaca, N.Y.: Cornell University Press, 1998).

44. Tun-jen Cheng, "The Economic Significance of Taiwan's Democratization," in Chao-cheng Mai and Chien-sheng Shih, eds., *Taiwan's Economic Success Since 1980* (London: Edward Elgar, 2001), 130–31.

45. For the 1992 figures see *Economic Daily,* 9 March 1995, and for the 1998 figures see the *Annual Report of the Kuomintang Central Finance Committee 1998–1999.*

46. The expansion of the party-owned business empire has not met so far with strong resistance from the private sector. To spread risk and mellow the resentment of private business, the KMT CFC avoided majority control in all new business ventures. Instead, major diversified business groups were invited to form joint ventures. Thus, through business tie-ups, the CFC has built up a seamless web of business partnerships and interlocking interests throughout the private sector. See Gan-lin Hsu, "Political Dominance or Market Logic—A Re-examination of the Party-owned Enterprises," *Taiwan Radical Sociological Review* 28 (1997) (in Chinese). This collusion of interest virtually made many diversified business groups the accomplice of Taiwan's dominant one-party regime.

47. We have borrowed the concept of "competitive clientelism" from Richard Doner and Ansil Ramsay, "Competitive Clientelism and Economic Governance: The Case of Thailand," in Sylvia Maxfield and Ben Ross Schneider eds., *Business and the State in Developing Countries.*

48. For the concept of "hard budget constraint," see Janos Kornai, *The Road to a Free Economy* (New York: W.W. Norton, 1990).

49. Stephan Haggard and Susan Collins, "The Political Economy of Adjustment in the 1980s."

50. Young Rok Cheong, Kap-Young Jeong, and Young-ryeol Park, "The Korean Financial Crisis: Causes, Impacts on FDI, and Implications for Central Asia," *Global Economic Review* 27 (Summer 1998): 37–58.

51. Peter Beck, "Foreign Direct Investment: From Exclusion to Inducement," *Joint U.S.-Korea Academic Studies* 9 (1999).

52. C. Fred Alford, *Think No Evil: Korean Values in the Age of Globalization* (Ithaca, N.Y.: Cornell University Press, 1999).

53. Thomas F. Cargill, "The Need for a New Financial Paradigm," *Joint U.S.-Korea Academic Studies* 9 (1999).

54. Ibid., 123.

55. Byung-sun Choi, "Financial Policy and Big Business in Korea: The Perils of Financial Regulation," in Stephan Haggard and Chung Lee, eds., *Politics of Finance in Developing Rim Countries,* 55–92.

56. Thomas F. Cargill, "The Need for a New Financial Paradigm," 124.

57. Mihae Lim Tallian, "Politics of Financial Reform in the Republic of Korea," Ph.D. dissertation, Graduate School of International Relations and Pacific Studies, University of California, San Diego (1999).

58. Chung-in Moon and Sang-young Rhyu, "Between Flexibility and Rigidity:

Understanding Economic Hard Times in Japan and South Korea," paper presented at the Annual Meeting of the American Political Science Association, Atlanta (September 1999).

59. Duck-Woo Nam, "The Financial Crisis in Korea," *Korea Economic Update* 9 (January 1998).

60. Mikyung Yun, "Foreign Direct Investment: A Catalyst for Change?" *Joint U.S.-Korea Academic Studies* 10 (2000).

61. Peter Beck, "Korea's Embattled *Chaebol:* Are They Serious About Restructuring?" *The Two Koreas in 2000: Sustaining Recovery and Seeking Reconciliation* (Washington, D.C.: The Korea Economic Institute, 2000).

62. For details on corporate reform, see ibid.; Ira Liberman, "Korea's Corporate Reform," *Korea Approaches the Millennium* (Washington, D.C.: The Korea Economic Institute, 1999); and Peter Beck, "Revitalizing Korea's *Chaebol,*" *Asian Survey* 38 (November 1998): 1108–32.

63. The established diversified business groups, aiming for the rising consumption power of the domestic market, expanded more vigorously into the service sector.

64. Tse-kang Leng, *The Taiwan-China Connection: Democracy and Development Across the Taiwan Straits* (Boulder, Colo.: Westview 1996); Yun-han Chu, "The Institutional Foundation of Taiwan's Industrialization: Exploring the State-Society Nexus," in Cheng-sheng Hu and Yun-peng Chu, eds., *The Economics and Political Economy of Development in Taiwan into the 21st Century* (London: Edward Elgar, 1999).

65. For a detailed account, see Chao-cheng Mai and Pei-cheng Chang, *Asian Financial Storm: Taiwan's Experience and Prospect* (Chung-hua Institute for Economic Research, mimeo, 1998).

66. The high-tech industries include four categories: power and electrical machinery (including informatic products), chemicals, biotech, and precision machinery.

67. Chien-chuan Wang et al, "The Role of SMEs in High-tech Industries" (Taipei: Chung-hua Institute for Economic Research, 1998) (in Chinese).

68. Yun-han Chu, "Surviving the East Asian Financial Storm: The Political Foundation of Taiwan's Economic Resilience," in T.J. Pempel, ed., *The Politics of the Asian Economic Crisis* (Ithaca, N.Y.: Cornell University Press, 1999).

69. In this case, Lin Kun-tzong, a candidate favored by the KMT, handily won the chairmanship after his rival, Sun Tao-chun, allegedly backed by Chen Shui-bian, withdrew from the race at the last minute. After he pulled himself out of the race, Sun announced his plan to organize a rival organization that will give greater recognition to the high-tech industries and the "new economy."

70. Linda Weiss, *The Myth of the Powerless State* (Ithaca, N.Y.: Cornell University Press, 1998).

71. Douglas C. North, *Institutions, Institutional Change and Economic Performance* (Cambridge: Cambridge University Press, 1990).

4

STATE-BUSINESS RELATIONS IN LATIN AMERICA

Eduardo Silva

Eduardo Silva *is associate professor of political science and a fellow of the Center for International Studies at the University of Missouri–St. Louis and a senior adjunct research associate of the North-South Center at the University of Miami.* He is author of The State and Capital in Chile *and coeditor of* Organized Business, Economic Change and Democracy in Latin America *and* Elections and Democratization in Latin America, 1980–85. *His articles on business-state relations have appeared in* World Politics, Comparative Politics, The Journal of Inter-American Studies and World Affairs, *and* The Bulletin of Latin American Research. *He also researches the issue of environment and development with a focus on forest policy.*

Economic and political crises provoke change because they call into question whether prevailing models and institutions can provide stable economic growth and legitimate political order. A cycle of political and economic calamities that culminated in the debt crisis of the early 1980s propelled Latin American countries to replace state-led, import-substituting industrialization, populism, and authoritarian regimes with free-market economic reform, fiscal sobriety, and political democracy. These changes renewed interest in business-state relations, mostly because the new economic model required the private sector to become the engine of economic growth. As the main provider of investment and employment, business was expected to play a key role in the implementation of free-market economic reforms; it had to step in where the state bowed out for the model to succeed. Given that the private sector bore this responsibility, the effect of economic reforms on the size and vitality of the private sector, as well as on its organization for production, became significant themes in business-state relations, albeit not the only ones. Analysts also examined how the structure of interaction between business and the state affected the private sector's capacity to implement free-market economic reforms. Free-market reforms certainly suggested a more arms-length relationship, but too little interaction may be detrimental to their success. State actors benefit from contacts with the private sector because it enables them to craft policies that elicit investor confidence, although too close a connection breeds collusion that can be harmful to economic stability. Therefore, the search for a system of interaction between business and the state that was functional for investor confidence and stable economic growth became a significant question. Equally important, business-state relations have a strong bearing on whether business elites support democracy or authoritarianism. This is a broader question than inquiries into the effects of democratization on the structure of business-state relations, but it is highly relevant given the region's cyclical embrace of alternative political regimes.

Uneasiness over the quality of the Latin American entrepreneurial spirit imbued these issues with an additional sense of urgency. As stressed above, the ultimate success of free-market economic reforms, and perhaps of democratization, hinges on the emergence of a dynamic private sector capable of supplanting the state as the engine of economic development. Unlike the prevailing view of East Asian entrepreneurs, however, until recently Latin American business elites were not considered up to the challenge. They were thought of as obstacles to economic and political modernization. State-led development and import-substituting industrialization (ISI) had created weak industrialists incapable of becoming dynamic, modernizing agents of change. At best, they were the weakest link in a triple alliance led by the state and transnational corporations. At worst, they used personal, family, and clientelist business-state relations to intransigently oppose necessary economic change, and supported repressive authoritarian regimes.[1] This "checkered past" reinforced the need to evaluate the extent to which economic and political crises have changed these patterns.

This chapter analyzes these themes in turn. The next section assesses how free-market economic reforms have affected key elements of Latin American business systems, such as the mix between public and private ownership, the relative importance of transnational corporations, the structure of ownership (family/corporate), and the coordination of firms in the economy (conglomeration). The third section examines how three ideal-type structures of business-state relations in Latin America differentially affect the management of economic transformation in the region. The fourth section analyzes the sources of the regime loyalties of Latin American business elites and evaluates whether the current structures of business-state relations offer sufficient inducement for them to support democracy. This section also explores how democratization has affected business-state relations with special emphasis on their place in the construction of broader systems of intermediation between state and society. Running like a thread through these sections is a treatment of how globalization has affected business-state relations and whether the reformed structures are converging on an Anglo-American model. The analysis will mostly draw on Argentina, Brazil, Chile, and Mexico for evidence. And, although the method employed in this chapter differs from that used in the chapter on East Asia, the evidence will also serve to disaggregate the "Latin American model," making it clear that, though Chile is a paradigmatic case, there are significant differences, as well as similarities, in the region.

Structural Adjustment and Business-System Change

As economic crisis, fiscal insolvency, and globalization propelled the dismantling of the developmentalist state, how state policy shaped the private sector emerged as a significant theme in business-state relations. The common view was that the developmentalist state generated weak, state-dependent private sectors.[2] Public enterprise dominated capital-intensive basic industries, utilities, and transportation in alliance with foreign companies that also controlled the consumer durable sector. The state supplied a large (sometimes the largest) share of credit, and its extensive regulation of imports, prices, finance, and foreign exchange tied national businesspeople to the "papa" state and stunted their entrepreneurial spirit.

With gathering force since the mid-1970s, and snowballing during the 1990s, political and, especially, economic crises and globalization induced Latin American states to implement structural-adjustment programs centered on free-market economic reforms to replace state-dominated, protected, and highly regulated economies. Key policies included privatization; extensive liberalization of finance, commerce, and trade; fiscal stability; deregulation; and unified exchange rates. In addition to producing macroeconomic stability, it was assumed that the emphasis on the market would stimulate the emergence of a robust, vibrant, and competitive private sector capable of taking the state's place. Many analysts also believed that Latin America's embrace of free-market economic reforms and the reduction in the economic role of the state signaled convergence on a neoliberal political economy centered on an Anglo-American model of capitalism.[3]

In other words, these assumptions postulated that market-oriented structural-adjustment programs had the capacity to significantly alter Latin American business systems, which, from an organizational perspective, can be understood as systems for the coordination and control of economic behavior.[4] This section undertakes a qualitative assessment of these assumptions on four dimensions of the business system. Two key characteristics of business systems focus on the structure of ownership. These are the mix between state and private enterprise, and whether families or shareholders control firms. A third significant feature of developing-country business systems, which is also tied to ownership structure, is the degree to which foreign or domestic capital participates in the private sector. A fourth important characteristic involves the mode of coordination among firms in the economy, meaning patterns of economic concentration in the form of conglomeration and the type of conglomeration (horizontal or vertical). The analysis of changes in ownership structure and patterns of economic concentration offers an entry point for assessing the degree to which the old dysfunctional Latin American business system has been restructured, primarily through policies of privatization and the liberalization of finance and trade. By the same token, how the region's firms have faced the pressures of international expansion in a global economy offers interesting contrasts with other regions.

The pre-crisis Latin American business system. During the period of import-substituting industrialization (ISI), Latin American business systems exhibited several well-known characteristics. One was a high degree of state enterprise. Many countries also established state-administered credit-based financial systems to provide investment funds for domestic firms and to implement industrial policy.[5] In this context, an industrial policy that subsidized credit and utilities and controlled foreign-exchange rates encouraged the emergence of industrial conglomerates or the expansion of old-line conglomerates into industry. In fact, many of Latin America's conglomerates had their origins during the ISI period, although some were founded earlier in the primary-product-export era.[6] Transnational corporations also began to set up subsidiaries to penetrate domestic markets, frequently at the behest of government policy makers seeking to boost investment and technology. High tariff barriers ensured inward-looking behavior for most firms not in the agro-mineral exporting sectors.

In addition to these characteristics, family and personal ownership was a prominent feature of Latin American business systems that extended to the control of conglomerates. Personal and family ownership was organized either formally or informally and governed financing, asset control, and the distribution of resources. This form of ownership provided great decision-making flexibility, which was especially useful during periods of economic and political uncertainty. The fact that most firms were limited, privately held enterprises that did not quote shares in open markets enhanced decision-making flexibility.

Conglomerate structure was also frequently vertical and organized around a flagship company. For example, the Monterrey Group in Mexico expanded from beer production to the bottling industry, metal sheeting, and corrugated cardboard manufacture. The Argentine group Bunge y Born started in cereal distribution and later went into food processing. Yet vertical integration could be combined with horizontal linkages, as occurred in Chile. For instance, the Edwards group combined newspaper publishing, insurance, banking, fishing, breweries, and more. The Matte group, among other activities, spanned banking, food processing, breweries, insurance, and construction.[7]

Latin American business systems in the wake of economic crisis and structural adjustment. The Latin American experience certainly corroborates the perception that economic and political crises provide powerful incentives for initiating structural-adjustment programs. Yet such crises are best thought of as necessary but not sufficient factors, because the cases differed markedly both in whether political leaders responded to such pressures with free-market reforms and in the timing, sequencing, and pace of reforms.[8] There were definitely leaders (Chile), laggards (Brazil), and quitters (Venezuela), although most countries began structural reforms some time between the second half of the 1980s and the early 1990s.

With few exceptions, Latin American nations have been implementing free-market economic reforms centered on fiscal restraint, macroeconomic stability, privatization, financial-sector liberalization, and opening to international competition. This suggests that economic policy and much of the legal-institutional support for markets in the region are converging on a neoliberal model. Moreover, it seems clear that structural-adjustment programs have generated some of the sweeping transformations of Latin American business that were postulated. For example, a substantial literature has shown that privatization, where rigorously applied, had the expected result of reducing the size of the state component of the business system and increasing that of the private sector.[9] As will be seen later on in this section, structural-adjustment policies also increased the presence of transnational corporations in national economies. Opening protected markets converted surviving businesses into more vital and competitive enterprises.

Yet not all of the changes have been so unidirectional, especially on the issue of convergence on Anglo-American models of neoliberalism. For example, privatization and financial-sector liberalization certainly transformed state-administered financial systems. Nevertheless, the process has not resulted in convergence on an Anglo-American capital-market-based financial system in which ownership based on publicly traded shares is separated from the management of firms. Obviously, some capital markets have emerged due to purchases made by publicly traded transnational corporations. Yet many of the national firms that participate in them only issue nonvoting stock and in percentages that are small compared to the overall value of the firm. Instead, family and personal ownership and closed-property firms that do not quote shares on stock exchanges still predominate.

Given the privatization of the banking system, and the absence of well-developed capital markets, one might conclude that Latin America is moving toward a private-bank credit-based financial system. Yet governments have kept interest rates at such high levels to attract international financial capital to bolster current account and reserve positions that many large-scale companies frequently find it ruinous to turn to their national banking systems for long-term investment funds. Consequently, large firms have often resorted to raising such funds abroad, for example, by issuing American Drawing Rights (ADRs) in the capital markets of the United States, or by dipping into retained earnings.[10] Furthermore, despite all of these changes, the underlying logic upon which the domestic private-sector side of the Latin American business systems rested has resisted fundamental alterations. Structural reforms have done little to change two central features of Latin American business systems: the structure of ownership and the form of coordination between firms in the economy. Then as now, as mentioned above, Latin American business systems are still fundamentally characterized by family or personal ownership. They also exhibit a high degree of concentration in vertical or horizontal patterns of conglomeration in virtually every economic sector. If anything, by increasing the size of the private sector, structural reforms have amplified these features.

In conjunction with inadequate regulatory environments, these characteristics can obstruct efficient and effective policy responses to periods of economic instability that so frequently occur during structural adjustment. Closed property and personal or family ownership, combined with conglomeration, produce a web of interlocking directorships based on strong family or personal loyalties. Firms within a conglomerate own each other's shares and loan each other money free from public scrutiny. Thus financial and asset transactions are frequently made on the basis of association rather than economic value. From a microeconomic perspective, these networks based on personal association could, and did, behave like market-distorting cartels. In addition to this negative feature, collusion within the inter-firm network of a business group can turn these arrangements into examples of crony capitalism, if one defines crony capitalism broadly to encompass more than collusion between government and business. In these features and behavior, Latin American conglomerates were not so different from the South Korean *chaebol* or the overseas-Chinese family-owned conglomerates in Southeast Asia.[11] The irony is that the difficulties created by this form of cronyism had manifested themselves some time before the East Asian crisis of 1997–99 popularized them. For whatever reason, however, their implications for other, more successful, regions were ignored.

Many free-market economic reforms, but especially privatization, generally favored conglomerates by creating new ones and giving existing ones opportunities to adjust and expand. Chile, during the military government of General Augusto Pinochet, was the first country significantly to privatize its economy during the 1970s. The less-than-transparent auctioning process generated powerful new conglomerates, especially the Cruzat-Larraín and the Vial/BHC groups. These conglomerates conducted aggressive, highly leveraged merger and acquisitions programs that allowed them to control the lion's share of assets in Chile. Their holdings spanned the financial sector, domestic and international commerce, real estate, insurance, and manufacturing. From their dominant position in the newly liberalized financial sector, these new conglomerates focused on gaining control of internationally oriented and import-competitive companies in addition to acquisitions in the nontradeable sector. More traditional conglomerates, such as the Matte and Luksic groups, among others, adjusted admirably to the opportunities that privatization and structural economic reform provided.[12] The top management of these, and other, conglomerates provided significant support for the military government's free-market economic reforms.[13]

As in much of the rest of Latin America, most of Mexico's large firms had been organized in family-owned conglomerates. These firms successfully adjusted to the free-market economic reforms of the 1980s and 1990s. Mexico began to privatize in the 1980s during the administration of Miguel de la Madrid and accelerated the process during Carlos Salinas de Gortari's term (1988–94). As in Chile, the process generated opportunities for traditional conglomerates to expand and for the emergence of new economic groups. Typically, these groups exhibit a structure of diversified investment with, among the largest conglomerates, the predominance of financial-industrial groups that also have holdings in commercial and service-related activities.[14] The financial component of this structure had its origins in the privatization of the banks, when many of the large industrial groups bought banks and other financial institutions. The privatization of public enterprises in transportation, telecommunications, steel, mining, agribusiness, and food processing allowed traditional and, especially, new conglomerates to expand into these economic sectors. New financial groups also sprang up and expanded rapidly as a result of bank privatization and general financial-sector liberalization.[15]

There were a number of important traditional and new conglomerates that benefited from privatization and other free-market reforms in Mexico. The largest traditional diversified financial-industrial conglomerates that successfully took advantage of structural adjustment were Visa (beverages and telephones), Vitro (glass and consumer durables), and Grupo Maseca (industrial maize). The most important new diversified financial-industrial conglomerates to emerge were Carso (telephones, tobacco, electrical, metallurgy, rubber, and mining) and Pulsar (agro-industry). Alfa is the best-known traditional group without a bank (food, steel, chemicals, petrochemicals, and telephones). The new financial-industrial Banamex-Accival group participated heavily in the privatization of the telephone industry, although it lost control of Banamex after the 1995 financial crisis.[16] In the process, Carlos Slim, the leading director of the Carso group, emerged as the richest new billionaire in Mexico and (as will be seen later) developed a powerful alliance with the Salinas administration.[17]

Privatization and free-market economic reforms in Argentina had much the same effect with respect to their impact on the private-sector component of the business system and the political management of the reform process. The efforts of past military governments and the Alfonsín administration notwithstanding, rapid privatization and a coherent structural-adjustment program did not get started until Carlos Menem's terms (1989–99).[18] According to Bisang, Argentine conglomerates are frequently family-controlled and are highly centralized in such important functions as financing, human-resources management, and decisions on acquisitions and mergers, while being operationally decentralized.[19] The Menem administration privatized more than 100 firms in its first three years. Unlike the process in Chile and Mexico, the Argentine conglomerates that participated in the purchase of those companies overwhelmingly tended to be well-established ones—conglomerates born in the import-substitution phase of the economy and even in the earlier primary-product-export period. These included Pérez Company in energy, petrochemicals, telephones, and highway tolls; Techint in energy, steel, telephones, and transportation; B. Roggio in transportation; and Socma and Bunge y Born in utilities. New conglomerates formed in the 1990s include CEI and the Exxel Group in communications, chemicals, paper, and various services.[20]

In Brazil, privatization has been on the policy agenda throughout the 1990s. It began during the administration of Fernando Collor de Mello (1990–92) and, after his impeachment, sputtered under Itamar Franco (1992–95), but, mainly because of the state's fiscal crisis, did not die. The governments of Fernando Henrique Cardoso (1995–present) breathed new life into the process, and a substantial amount of privatization has taken place during his tenure.

As in the other cases, privatization spurred a boom in mergers and acquisitions that had significant effects on Brazil's economic groups and the strategies they employed to take advantage of the opportunity. A number of conglomerates concentrated on vertical integration, such as the Gerdau group in specialty steel and the Klabin group in pulp and paper. Others expanded rapidly and diversified. This was the case with the Grupo Vicunha, which, from its base in textiles and commercial activities, aggressively expanded into steel and utilities. Meanwhile, the Suzano conglomerate, a giant in pulp and paper, expanded its holdings in the petrochemical sector. Finally, other conglomerates, such as the well-established Votorantim group, used privatization as a means to continue its traditional pattern of diversification, with holdings in cement, metallurgy, pulp and paper, agribusiness, the chemical industry, and banking.[21]

The free-market reform-induced process of conglomerate adjustment and restructuring affected the traditional ownership patterns of Brazil's economic groups, but did not revolutionize them. Brazil's conglomerates were, in the main, family-controlled economic groups, although many also had highly professional managerial organization.[22] The complicated ownership structure of many privatized state enterprises forced some changes in that ownership style. Frequently, investment groups in which several conglomerates participated, often in conjunction with international corporations, bought the large public enterprises auctioned by the state. As a result, management had to be coordinated between the controlling shareholding groups. Overall, however, family-controlled conglomerates remained the norm.[23]

By the year 2000, in all cases, privatization, financial and trade liberalization, and deregulation had substantially increased the participation of transnational firms in the financial sector, mining, utilities, telecommunications, pulp and paper, port management, petrochemical sectors, and other industries. In many instances, domestic business groups were in partnership with foreign concerns, frequently in a minority position. Sometimes, as occurred in Brazil, the arrival of new international companies and the consortia they formed with domestic capital pushed old-line domestic conglomerates down in the national rankings of great economic groups. The international firms certainly diluted the tendency toward family-controlled, closed-property economic groups in Latin America by introducing more Anglo-American styles of business-system organization. But they did not displace family control as the principal means of organizing ownership in the domestically owned business system, although, of course, most had adopted professional management practices.

Overcoming economic crisis, restoring investor confidence—especially in the foreign sector—and the political management of free-market economic reforms, all of these factors influenced privatization in the cases examined above. Yet in the case of the countries that privatized first, Chile and Mexico, financial crises after structural adjustment forced the states to intervene in the financial systems of their countries. The economic and political management of those crises, especially in the case of Chile, deeply affected many of the financially centered conglomerates that had been formed in the initial waves of privatization.

Chile suffered one of its worst economic downturns between 1982 and 1983. The debt crisis that rocked Mexico placed a severe strain on Chile's fixed foreign-exchange policy and contributed to a strong liquidity crunch. The government responded with various policy measures to ease the stress on Chile's currency and financial system. In the end, however, it was forced to place major banks and non-bank financial institutions in receivership, effectively dismantling some of the major new conglomerates that had formed during the military government. The targeted conglomerates suggested that the intervention was part of a political strategy for managing the crisis.[24]

Most of Chile's conglomerates had expanded through a strategy of highly leveraged acquisitions. The largest, Vial and Cruzat-Larraín, had acquired a substantial share of Chile's financial institutions, through which they financed many of the operations of the firms they controlled. Ownership based on family control and close personal ties among friends, coupled with interlocking directorships, led to a pervasive policy of hiding accumulating nonperforming loans in companies with untenable debt-to-equity ratios. When the government attempted to ease Chile's liquidity crunch, these two conglomerates used their market power to soak up most of the dwindling credit, endangering the solvency of many other economic groups and independent large companies.

These two conglomerates, and allied economic groups, did more than threaten the finance ministry's desperate attempts to keep the currency and financial system from collapsing. Their use of market power to thwart the economic authorities' policy was fueling an economic crisis that threatened the cohesiveness of the business community's heretofore solid support for the military government's free-market economic reforms. Thus, in 1983, it was clear that the government would have to intervene in the financial system to keep the country from sinking into economic chaos. But the decision to concentrate on the financial institutions of the Cruzat-Larraín and Vial groups was at least partially politically motivated. The authorities wanted to dismember those two because of the challenge they posed to the economic and political management of the crisis. That goal was achieved by placing under government control the financial institutions that owned the nonperforming loans of over-leveraged holding companies. Javier Vial was tried, convicted, and given a light prison sentence. Manuel Cruzat was reprieved for cooperating with the authorities in untangling the ownership and debt-structure maze of his myriad holdings.

When the Chilean military government placed major financial institutions into receivership it wound up in de facto control of many of the leading corporations of the Chilean economy. This was because Chile's largest firms depended on bank credit for most of their long-term financing and because of their interconnection through the conglomerate structure. It is ironic that a government committed to free-market economic reform had the opportunity, if it wished, to intervene extensively in the economy and reassert public ownership.

By some accounts, there was a strong current in the military government that wanted to exercise that option. Yet General Pinochet and his closest advisors never deviated from the neoliberal path. Instead, they introduced some pragmatic reforms to the model, including capital-account controls to encourage long-term over short-term investment and a reflationary economic policy. More importantly for our purposes, by controlling the debt-restructuring process, the economic authorities influenced which companies and conglomerates weathered the storm better than others. The conglomerates that fared best were those that had exercised more prudence in the amount of debt they incurred to expand their holdings. Diversified conglomerates such as Angelini, Matte, and Luksic grew at a rapid rate.

The state-led private-debt restructuring process also deliberately encouraged Chilean conglomerates to associate with transnational corporations or conglomerates in the second half of the 1980s. These foreign consortia had the financial wherewithal to absorb the high levels of debt with which the companies they bought were saddled. For example, the Carter-Holt-Harvey group (New Zealand) allied with Angelini in the forest and fishing industries. The Fletcher Challenge group, also from New Zealand, allied with the Matte conglomerate in the purchase of highly leveraged assets in the forestry sector. The Luksic conglomerate joined forces with the Paulaner group (Germany) in the beverages sector (beer). [25] Last, but not least, the privatization of utilities (electricity, telephones, sewer systems, ports, transportation, and so on) and of state-owned steel and non-copper mining industries, beginning in the 1980s and continuing through 2001, led to the formation of new, foreign-led, vertically integrated economic groups dominated by Spanish, U.S., Swiss, and Dutch capital. The process by which these public enterprises were sold frequently lacked transparency. In a number of cases, the directors of the public firms (appointed by the government, whether military or civilian) were also major partners in their purchase.[26]

Mexico's conglomerates also suffered from a similar economic crisis in 1994. This was the Mexican peso crisis, with its subsequent "Tequila Hangover" for other Latin American economies, especially Argentina and Brazil. Rapid accumulation of short-term debt during the Salinas administration—again, in the absence of capital controls—led to a run on reserves held by the Mexican Central Bank. This put pressure on the peso and contributed to the meltdown of Mexico's financial system.[27] As occurred in Chile, the government intervened by placing a significant portion of the financial system in receivership, and in some cases turned them over to foreign financial institutions, a tactic not used in Chile. Also unlike Chile, private-sector debt restructuring did not lead to the dismemberment of major conglomerates. Traditional and new diversified conglomerates lost control of their financial institutions and proceeded to restructure without them. But those conglomerates remained powerful, rather than suffering liquidation. Thus, for example, the Grupo Desc lost control of the Grupo Financiero InverMexico and the Grupo Vitro gave up the Grupo Financiero Serfin. Like Chile, however, high levels of debt forced some Mexican conglomerates to seek foreign partners or spin whole companies off to transnational corporations. Philip Morris gained control of Cigatam from the Carso group and British American Tobacco bought Cigarrera La Moderna, which had been part of the Pulsar group.[28]

Regional integration and Latin American business systems. How have regional economic-integration initiatives affected national business systems in Latin America? The turn toward open regionalism by Latin American governments, as expressed in the North American Free Trade Agreement (NAFTA) and the Common Market of the South (MERCOSUR), has accelerated the international expansion of the largest conglomerates of Mexico, Argentina, Brazil, and Chile. It has quickened the pace with which some Latin American conglomerates have jointed the ranks of global transnational corporations. Open regionalism assumes that globalization and regionalism are simultaneous developments. In this context, regional economic interdependency is a means to increase competitiveness in international markets, and a strategy of defense against protectionism in other regions of the world. Open regionalism promotes the regional expansion of private capital, especially among the newly privatized firms.[29] The conglomerates, often in alliance with international companies (or subordinate to them), possess investment capabilities that place them in a privileged position to take advantage of regional economic liberalization. Labor-code reforms that complement economic liberalization, especially labor flexibility and the weakening of collective-bargaining rights, also encourage regional expansion.[30] For these conglomerates, foreign acquisitions are becoming a significant element of their overall operations. Most of their flagship companies produce mature intermediate and finished goods. Foreign direct investment becomes a means to extend their lifecycle and improve profitability through the acquisition of financing, technology, and managerial and operational know-how. The process is accomplished by purchasing assets, building new plants and equipment, and associating with other transnational corporations.[31]

What are some of the characteristics of the process in Argentina, Brazil, Chile, and Mexico? The expansion of Argentine conglomerates abroad has concentrated on MERCOSUR countries, especially Brazil, frequently in partnership with local firms, and has followed three main models. Some conglomerates establish distribution companies abroad that they source from Argentina. Acindor, Bunge y Born, and Alpargatas, among others, have applied this strategy. Others establish their control over production processes and distribution in key market segments, such as pharmaceuticals and milk products. In a third approach, firms that already had a presence abroad take advantage of regional integration to broaden their range, such as Bunge y Born and SOCMA in Brazil. In a

separate process, firms in the newly privatized Argentine energy industry penetrate markets in other energy-producing countries, whether or
not they are in regional trading blocs, by building alliances with host-
country firms. This has been the case with SCP in Bolivia and Pérez
Compac in Venezuela and Ecuador, and YPF has gained access to distribution networks in Chile and Peru.[32]

Brazilian conglomerates expanded at an aggressive rate in 1990s.
According to a study by the National Economic and Social Development Bank of Brazil of 114 subsidiaries established in Latin America by
Brazilian conglomerates, 75 were in MERCOSUR countries. In the majority of the cases (64 percent), Brazilian firms bought existing assets,
often in conjunction with host-country firms. The remaining cases involved the establishment of new assets. Economic groups specializing
in the mining, assembly, pulp and paper, and food-processing industries
tended to invest in distribution centers. Conglomerates concentrating on
metallurgy, transportation materials, chemicals, and construction frequently built new production units.[33] Furthermore, Petrobras's incomplete
privatization has contributed to the emergence of a regional shareholder-
driven energy company. In addition to regional expansion, Brazilian
economic groups have also invested in the United States and Europe.

Chile's leading economic firms have invested mainly in Peru and
Argentina. In the mid-1990s, some announced plans to expand into Brazil
as well. The Matte and Angelini conglomerates bought assets in these
countries to establish a presence in the pulp and paper and wood-panel-
ing industries. But the most publicized foreign investments by
Chilean-based firms are to be found in the energy sector. The Grupo
Enersis, a Spanish-controlled conglomerate that emerged from the
privatization of Chile's energy sector, has made large investments in
Argentina and Peru and has also penetrated into Mexico, Venezuela,
Brazil, and Colombia. The Asian economic crisis negatively affected
the foreign holdings of Chilean firms, because economic slowdown reduced their profitability. As a result, these and other conglomerates pared
down their foreign-acquisitions programs by selling assets, especially
in Argentina. Yet this did not deter them from purchasing attractively
priced assets when available.[34]

Entry into NAFTA coupled with economic and financial liberalization stimulated both new and established Mexican conglomerates to
invest abroad.[35] According to Garrido, foreign direct investment is part
of a proactive strategy to meet international competition in open markets head-on. It allows the flagship firms of Mexican conglomerates to
increase their size while maintaining acceptable levels of profitability.
Most of the firms produce mature intermediate or finished-good products.[36] Expansion abroad allows them to extend the lifecycle of these
mature products and to compete in regional and global markets in mature product lines.

Where have Mexican conglomerates invested? All of them expanded into the United States, with Central America and South America (in that order) as the next favored destinations of Mexican capital. These included diversified conglomerates such as Alfa (petroleum-polyester fibers), Carso (communications), Desc (food processing), Visa (beverages), and Vitro (glass). Vertically integrated economic groups also invested in the United States and tended to expand into Central and South America with more frequency than the diversified ones. Some of the prominent enterprises in this category included Bimbo (Bread), Cemex (cement), Dina (trucks and buses), Geo (construction), Gruma (food processing), Grupo Posada (hotels), and Televisa (Media). A few large firms have also set up shop in Europe, and only Cemex has made significant investments in Asia.[37]

Conclusion. Economic reforms in Latin America suggest convergence on a neoliberal model in terms of policy and legal-institutional patterns. Yet on a more sociological basis (considering ownership forms and linkages across firms) the domestic component of Latin American business systems diverges from Anglo-American shareholder models in which ownership and management are separated. Instead, personal and family ownership, the closed-property firm, and interlocking directorships in conglomerates prevail, as do banks rather than capital markets as the major source of financing for long-term investment. The ownership characteristics facilitate decision making in chronically uncertain business climates. Yet they also make cronyism possible, although the introduction of professional management practices may abate that danger. Privatization has had important impacts as well. First, the increased presence of foreign firms strengthens Anglo-American shareholding practices and professional managerial practices, thus diluting the extent to which Latin American countries exhibit distinct business systems. Second, if not carefully managed, privatization may stimulate the too-rapid expansion of conglomerates on risky financial premises. This contributes to the eruption of economic crises and can make the management of such crises more difficult. Third, Latin American firms prefer to expand within the confines of regional economic blocs rather than enter the markets of developed nations. Fourth, some of the cases suggest limits to which the state is willing to privatize, as evidenced by continuing difficulties in extricating the state from enterprises it has long controlled, as has occurred in the Chilean and Brazilian energy sectors.[38]

Economic Change and Recasting Business-State Relations

Free-market economic restructuring suggests the construction of a more arms-length relationship between business and the state than that which occurs in mixed economies with strong industrial policies.[39] This assumption, however, should not obscure the fact that in both market and mixed economies good policy design by itself does not necessarily lead to optimum results. Whether businesspeople invest, and what they invest in, also depends on how they react to the signals government officials send. Schneider and Maxfield and Evans argue that in some measure this hinges on the quality of the relationship between businessmen and state officials.[40] Where it is mired in bitter antagonism, no policy design, no matter how correct, elicits the desired response from the private sector. By the same token, if the relationship is too cozy, it may degenerate into collusion, also known as crony capitalism. Both East Asian and Latin American cases have shown that this leads to an inefficient allocation of scarce resources through corruption and that it obstructs the management of economic change. Moreover, the relationship between businessmen and state officials is crucial for investment and production because, among other factors, it influences the private sector's confidence to commit resources. When business elites are involved in the policy process they will trust that solutions to thorny policy issues will be reasonable and stand a chance of actually working. By the same token, dense networks of communication between state officials and the private sector provide important information to policymakers on what policies businesspeople are likely to find workable.[41]

During the ISI period, the combination of state enterprise, state-administered credit-based financial systems, and industrial policy contributed to strong, particularistic ties between state actors and the directors of conglomerates and large firms. Important businesspeople sought advantages for their firms in relationships with state officials that sometimes turned collusive. Under this arrangement, the representatives of large firms behaved in a manner congruent with their narrow economic interests. They tended to advocate policies that benefited them without much considering the effects on the larger economic problems facing the nation. The benefits sought frequently took the form of rent seeking or of enhancing the firm's competitive advantage.

A similar situation characterized the state's relationship with organized business interest groups. During the ISI period, the state had generated a proliferation of agencies (including public enterprises) that managed differential industry-specific prices for financing, trade, commerce, energy, transportation, tax incentives, and other economic activities. As predicted by Olson, under these circumstances individual business associations tended to form distributional coalitions with government agencies to obtain and protect rents.[42] These actions frequently made it difficult for economic officials to craft coherent policy packages and promoted economic inefficiency through directly unproductive activities.

Waves of economic and political crises and restructuring over the past 25 years have recast business-state relations in Latin America. The structures of business-state relations that emerged from these complex processes of change depended on many factors. Yet one key factor was how state actors used business groups to generate private-sector support for free-market economic reforms and to consolidate their rule. Moreover, privatization was a key component for building a more robust, or at least bigger, private sector. Consequently, privatization policy played an important role in the reconstruction of business-state relations throughout much of Latin America, with, as will be seen, both positive and negative results for the management of economic change.

Lessons from the Chilean case. Chile has the longest sustained experience with free-market economic restructuring, beginning in the middle of the 1970s. Chile also offers two contrasting, well-defined models for reconstructing business-state relations, one that proved dysfunctional for the management of economic change and one that was much better suited for the task. In Chile, as elsewhere in Latin America, state actors were responsible for setting reform agendas and initiating adjustment programs. Therefore, our analysis of the restructuring of business-state relations in Chile begins with an examination of the reorganization of the state for economic management. Those characteristics also apply to most other Latin American cases that have undertaken sweeping, rapid free-market economic reforms, such as Mexico and Argentina, although, as will be seen, they do not apply to Brazil.

After the armed forces overthrew Salvador Allende and ended democratic rule in Chile in September 1973, the new military government, among other tasks, spent the next few years building a centralized, cohesive state structure for economic management. It established a clear hierarchy of ministries in economic affairs (headed by the Ministry of Finance and the Central Bank) that helped to generate a cohesive policy package. The lead ministries acted as gatekeepers and the delegation of authority from them to other agencies contributed to policy coherence. This hierarchical system also reduced the porosity of state institutions to particularistic interests, giving policy makers significant autonomy from social forces. Thus effective levels of influence by outsiders in the policy process, particularly in agenda setting and policy formulation, were tightly circumscribed. In addition to these features, technocrats that shared neoliberal ideals and held postgraduate degrees in economics staffed lead ministries and economic-planning departments. These were the so-called Chicago boys, because many of them had their graduate degrees from the University of Chicago economics department.[43] Their like-mindedness contributed to policy cohesion.

Most of the features of this structure were functional for the management of rapid economic transformation along free-market lines. One element, however, was not. That was the ideological rigidity of the Chicago boys and their relative lack of professional experience in government service. This feature, in turn, formed part of a system of interaction of the state with the private sector that proved highly dysfunctional for the management of free-market economic restructuring. The system of interaction produced changes in the patterns of conglomeration that contributed to the economic crisis of 1981–83 described in the previous section.

Between 1975 and 1981, the Chilean state's cohesive, centralized, and autonomous economic agencies, staffed by like-minded technocrats, established a close relationship with the directors of a subset of new Chilean conglomerates (headed by the Cruzat-Larraín and the Vial groups), all the while routinely turning away the representatives of business organizations.[44] The directors of these new conglomerates offered the Chicago boys crucial private-sector support for radical economic restructuring because they provided a means to implement that policy. As previously discussed, the new conglomerates used privatization and financial-sector liberalization to crush competitors and to establish their dominance in the most dynamic sectors of the new market-driven economy via a strategy of highly leveraged acquisitions and mergers. It should be added, however, that the privatization process suggested collusive behavior (cronyism) between the state and the directors of the new conglomerates. The Chilean privatization program was not very transparent and, by all accounts, the state sold off blocks of shares (or percentages of the state's ownership) at far below market-value prices. The fact that the directors of these newly rising conglomerates with connections to the Chicago boys bought so many of those companies raised suspicions that they were pre-selected buyers.[45]

The negative consequences of this mode of conglomerate expansion in the context of personal or family ownership, and in the absence of adequate state regulation of financial markets, have already been described. Yet this particularistic style of interaction between the state and the private sector for economic management suggests additional general conclusions as well. Rapid economic liberalization with an emphasis on neutral policy instruments leaves virtually all aspects of policy implementation to the private sector. If policy makers only consult with a narrow group of businesspeople interested in rapid expansion and short-term financial gain, policy may be disproportionately skewed in their favor with little or no attention to the contributions of other sectors of the economy. Thus overall investment figures may remain low, in part, because businesspeople excluded from the policy loop are uncertain of their chances in the new development model. Consequently, balanced economic growth may become compromised and the management of economic problems may become more difficult.

In Chile, the economic crisis unleashed by the implementation of radical reform, aggravated by the particularistic, firm-centered system

of interaction between the state and business, generated a political crisis for the military government in 1983. Massive monthly mobilizations
calling for redemocratization began in May, and the private sector,
wracked by bankruptcy, debt, and economic depression, clamored for a
more flexible, pragmatic approach to free-market economic restructuring. By 1984, the military government had regained firm political control
and orchestrated a thorough restructuring of business-state relations.

   This system of interaction was more functional for the generation of
cohesive policy packages supported by a broader spectrum of the private sector than previously. The state retained most of its previous
attributes; its organization for economic management remained cohesive, centralized, highly autonomous, and staffed by technocrats, with
one important difference. The technocrats, while still trained in neo-
classical economics, were more pragmatic and flexible in their approach
to policy problems than the Chicago boys. They were committed to free-
market economics, but were also willing to break with orthodoxy if
necessary. The nature of the interlocutor on the business side also
changed. Instead of linking up with firms, state agencies primarily dealt
with organized businesses, of which the most important was Chile's
encompassing business association, the Confederación de la Producción
y Comercio (CPC).[46]

   The involvement of the CPC and its member associations (the umbrella organizations for the industrial, agricultural, commercial, mining,
construction, and financial sectors) on a regular basis in the later stages
of the policy process generated broad-based private-sector support for
the government's economic policies. As an encompassing business organization, the involvement of the CPC ensured that the general interests
of business would be attended to—the very interests that are crucial to
maintaining confidence in government economic policy making and to
inducing investment from the private sector. The state opened multiple
channels of interaction that allowed the private sector to inform state
officials of the conditions under which proposed state economic policy
would work best to induce renewed investment. These channels included
high-level meetings with top policy makers during the early stages of
policy making, to iron out major issues. After that, regularized meetings between the technical staff of the relevant government agencies
and the technical staff of the encompassing organizations' relevant member associations—the sectoral peak associations—smoothed out more
technical points. In this way, more professionally and technically competent sectoral peak associations ameliorated the distributional conflicts
and unproductive behavior ascribed to business interest groups.[47]

   This style of interaction between business and state officials in Chile
has contributed to investment in production since 1984 through a dual
process which built confidence that policy would address the needs of
the economy and of the firms in various economic sectors. On the one

hand, Chilean businessmen have felt confident that solutions to national economic problems would not be at the expense of their interests. On the other hand, policy makers have benefited in policy design. They get a much better idea of how business elites will react to a policy. This arrangement characterized the last seven years of the military government, continued after its end in 1990, and is still operating as of this writing. In the new democratic period this arrangement also helped to smooth a potentially conflictive relationship between the private sector and the governments of center-left Concertación de Partidos por la Democracia (CPD), which has governed Chile since 1990. This was because the CPD was a coalition of parties that had formerly constituted the political opposition to the dictatorship and had been vilified by the business sector during the military government. Tax and labor-code revisions, environmental policy, and negotiation over regional integration have been highly visible issue areas in which the above-described interaction between business and the state has been put into action in the administrations of Patricio Aylwin (1990–94), Eduardo Frei Ruiz-Tagle (1994–2000), and Ricardo Lagos (2000–present).[48]

Business-state relations in Mexico, Argentina, and Brazil. The Chilean case offered two neatly contrasting arrangements for business-state relations in Latin America. Both featured a cohesive, centralized, and highly autonomous state staffed by technocrats. The major difference lay in the type of business actor that the state predominately associated with and the structure of interaction between the state and the private sector. In one type, state actors had a particularistic relationship with the directors of a handful of new conglomerates. Moreover, state actors used privatization policy to expand those conglomerates rapidly in the interest of building immediate support for the free-market economic model. This relationship proved unstable. The subsequent model of interaction between business and the state emphasized business peak associations, and especially the encompassing association, as the main private-sector interlocutor with the state in a more regularized and institutionalized setting. This system proved more functional for economic growth and stability. It must be stressed that this system did not exclude interaction between firms (especially those of leading conglomerates) and the state. To the contrary, what made it work was the fact that all of the major Chilean firms were members of the sectoral peak associations and of the CPC. Yet the representation of their interests, through their organizations and on technical grounds, forced them to agree on minimum common positions, thus removing many of the negative features of more particularistic relations.

Mexico exhibits features of both of the ideal typical arrangements for business-state relations suggested by the Chilean case. The fact that Mexican business groups were officially linked to the state via a state-corporatist system of interest-group articulation certainly complicates the issue.[49] Yet on many major issues, and increasingly so since the beginning of the 1990s, the important business-state interactions have taken place outside the official corporate structure.[50] Consequently, the analysis that follows below focuses on those extra-official linkages, which fall into two broad categories. First, in some instances, business-state relations predominately entail interaction between state actors and the directors of Mexico's principal conglomerates. Second, on other occasions, they may involve negotiation with functional equivalents of encompassing business associations that emerged independently of the corporatist structure. In both instances, the state structure for economic management is reasonably centralized, cohesive, relatively autonomous, and staffed by technocrats.

Privatization policy offers the best example in Mexico of the consequences of a particularistic relationship between state actors and institutions with a set of conglomerates bent on rapid expansion. Carlos Salinas de Gortari's administration (1988–94), which had publicly declared its support for Mexico's large-scale firms and conglomerates, presided over the bulk of privatization efforts in Mexico.[51] During his six-year term, 939 public enterprises were either spun off to the private sector or liquidated, leaving only 216 entities under public ownership when Salinas left office in 1994. By all accounts, the privatization process, especially the transfer of non-financial enterprises, was not a transparent one. The state sold blocks of shares to the flagship firms of major conglomerates, frequently on very favorable terms to the buyer. The process seemed more geared toward building a source of support for state-led economic reforms and for Salinas personally, rather than the integrated development of the Mexican economy. As in the Chilean case, this was especially true with regard to favoritism for the new conglomerates. As mentioned previously, the rise of Carlos Slim and his close alliance with Salinas personified that process as did a small dinner party early in 1993 to which Salinas invited, among others, Carlos Slim, Carlos Hernández (of the Banamex group), Emilio Azcarraga (communications giant Televisa), and Adrián Sada (Monterrey group). Many of them acquiesced to Salinas's request for a 25 million dollar contribution to the PRI's upcoming presidential campaign. When news of the dinner was leaked to the press, however, the resulting scandal persuaded the donors to cancel their contributions. In addition to building support for the administration, in some instances the favoritism displayed toward some of the economic groups also responded to the personal economic interests of high government officials.[52]

As seen in the previous section, rapid expansion of new conglomerates on the basis of highly leveraged purchases had the same negative impact on economic stability that occurred in the Chilean case. The difference was that the Mexican government restructured the conglomerates instead of destroying them. Perhaps this more moderate stance was due to the fact that Mexico's new conglomerates never challenged the more established economic groups or the state to the degree that occurred in Chile, and they never gained such a commanding, dominant position within the national economy that the new Chilean conglomerates obtained.

Whether this particularly unhealthy relationship between the state and the Mexican private sector was an aberration in the process of Mexico's free-market economic restructuring remains to be seen. Concomitant with it, however, the economic crises of the 1980s and structural adjustment in the 1990s also generated a new relationship with organized business. The directors of Mexico's most prominent firms founded a voluntary association called the Consejo Mexicano de Hombres de Negocio (CMHN) in the 1960s as a vehicle to represent the interests of large-scale business, something that official state corporatism had neglected. To counter perceived threats to large-scale business in the early 1970s (resurgent populism), the CMHN founded Mexico's version of an encompassing business organization, the Consejo Coordinador Empresarial (CCE), which articulated demands for free-market economic reforms. Miguel de la Madrid's administration (1982–88), which began Mexico's process of economic stabilization cum restructuring, turned to the CCE and the CMHN to gain political support for its stabilization program and to restore business confidence. These organizations also supplied information on the effects of price controls and monitored those controls. Mexico's financial-sector organizations have performed similar information-supply and monitoring functions in the National Banking and Securities commission that was created in 1996 in the wake of Mexico's most recent economic crisis. By the same token, the CCE created a spin-off organization, the Coordinadora Empresarial de Organismos de Comercio Exterior (COECE), to build political support for NAFTA and to provide critical information to government officials negotiating the treaty.[53]

The relationship between the state and business peak and encompassing associations built private-sector political support for economic stabilization and restructuring and provided effective information-gathering and monitoring services for much the same reason they did in Chile. These organizations did not exclude large-scale firms from the policy process. To the contrary, the associations successfully completed their functions because large-scale firms (many of them the principal firms of leading conglomerates) dominated them. The advantage for stability was threefold. First, the most important businesspeople of Mexico had to negotiate common positions, thus avoiding the worst evils of particularism. Second, organizations such as the CMHN spent considerable sums upgrading the research capacity of key associations, such as the CCE. Third, these elements added a measure of transparency to the interaction between business and the state, at least among the most economically significant members of the private sector.

Argentina offers a sharply contrasting case to both Chile and Mexico. After disastrous flirtations with free-market economic restructuring during the military government of 1976–82, and failed experimentation with heterodox adjustment after redemocratization under Raúl Alfonsín (1983–89), Argentina began a sustained economic stabilization and free-market reform program during the two consecutive administrations of Carlos Menem (1989–2000). That program continued under President Fernando de la Rúa (1999–2001). In this complex sequence of change, the features of business-state relations most relevant for the management of recent economic transformations were forged during the governments of Carlos Menem.

Unlike Chile and Mexico, the Argentine case offers an example where state actors established an enduring, direct, and unmediated relationship with the nation's principal conglomerates as the predominant form of interaction between business and the state. Upon taking office in 1989, Menem, leader of the Justicialista party—the once-archetypical and frequently banned populist political party of Juan Domingo Perón—decided that orthodox economic stabilization and neoliberal reforms were the solution to Argentina's deep economic crisis.[54] From the very beginning, Menem established close relations with Argentina's leading conglomerates as a means of regaining the Argentine private sector's confidence and support for his economic policies. This was evidenced by his choices for his administration's economic team, headed by Minister of Economy Manuel Roig of the Bunge y Born conglomerate, one of Argentina's leading established economic groups. After some initial success, the Bunge y Born economic plan ultimately failed to stabilize the economy and a more technocratic figure, Domingo Cavallo, replaced Roig as minister of economy. The central feature of Cavallo's stabilization plan, fixing the price of peso in relation to the dollar with unrestricted convertibility, proved durable until the end of 2001. He also proceeded with the free-market restructuring of the Argentine economy, of which privatization was a central feature.

Privatization policy under Menem's government offers a window into the essence of unmediated relations between the state and the private sector during Argentina's crucial economic restructuring period. To be sure, the scale of foreign investment in the privatization process (especially Spanish and not always by private companies) was large. As political leaders had done in Chile and Mexico, however, Menem also used privatization as a tool for the political management of free-market economic reforms, specifically as a means to obtain political support from big business. Like in Chile and Mexico, the divestiture process was not transparent since the state often brokered blocks of shares instead of selling them in open markets. This meant that buyers were frequently pre-selected and, as seen in the previous section, leading Argentine conglomerates benefited greatly from the process. Moreover, the public-utilities sector, transportation, and other services were unusually lucrative for the conglomerates. The state sold the public enterprises in those monopolistic sectors before it established a regulatory framework and set rates for the privatized economy. As a result, private firms set their own rates and then negotiated regulation with the government from a position of strength, reaping large profits in the bargain. In return for these practices, once the principal conglomerates were convinced that Menem was going to win his reelection bid in 1995, they generously funded his campaign. In short, although initially skeptical, the relationship between Menem and the conglomerates strengthened, surpassing even the level of support they had once extended to the military governments of 1976–83.[55]

Although Argentina lacks an enduring encompassing business association like Chile's CPC or Mexico's CCE, it does have well-established powerful sectoral organizations, such as the Unión Industrial Argentina (UIA), which represented the interests of large-scale firms. Unlike the case in Chile and Mexico, however, there has been little for them to do in the 1990s and early 2000s due to the absence of social pacts to manage inflation, the success of the economic stabilization program, and the benefits of privatization and economic liberalization for large-scale firms.[56] Under these circumstances, sectoral peak associations that represented large-scale business, such as the UIA, took a back seat to direct representation via the firms that dominated the association.

Although they failed in Chile, unmediated relations between the state and big business as the principal form of interaction probably succeeded in Argentina because the state turned to well-established conglomerates as part of Menem's strategy to build political support from recognized business elites. By contrast, in Chile, and partially in Mexico, political leaders used privatization to foment new conglomerates in an effort to quickly create new business elites capable of competing with established ones. Thus, in the context of closed property, personal or family ownership, and interlocking directorships, rapid conglomerate expansion involved an element of financial recklessness in merger-and-acquisitions practices not present in Argentina. In Chile and Mexico those practices contributed to financial crises. In Chile, the crisis forced the private sector to turn to its business organizations to forge a consensus and political leverage to overcome the crisis. It remains to be seen how Argentine conglomerates will weather their nation's financial crisis, which began in December 2001.[57]

Brazil offers yet another variant of how business-state relations are structured in Latin America. Until recently, Brazil was typically considered a case in which conditions impeded the formulation and implementation of a coherent package of policies for economic transformation or for the generation of business confidence. Those conditions include a decentralized, fragmented state structure, where the state lacked cohesion and autonomy, making it relatively porous to social groups, especially business groups. The myriad of ministries, state governments, and parapublic agencies all offer points of entry to business interests. Kurt Weyland documents how, in the absence of an encompassing business association, business interests approach this porous state to gain particularistic benefits.[58] This certainly hinders the progress of free-market economic reforms in Brazil. The situation was particularly acute under President José Sarney (1985–90), but was brought somewhat under control during Fernando Collor's short-lived administration (1990–92), if for no other reason than because Collor limited interaction to interests loyal to him. Although conditions improved during Fernando Henrique Cardoso's government (1995–present), privately business groups seek to avoid paying the costs of macroeconomic stabilization and state reform. Schneider adds that the interaction between business and the state is largely limited to firms and state officials.[59] This reinforces the lack of collective action or consensus politics among businesspeople. It accentuates the search for particularistic benefits that undermine policy coherence and the implementation of free-market economic reforms.

A more benign view of the same situation recognizes that Brazilian presidents lack the degree of insulation from societal and political pressures that exists in Chile, Mexico, and Argentina. Where others see only the ill effects of Brazil's fragmented state, however, this interpretation argues that President Cardoso has made slow but coherent strides in advancing a neoliberal reform agenda that includes economic stabilization, trade opening, and privatization. Where other analysts see particularistic interests at work diluting free-market restructuring, these observers see examples of patient bargaining by the executive with political and social groups to keep the reforms on course. Thus, for instance, business groups may negotiate exceptions for themselves in trade policy, but trade liberalization continues to be the general policy.

More than any other policy, however, and as occurred in the other three cases, the Cardoso administration used privatization as a tool for the political management of free-market economic reforms. In the Brazilian case, privatization was also used as a means to gain political support for constitutional reform. Unlike in the other three cases, privatization favored domestic capital and the process was conducted in a relatively transparent style that suggests more stable business-state relations and conglomerate expansion.

For a number of reasons, foreign companies initially showed little interest in privatization in Brazil. Early efforts depended heavily on participation by national business groups. Only after the *Real* Plan stabilized the Brazilian currency and after it had survived the Mexican financial crisis of 1994 did international investors gain interest between 1997 and 1998. That the highly lucrative utilities, telecommunications, and mining sectors would be sold off boosted their attention. To retain the Brazilian private sector's confidence and support, in a number of cases the Cardoso administration structured the sale of major state enterprises in ways that assured a major role for domestic business groups. This was particularly true of the divestiture of the CVRD, Telebrás, and Petrobrás. Thus privatization was one of a number of free-market economic reforms Cardoso hoped would form the basis for business support for his government, a goal he largely attained.[60]

In contrast to the other three cases, a more transparent and institutionalized relationship between the state and business prevailed in the procedure for privatization. Many of the irregularities, rule bending and breaking, and collusion that characterized the early process in Chile and Mexico, and that were pervasive in Argentina, were largely absent in Brazil. According to Goldstein and Schneider, this was because the institution that guided the process (the Banco Nacional de Desenvolvimento Economico y Social) constituted one of the pockets of efficiency within the Brazilian state.[61] Staffed with capable professionals, bids were open to scrutiny, regulatory mechanisms preceded sales, and companies up for divestiture had stabilized their financial and operating conditions.

Conclusion. Neoliberal reforms suggest the construction of a more arms'-length relationship between business and the state. This is because state actors dominate the policy process and because the market becomes the relevant arena for firms.[62] Nevertheless, arm's-length does not mean nonexistent. Good policy design and the management of economic change are affected by the structure of business-state relations that emerges from the process of economic and political reform. With respect to state structure, the Chilean, Mexican, and Argentine cases suggest that management of rapid economic change benefits from a cohesive, centralized state that enjoys significant autonomy from social and political forces. The Brazilian case confirms that a more fragmented state structure slows down the reform process and makes it more gradual, but it does not necessarily mean that a comprehensive reform package cannot be conducted.

Which business actors state officials interacted with, and how that interaction was structured, also affected the management of economic change. Privatization proved to be a pivotal policy issue area for the initial reconstruction of business-state relations, especially in relation to large-scale firms (or "big business"). First of all, political leadership used privatization as an instrument to build political support among big business for structural adjustment, a means to counter entrenched segments of the ruling party, the state apparatus, or less competitive business groups.[63] With the partial exception of Brazil, however, the process did little to improve transparency in business-state relations. To the contrary, it often encouraged favoritism and particularistic relations. It was common for the directors of the key flagship holding companies of conglomerates to enjoy privileged access to the sales, which rarely were carried out in open markets. Instead, privatization agencies frequently pre-selected buyers, and the auctioning process often discriminated in favor of conglomerate flagship companies. In the worst cases, directors of the privatizing agencies and even high political figures benefited from their involvement in the auctions.

Second, the cases examined here suggest that in and of themselves these features of the privatization process did not spell disaster for the management of economic change. In some cases they did and in others they did not. The difference lay in the type of conglomerate the state gave preference to. Chile and Mexico exemplified conditions that hindered the management of economic change. State actors relied on new conglomerates that expanded rapidly via a strategy of highly leveraged acquisitions and mergers. These new conglomerates took advantage of privatization, financial liberalization, deregulation, and trade opening to grow at a breakneck speed in efforts to dwarf their competition (usually more established conglomerates and firms). In the end, their bad debt-to-equity ratios did not allow them to survive national financial crises. In fact, they contributed to making those crises even worse. By contrast, the Argentine and Brazilian cases suggest that alliances between the state and established conglomerates proved to be much more stable for the management of economic change. These conglomerates pursued more conservative expansion policies because they already dominated their sectors. In short, business-state relations founded on interaction with established, secure multisector conglomerates resulted in more stable political support for the management of economic change than did the state's reliance on building up new, competing business elites. Of course, it remains to be seen whether the Argentine pattern, with its lack of transparency and allegations of corruption, will survive severe economic crisis, although the odds are in the conglomerates' favor given that they have done so in the past. The Brazilian case offers a potential test of a more stable structure of business-state relations, since the privatization process involved established conglomerates under more transparent conditions.

The four cases examined in this section also make it clear that there is no "Latin American" model of business-state relations. Instead, as the Korean and Taiwanese cases did in the chapter on East Asia, they offer criteria by which to disaggregate patterns of business-state relations. Distinguishing cases on the basis of differences in the characteristics of the state and of business actors seems a useful point of entry for categorizing modes of business-state relations in Latin

America.[64] Chile and Mexico share two important characteristics. State organization for economic management is cohesive, centralized, relatively insulated from political and social pressure, and staffed by competent technocrats. On major policy issues, state institutions and actors interact in meaningful ways with the heads of leading conglomerates and with technically competent business organizations ranging from encompassing to sectoral associations. Although Argentina offers an example of a state that basically shares the same attributes as Chile and Mexico, on the most important policy issues state institutions and actors consult mainly with the directors of the main conglomerates, relegating business organizations to a more minor role than was the case in Chile and Mexico. Finally, Brazil reveals a model in which a fragmented state structure interacts with both the heads of major firms and with highly defensive sectoral business organizations.

Business and Democracy in Latin America

The literature is clear that, in market economies, business support for a regime—whether democratic, authoritarian, or some intermediate form—is vital for political stability. At its root, the power of business rests on its capacity to influence the public functions of employment and investment. Its decisions in these areas affect economic growth, which, in turn, is central for the political health of governments. If it finds a particular form of government intolerable, it may exacerbate economic crises and form political coalitions with antisystem forces to bring down the regime.[65]

Given the structural power of businesspeople, analysts have been interested in their democratic proclivities. With ample evidence to back it, the early literature on business and democracy of the 1960s and 1970s concluded that socioeconomic elites were inherently antidemocratic. Economic modernization weakened established elites (landowners) and rendered new ones (industrialists) too feeble to defend their vital interests in democratic regimes dominated by coalitions of middle classes, labor groups, and center-left political parties.[66] Cresting in the 1980s, the tidal wave of democratization that swept Latin America, and the fact that the private sector displayed remarkable little yearning for the restoration of authoritarian rule, called those earlier conclusions into question. This section examines some of the reasons for private-sector support of democracy, and it evaluates whether pluralist or more corporatist systems of interest group intermediation are likely.

The regime loyalties of businesspeople. Recent literature on democratization agrees that businesspeople have no intrinsic allegiance to either authoritarianism or democracy. Their first loyalty is to the maintenance of a good business climate and stable rules of the economic game. For example, during recent dictatorships, economic crises created tensions in authoritarian coalitions that business elites were a part of, prompting them to join coalitions that supported democracy. Inclusion in the policy-making process was an additional key condition that affected the regime loyalties of business elites.[67] Such inclusion gives them confidence that, in general, government policy will be beneficial to them: It provides a measure of stability and predictability. Authoritarian governments between 1964 and 1989 often failed to provide these conditions, which exacerbated the frustration of business with hard economic times. By contrast, beginning in the 1970s, postauthoritarian democratic regimes, more in need of private investment, offered big business the possibility of inclusion in the policy-making process. Decline in the "threat from below" was another reason that made it possible for businesspeople to be less afraid of democracy.[68]

In a few cases, such as Chile and Mexico, businesspeople were initially more ambivalent about democratization. In part this was because of inclusion in the policy-making process under authoritarianism. Tirado showed that business elites in Mexico did not necessarily support democratization, even though they helped strengthen the conservative opposition political party.[69] Instead, they were content to stop at political liberalization once the Mexican executive restored their access to and influence on policy making. Silva argued that Chilean businesspeople wanted Pinochet to continue authoritarian rule at least in part because between 1983 and 1985 the military government reestablished broad private-sector access to the policy process.[70]

As democracy became the norm in the 1990s, businesspeople have developed more interest in questions such as "what kind of democracy" than in the old debate over democratic versus authoritarian rule. As a collectivity, they want "business-friendly" democracies. Bartell and Payne noted that entrepreneurs use their privileged structural position in the economy and their organizational strength to limit democracy.[71] They unabashedly support undemocratic institutions embedded in many of Latin America's democracies that protect their interests from "mob rule." These institutions usually consist of authoritarian enclaves and unbalanced executive-legislative relations. They concentrate power in the executive and restrict effective access to the policy-making process to business elites and more or less limit participation by the rest of civil society.[72] Moreover, businesspeople are well placed to fight for these conditions, in addition to the maintenance of business-friendly policy outcomes. Among other tactics, they threaten capital flight, finance pro-business candidates, use their control of the media to stir up public opinion, and lobby hard during the policy process.

In sum, for the moment, it seems that business elites have little to fear from democracy and have come to that conclusion themselves. The catalysts for antidemocratic mobilization—the strength of leftist politi-

cal parties and labor unions—are in disarray. In some cases the democracies have formal institutional constraints on political forces that once
constituted a threat from below. In others, conservative political parties
or neopopulist leaders that support free-market economic reforms dominate the political system and offer adequate protection for the key
interests of business. Where neither institutional constraints nor conservative political parties exist to comfort business fears, governing parties
committed to market-oriented policies and weak political opponents can
assuage insecurities. From the point of view of capital, greater participation in the policy process by business elites and the relative exclusion
of other groups significantly enhance their support for democracy by
reinforcing the belief that it is the "right kind" of democracy.

This picture, and the political discourse of business in general, corroborates concern by a number of analysts that support for democracy
in Latin America by socioeconomic elites is tentative. It seems contingent on the presence of "democracy with adjectives" with its myriad
obstructions to deepening democracy and the extension of democracy's
egalitarian ideals. In the past, progress on the egalitarian front came
from pressure for greater inclusion in the political system by the middle
classes, labor, peasants, and shantytown dwellers. In the future, they
will have to act again. The concern is that relatively inflexible business
elites, who are only interested in democracy as long as it promotes their
idea of a good business climate, may react as they so frequently have in
the past by turning against democracy. Yet attention to the concerns of
other social sectors does not have to be threatening to business elites.
There is no reason why many issues cannot be part of the normal give
and take of democratic politics as long as extremes and polarization can
be avoided, and as long as business elites are included in the policy
process and compromises can be reached.

Democracy, societal corporatism, and pluralism. Democratic stability, and the loyalty of business elites to democratic regimes, depends,
in part, on how systems of interest intermediation between state and
society affect the conditions for democratic consolidation and governance. Consolidation usually involves overcoming the authoritarian
enclaves of current democracies, limiting the executive branch's power,
and improving the quality of societal participation in policy making.
Governance addresses improvements in the efficacy and efficiency of
political institutions to craft and implement policy and the establishment of the rule of law.[73] The institutions that articulate and mediate the
relationship between social groups and the state can contribute to conflict resolution or exacerbation.

Societal corporatism or neo-corporatism has long attracted scholars
as an institutional vehicle for democratic consolidation and governance.
Corporatism refers to a system of interest intermediation in which the

government recognizes the associations of the functional groups of society as the legitimate representatives of social groups in the policy-making process.[74] In practice, corporatism involves negotiation and tripartite bargaining between state agencies, organized business, and organized labor. Policies that affect general interests bring together ministers (or the presidency) and the encompassing organizations of business and labor, or, in their absence, the relevant sectoral peak associations of business and industry-wide unions. Because all of the most important affected interests are present, tripartite bargaining is expected to improve policy consensus and, therefore, policy implementation.

Although others have recognized the difference, it was Peter Katzenstein who most clearly identified the distinction between state and societal corporatism.[75] In state corporatism, the government officially charters, and frequently organizes, the representative associations of social groups, as occurred in Brazil and Mexico, and to a lesser extent in Argentina. Under these circumstances, social organizations usually become instruments of government control. This is particularly true in the case of labor, but may apply more subtly to business interests as well. Because of this feature, analysts do not look to state corporatism as a tool for democratic consolidation and governance. Nevertheless, the evidence suggests that a state-corporatist political system's degree of centralization has an effect on the formation of encompassing business associations. Highly centralized ones, such as Mexico's, encourage them because business groups need centralization to protect their interests. More decentralized political systems, such as Brazil's, have the opposite effect.

By contrast, many analysts have a normative preference for societal corporatism as an instrument for consolidating democracy and improving democratic governance. In this system of interest intermediation, the state recognizes specific organizations as the legitimate representatives of well-defined social groups, principally labor and the private sector. But it does not license, charter, or directly organize them or become involved in their internal governance. Instead, social organizations evolve according to their independent interactions. That dynamic determines the levels of aggregation of organized interests and their hierarchy, meaning which ones dominate. State actors then simply deal with them.

The normative preference for this system of interest intermediation stems from two closely related sources. First, the absence of state control of organized interests creates space for a crucial feature of democracy: a vibrant civil society. Second, the institutionalized tripartite negotiating system of societal corporatism provides a meaningful channel for the participation of civil society in public policy. Tripartite bargaining, in turn, enhances consensus-building among class-based groups and the state, thus decreasing the likelihood of politically and economically debilitating polarization and increasing the chances for effective policy implementation. Streeck and Schmitter extended the idea even further. Because of the representative legitimacy of the organizations involved, private-interest governance could alleviate much of the pressure on public policy making, reduce tension between the private and the public sector, and improve policy implementation.[76] A strongly organized, vibrant civil society could regulate itself and monitor compliance with policy without the need for government intervention in many instances.

The interest in societal corporatism notwithstanding, Haggard and Kaufman correctly concluded that, with perhaps one or two partial exceptions (Chile, for example), the conditions for it are not ripe in Latin America. By extension, private-interest governance is even more of a dream. Societal corporatism requires strong, centralized encompassing organizations in both business and labor. If Silva and Durand are right, one might argue that the trend toward encompassingness in the private sector is an encouraging institutional development on the road to societal corporatism. But that institutional requirement is woefully underdeveloped in the labor sector and is likely to remain so for a long time.[77] Moreover, societal corporatism requires a greater degree of institutionalization of state-society relations. With the partial exception of Chile this is not the pattern in the cases examined in this volume. Finally, even if we limited the concept to business-state relations, in the hope of including a stronger organized labor movement in the future, again only Chile seems a likely case for success at the moment.

The fate of *concertación* attempts between the state, the private sector, and labor over free-market economic reforms in a number of cases, such as Mexico, Argentina, and Brazil, bears out these observations. In the mid-1980s, Dos Santos and others believed *concertación* might develop into societal corporatism, or something very much like it.[78] But, in the end, *concertación* proved to be a short-lived *ad hoc* arrangement. Once the economic policy pact had been approved, further negotiation (much less institutionalized bargaining mechanisms) was not forthcoming. In addition to this shortcoming, labor was placed in a thoroughly subordinate role to business interests.

Instead of societal corporatism, Latin America may perhaps be developing a system of interest intermediation closer to the U.S. pluralist model than anything else, although it lacks essential elements. Furthermore, this trend appears to have occurred more by default than by design since it simply fills the void left by the demise of state corporatism, the dismantling of production boards with the death of industrial policy, and marked difficulties with the construction of societal corporatism. As in the U.S. pluralist model of interest-group intermediation, voluntarily organized social groups—interest groups—with varying power resources press their demands on the political institutions of the executive and legislative branches of the government relevant to their problem.[79] Which interest groups participate, their level of aggregation, the political institutions they approach, and other features are not regulated, codified, authorized, required, or institutionalized. Interaction occurs on the basis of felt need, and it is expected that the associations with the best organization and capacity for resource mobilization will prevail. Of course, pluralist theory assumes that interests on several sides of the issue will have effective levels of organization. Moreover, because policy makers bargain and negotiate separately with those interest groups, policy is supposed to reflect a salutary compromise among conflicting demands. In Latin America, however, the power asymmetry among groups is far greater than in the United States, and the range of organized interests is significantly lower. Hence, key assumptions behind the expectation that the "invisible hand" of interest group interaction will produce positive outcomes do not apply to Latin America.[80] Another essential feature of U.S.-style pluralism is also absent in Latin America. U.S. pluralism assumes the existence of an effective and independent legal system so that rival interests can, if necessary, litigate their differences without reference to the state. In Latin America, this may be even harder to construct than societal corporatism.

Despite these shortcomings, or, even more unfortunately, perhaps because of them, this inchoate Latin American version of pluralism may persist due to the fact that in many countries significant business and political elites believe it best serves their immediate interests. From the perspective of shortsighted business elites, this system offers them a significant advantage over other social groups. Because Latin American political leaders are implementing free-market economic policies, large-scale business interests enjoy preferential access to the policy-making process and superior power resources. Solid connections to strong conservative political parties, where present, bolster the private sector's power resources. Where such parties are weak, legislatures often have limited impact on the policy process. Given these power asymmetries, all else being equal, business elites are not keen on systems of interest intermediation that formalize bargaining because these might grant competing social groups (primarily labor and other social movements) capabilities for effective participation in the policy process that they currently lack. All else being equal, business leaders seem to prefer a system of interest intermediation that provides them with an exclusive relationship of close collaboration with the government.

This more pluralist rather than societal corporatist system of interest intermediation has also suited political leaders. Many of Latin America's new democracies exhibit a strong centralization of authority, high insulation of policy makers, and wide discretionary powers of the executive branch. Political leaders have used their powers to push free-market economic reform, but they have also had to craft support coalitions to do so.[81] Strong presidencies, together with these more pluralist-like systems of interest intermediation, give political leaders a freer hand in the choice of allies than societal corporatism. The combination also facilitates the fragmentation and disruption of the opposition more than societal corporatism.

Settling for this truncated or incomplete Latin American style of pluralism may have been functional for the implementation of free-market economic reforms and for the establishment of business-friendly democracies in the short term. Yet it is fraught with instability in the longer run because it is not functional for the consolidation of market economies or political democracy. Where business-state relations are concerned, it blocks the construction of the structural arrangements that mitigate cronyism. If businesspeople enjoy more or less exclusive access to policy makers for prolonged periods of time, that relationship can become incestuous, regardless of the presence of optimum conditions for productive collaboration. In the worst of cases, it could perpetuate a condition of unmediated business-state relations (what the World Bank refers to as "state capture"), as has been the case in Argentina under Menem and of some East Asian cases (notably Korea) that have recently suffered from economic crisis. In addition to contributing to economic instability (as unmediated business-state relations did in Chile in 1982–84 and in Mexico after 1994), this undeveloped Latin American version of pluralism can also be a factor in the generation of political instability. It has the potential to reinforce brittle institutions that may crumble under the backlash of long-repressed concerns by excluded sociopolitical groups, another perennial problem of Latin American polities.

Framed this way, Evans's exhortations to broaden effective access to the policy-making process to include social groups whose interests potentially conflict with business may be the best way to avoid descent into crony capitalism in state-business relations.[82] Such arrangements, if nothing else, create pressure for transparency in policy making. In the Latin American context, this probably requires a redoubling of efforts to construct societal corporatism or some variant of it. This would seem a more feasible task than building the effective, independent legal system and the vibrant civil society required for full-scale pluralism. Perhaps more pragmatic business leaders who take the long view can be persuaded of the utility of such a course of action and see the advantage in avoiding the ills of crony capitalism for sustained, balanced economic development. They may also realize that it may be the best way to avoid conflicts within the business community resulting from tension over who is "in" and who is "out" of the policy loop, especially when there is no recourse to a legal system to block unfavorable policy outcomes. Those divisions can lead to surprising political alliances with uncertain outcomes. Such business leaders may be more receptive to efforts by political leadership to construct more inclusionary forms of policy making. If short-term views and narrow political and economic interests prevail, however, then the currently emerging dysfunctional system of pluralist interest intermediation and "democracy with adjectives" may persist. Under these circumstances, exclusionary business-state relationships that seem functional for economic reform today run the risk of contributing to economic and political difficulties in the future, as was demonstrated in both Latin America and East Asia during the 1980s and 1990s.

NOTES

The author thanks Laurence Whitehead and Ben Ross Schneider for their commentary on earlier drafts of this paper. He is also indebted to Celso Garrido and Ben Ross Schneider for promptly sharing the results of their latest research, and to David Fistein and Rosemary Makano for their able research assistantship. All remaining errors and omissions are the author's responsibility.

1. For these views on business elites, see Fritz Wils, *Industrialists, Industrialization and the Nation-State in Peru* (Berkeley: Institute of International Studies, University of California–Berkeley, 1969); William Canak, "The Peripheral State Debate: State Capitalism and Bureaucratic-Authoritarianism in Latin America," *Latin American Research Review* 19 (1984): 3–36; Peter Evans, *Dependent Development: The Alliance of Multinational, State, and Local Capital in Brazil* (Princeton: Princeton University Press, 1979); Guillermo O'Donnell, *Modernization and Bureaucratic-Authoritarianism: Studies in South American Politics* (Berkeley: Institute of International Studies, University of California–Berkeley, 1973).

2. See, for example, Fernando Henrique Cardoso, *Las ideologías de la burguesía industrial en sociedades dependientes: Argentina y Brasil* (Mexico: Siglo XXI, 1971); Fernando Henrique Cardoso and Faletto Enzo, *Dependency and Development in Latin America* (Berkeley: University of California Press, 1979).

3. Francis Fukuyama and Marwah Sanjay, "Comparing East Asia and Latin America: Dimensions of Development," *Journal of Democracy* 11 (October 2000): 80–94, advance convergence arguments.

4. For business systems, see Richard Whitley, *Divergent Capitalisms: The Social Structuring and Change of Business Systems* (Oxford: Oxford University Press, 1999); Gordon Redding, "Changes in Business-State Relations in Alternative Systems of Capitalism," paper presented at the conference on "State, Market, and Democracy in East Asia and Latin America," organized by the International Forum for Democratic Studies (United States), the Institute for National Policy Research (Taiwan), and the Centro de Estudios Públicos (Chile), Santiago, Chile, 11–13 November 1999.

5. For a definition of state-administered credit-based, private-bank credit-based, and capital-market-based financial systems and their political consequences, see John Zysman, *Governments, Markets, and Growth: Financial Systems and the Politics of Industrial Change* (Ithaca, N.Y.: Cornell University Press, 1983).

6. Celso Garrido and Wilson Peres, "Las grandes empresas y grupos industriales latinoamericanos en los años noventa," in Wilson Peres, ed., *Grandes empresas y grupos industriales latinoamericanos: Expansión y desafíos en la era de la apertura y la globalización* (Mexico: Siglo veiniuno editors, 1998), 30–33.

7. Fernando Dahse, *El mapa de la extrema riqueza* (Santiago: Aconcagua, 1979).

8. See, for example, Javier Corrales, "Do Economic Crises Contribute to Economic

Reform? Argentina and Venezuela in the 1990s," *Political Science Quarterly* 112 (Winter 1997–98): 617–44.

9. For privatization and its effects, see Luigi Manzetti, *Privatization South American Style* (Oxford: Oxford University Press, 1999); William Glade, *Bigger Economies, Smaller Governments: Privatization in Latin America* (Boulder: Westview Press, 1996); Werner Baer and Birch H. Melissa, eds., *Privatization in Latin America* (Westport: Praeger, 1994); Meredith Brown and Ridley Giles, eds., *Privatization: Current Issues* (London: Graham and Trotman, 1994).

10. Evidence for divergence can be found in J.P. Morgan, "Privatization in Latin America: One Step in an Ongoing Global Process," in Meredith Brown and Giles Ridley, eds., *Privatization: Current Issues*; Celso Garrido and Wilson Peres, "Las grandes empresas y grupos industriales latinoamericanos"; Luigi Manzetti, *Privatization South American Style*; Sebastian Edwards, "On Crisis Prevention: Lessons from Mexico and East Asia" in Alison Harwood, Robert E. Litan, and Michael Pomerleano, eds., *Financial Markets and Development: The Crisis in Emerging Markets* (Washington, D.C.: The Brookings Institution Press, 1999); Andrea Goldstein and Ben Ross Schneider, "Big Business in Brazil: States and Markets in the Corporate Reorganization of the 1990s," paper presented at the Workshop on Brazil and South Korea, Institute of Latin American Studies, University of London, 7–8 December 2000; Celso Garrido, "The Large Private National Mexican Corporations in the Nineties: Elements of a Problematic Profile," paper presented at the 18th World Congress of the International Political Science Association, Quebec, Canada, 1–5 August 2000.

11. Gary Hamilton, "Asian Business Networks in Transition," in T.J. Pempel, ed., *The Politics of the Asian Economic Crisis* (Ithaca: Cornell University Press, 1999), 46–47.

12. Fernando Dahse, *El mapa de la extrema riqueza*.

13. Eduardo Silva, *The State and Capital in Chile: Business Elites, Technocrats, and Market Economics* (Boulder: Westview, 1996).

14. Celso Garrido, "The Large Private National Mexican Corporations in the Nineties."

15. Celso Garrido and Wilson Peres, "Las grandes empresas y grupos industriales latinoamericanos."

16. Celso Garrido, "The Large Private National Mexican Corporations in the Nineties."

17. For Carlos Slim, see Celso Garrido and Wilson Peres, "Las grandes empresas y grupos industriales latinoamericanos," and Howard Handelman, *Mexican Politics: The Dynamics of Change* (New York: St. Martin's, 1997), 103.

18. Luigi Manzetti, *Privatization South American Style*.

19. Roberto Bisang, "La estructura y dinámica de los conglomerados económicos en Argentina."

20. *Ibid.*

21. For Brazilian conglomerates, see Regis Bonelli, "Las estrategias de los grandes grupos brasileños" in Wilson Peres, ed., *Grandes empresas y grupos industriales latinoamericanos*.

22. *Ibid.*

23. Luigi Manzetti, *Privatization South American Style*; Andrea Goldstein and Ben Ross Schneider "Big Business in Brazil."

24. This and the following analysis of the effects of economic crisis and conglomerate structure is based on Eduardo Silva, *The State and Capital in Chile*.

25. The process usually involved joining forces to buy the highly leveraged assets of key holding companies that were temporarily under state control because they had been part of the dismembered conglomerates, such as COPEC, Compañía Cevercerías Unidas, and INFORSA. See Patricio Rozas and Gustavo Marín, *El mapa de la extrema riqueza 10 años después* (Santiago: CESOC, 1988), 50–176.

26. These new trends in conglomeration are documented by Hugo Fazio, *Mapa actual de la extrema riqueza en Chile* (Santiago: LOM, 1997); Hugo Fazio, *La transnacionalización de la economía chilena* (Santiago: LOM, 2000).

27. For the Mexican financial crisis, see Andrés Velasco and Cabezas Pablo, "Alternative Responses to Capital Inflows: A Tale of Two Countries," in Miles Kahler, ed., *Capital Flows and Financial Crises* (Ithaca: Cornell University Press, 1998); and William C. Gruben, "Mexico: The Trajectory of the 1994 Devaluation," and Carlos Elizondo, "Mexico: Foreign Investment and Democracy," in Leslie Elliott Armijo, ed., *Financial Globalization and Democracy in Emerging Markets*. (New York: St. Martin's, 1999).

28. Celso Garrido, "The Large Private National Mexican Corporations in the Nineties," 16–17.

29. Jilberto Fernández, E. Alex, and Barbara Hogenboom, "The Politics of Open Regionalism and Neo-Liberal Economic Integration in Latin America: The Case of Chile and Mexico" in E. Alex, Jilberto Fernández, and André Mommen, eds., *Regionalization and Globalization in the Modern World Economy* (London: Routledge, 1998), 254.

30. Jilberto Fernández and E. Alex, "América Latina: El debate sobre los nuevos grupos económicos y conglomerados industriales después de la reestructuración neoliberal," *European Review of Latin American and Caribbean Studies* 69 (October, 2000): 97–108.

31. Celso Garrido, "El liderazgo de las grandes empresas industriales mexicanas," in Wilson Peres, ed., *Grandes empresas y grupos industriales latinoamericanos*, 51.

32. Roberto Bisang, "La estructura y dinámica de los conglomerados económicos en Argentina," 110–12

33. Regis Bonelli, "Las estrategias de los grandes grupos brasileños," 234–35.

34. Hugo Fazio, *La transnacionalización de la economía chilena* (Santiago: LOM, 2000).

35. Celso Garrido, "El liderazgo de las grandes empresas industriales mexicanas," 447–48.

36. Celso Garrido, "The Large Private National Mexican Corporations in the Nineties."

37. *Ibid.*

38. The same reluctance to privatize exists in some of the East Asian cases, such as Taiwan.

39. For this argument, see Laurence Whitehead, "Comparing East Asia and Latin America: Stirrings of Mutual Recognition." *Journal of Democracy* 11 (October 2000): 65–79.

40. Ben Ross Schneider and Sylvia Maxfield, "Business, the State, and Economic

Performance in Developing Countries," and Peter Evans, "State Structures, Government-Business Relations, and Economic Transformation," in Sylvia Maxfield and Ben Ross Schneider, eds., *Business and the State in Developing Countries* (Ithaca: Cornell University Press, 1997).

41. See, for example, Peter Evans, "The State as Problem and Solution: Predation, Embedded Autonomy, and Structural Change" in Stephan Haggard and Robert R. Kaufman, eds., *The Politics of Economic Adjustment* (Princeton: Princeton University Press, 1992); Peter Evans, *Embedded Autonomy* (Princeton: Princeton University Press, 1995).

42. For distributional coalitions, see Mancur Olson, *The Rise and Decline of Nations* (New Haven: Yale University Press, 1982).

43. For the Chicago boys, see Patricio Silva, "Technocrats and Politics in Chile: From the Chicago Boys to the CIEPLAN Monks," *Journal of Latin American Studies* 23 (May 1991): 385–410; Juan Gabriel Valdés, *La escuela de los Chicago: Operación Chile* (Buenos Aires: Grupo Editorial Zeta, 1989); and Jeffrey Puryear, *Thinking Politics: Intellectuals and Democracy in Chile* (Baltimore: The Johns Hopkins University Press, 1994). The professionalism and expertise of technocrats who are political appointees to high economic office in Latin America make them the functional equivalent of meritocratic career officials in the classic Weberian bureaucracy.

44. Eduardo Silva, *The State and Capital in Chile.*

45. Insider information about the timing and sequencing of financial sector liberalization also raised suspicions of collusive behavior between the state and the directors of the new conglomerates. The latter got a head start in setting up private financial institutions authorized to borrow freely from international markets. See Eduardo Silva, *The State and Capital in Chile.*

46. An encompassing business association is an umbrella organization that has as its members all of the most important economic sector-specific peak associations, such as industry, agriculture, commerce, and finance.

47. For this analysis see, Eduardo Silva "Business Elites, the State, and Economic Change in Chile," in Sylvia Maxfield and Ben Ross Schneider, eds., *Business and the State in Developing Countries*; see also Ben Ross Schneider and Sylvia Maxfield "Business, the State, and Economic Performance in Developing Countries."

48. See Eduardo Silva, "Capital and Lagos' Presidency: Business as Usual?" *Bulletin of Latin American Research* (forthcoming).

49. For business-state relations in Mexico, see Sylvia Maxfield and Ricardo Anzaldúa, eds., *Government and Private Sector in Contemporary Mexico* (San Diego: Center for U.S.-Mexico Studies, 1987). A definition of state corporatism follows in this chapter, see the section on "Business and Democracy in Latin America."

50. The extra-official linkages had, arguably, already surpassed the "official" ones in importance in the 1980s, as evidenced by the policy debates over Mexico's entry into the General Agreement on Trade and Tariffs.

51. Ricardo Tirado, "Mexico: From the Political Call for Collective Action to a Proposal for Free Market Economic Reform," in Francisco Durand and Eduardo Silva, eds., *Organized Business, Economic Change, and Democracy in Latin America* (Coral Gables: North-South Center Press at the University of Miami, 1998), 197.

52. For these actions, see, Howard Handelman, *Mexican Politics: The Dynamics of Change,* 103–4 and Celso Garrido, "El liderazgo de las grandes empresas industriales mexicanas."

53. For these data on Mexican business organizations, see Alicia Ortiz Rivera, "El Consejo Mexicano de Hombres de Negocios: Organo de acción política de la élite empresarial," and Alejandra Salas-Porra, "Policy Networks in the Mexican Financial Sector," both papers presented at the 18th World Congress of the International Political Science Association, Quebec, Canada, 1–5 August 2000; Andrea Goldstein and Ben Ross Schneider, "Big Business in Brazil"; Ricardo Tirado, "Mexico: From the Political Call for Collective Action to a Proposal for Free Market Economic Reform"; and Strom Thacker, "NAFTA Coalitions and the Political Viability of Neoliberalism in Mexico," *Journal of Inter-American Studies and World Affairs* 41 (Summer 1999): 57–89.

54. For Carlos Menem's policies, see William C. Smith, *Authoritarianism and the Crisis of the Argentina Political Economy.* (Stanford, Calif.: Stanford University Press, 1991).

55. For conglomerates and Memem, see Luigi Manzetti, *Privatization South American Style,* 83 and 95.

56. For this interpretation, see Carlos H Acuña, "Political Struggle and Business Peak Associations: Theoretical Reflections on the Argentine Case," in Francisco Durand and Edwardo Silva ,eds., *Organized Business, Economic Change, and Democracy in Latin America.*

57. For this view see, Eduardo Silva, *The State and Capital in Chile.* During the Chilean economic crisis of 1982–84, the more established conglomerates fared better than the new ones. In part that was because they had been more conservative in their expansion strategies. Afterwards, they benefited from the re-privatization of the assets of the dismantled new conglomerates that the state had placed in receivership.

58. Kurt Weyland, "The Brazilian State in the New Democracy," *Journal of Inter-American Studies and World Affairs* 39 (Winter 1997–1998): 63–94.

59. Ben Ross Schneider, "Organized Business Politics in Democratic Brazil," *Journal of Inter-American Studies and World Affairs* 39, (Winter 1997–1998): 95–127

60. For transnationals and privatization in Brazil, see Luigi Manzetti, *Privatization South American Style,* 174–98; and Peter Kingstone, "Corporatism, Neoliberalism, and the Failed Revolt of Big Business: Lessons from the Case of IEDI," *Journal of Inter-American Studies and World Affairs* 40 (November 1998): 73–96.

61. Andrea Goldstein and Ben Ross Schneider, "Big Business in Brazil."

62. See, for example, Robert H. Bates and Anne O. Krueger, "Generalizations Arising from the Country Studies," in Robert H. Bates and Anne O. Krueger, eds., *Political and Economic Interactions in Economic Policy Reform: Evidence from Eight Countries* (Oxford: Blackwell, 1993).

63. Stephan Haggard and Robert R. Kaufman, *The Political Economy of Democratic Transitions* (Princeton: Princeton University Press, 1995).

64. See, for example, Sylvia Maxfield and Ben Ross Schneider, eds., *Business and the State in Developing Countries* (Ithaca: Cornell University Press, 1997).

65. For the structural power of capital, see Charles Lindblom, *Politics and Markets* (New York: Basic Books, 1977); Adam Przeworski and Michael Wallerstein, "Structural Dependence of the State on Capital," *American Political Science Review* 82 (March 1988): 11–29; and Stephan Haggard and Robert R. Kaufman, *The Political Economy of Democratic Transitions.*

66. Barrington Moore, Jr., *The Social Origins of Dictatorship and Democracy: Lord and Peasant in the Making of the Modern World* (Boston: Beacon, 1966); Guillermo O'Donnell, *Modernization and Bureaucratic-Authoritarianism.*

67. For the effects of exclusion and inclusion, see Stephan Haggard and Robert R. Kaufman, *The Political Economy of Democratic Transitions, 7–8*; Catherine Conaghan, *Restructuring Domination: Industrialists and the State in Ecuador* (Pittsburgh: Pittsburgh University Press, 1988); Catherine M. Conaghan and James M. Malloy, *Unsettling Statecraft: Democracy and Neoliberalism in the Central Andes* (Pittsburgh: Pittsburgh University Press, 1994); Leigh A. Payne, *Brazilian Industrialists and Democratic Change* (Baltimore: Johns Hopkins University Press, 1994).

68. Eduardo Silva and Francisco Durand, "Organized Business and Politics in Latin America," in Francisco Durand and Eduardo Silva, eds., *Organized Business, Economic Change, and Democracy in Latin America.*

69. Ricardo Tirado, "Mexico: From the Political Call for Collective Action to a Proposal for Free Market Economic Reform."

70. Eduardo Silva, *The State and Capital in Chile.*

71. Ernest Bartell, C.S.C., and Payne A. Leigh, eds., *Business and Democracy in Latin America* (Pittsburgh: University of Pittsburgh Press, 1995).

72. See, for example, Dietrich Rueschemeyer, Evelyn Huber Stephens, and John D. Stephens, *Capitalist Development and Democracy* (Chicago: University of Chicago Press, 1992); Guillermo O'Donnell, "Delegative Democracy," *Journal of Democracy* 5 (January 1994): 55–69; David Collier and Steven Levitsky, "Democracy with Adjectives: Conceptual Innovation in Comparative Research," *World Politics* 49 (April 1997): 430–51.

73. For democratic consolidation and governance issues, see Scott Mainwaring, "Democracy in Brazil and the Southern Cone: Achievements and Problems," *Journal of Inter-American Studies and World Affairs* 37 (February 1995): 113–79; Juan J. Linz, *The Breakdown of Democratic Regimes: Crisis, Breakdown, and Reequilibration* (Baltimore: John Hopkins University Press, 1978); Abraham F. Lowenthal and Jorge I. Domínguez, "Introduction: Constructing Democratic Governance," in Jorge I. Domínguez and Abraham F. Lowenthal, eds., *Constructing Democratic Governance: South America in the 1990s* (Baltimore: Johns Hopkins University Press, 1996).

74. This definition of corporatism is from Philippe C. Schmitter, "Still the Century of Corporatism?" *The Review of Politics* 36 (January 1974): 85–131.

75. For these distinctions, see Philippe C. Schmitter, "Still the Century of Corporatism?"; Alfred Stepan, *The State and Society: Peru in Comparative Perspective* (Princeton: Princeton University Press, 1978); and Peter J. Katzenstein, *Small States in World Markets: Industrial Policy in Europe* (Ithaca: Cornell University Press, 1985).

76. Wolfgang Streeck and Philippe C. Schmitter, eds., *Private Interest Government: Beyond Market and State* (Beverly Hills: Sage, 1985).

77. Stephan Haggard and Robert Kaufman, *The Political Economy of Democratic Transitions*; Eduardo Silva and Francisco Durand, "Organized Business and Politics," in Francisco Durand and Eduardo Silva, eds., *Organized Business, Economic Change, and Democracy in Latin America.*

78. Mario Dos Santos, *Concertación y democratización en América Latina* (Buenos Aires: Centro Latinoamericano de Ciencias Sociales, 1987).

79. For pluralism, see Robert Dahl, *Pluralist Democracy in the United States* (Chicago: Rand McNally, 1967); Robert Dahl, "Pluralism Revisited," *Comparative Politics* 10 (January 1978): 191–203.

80. There is, of course, also doubt in some quarters whether pluralism produces those salutary effects in the United States itself.

81. See, for example, William C. Smith and Carlos H. Acuña, "The Political Economy of Structural Adjustment: The Logic of Support and Opposition to Neoliberal Reform," in William C. Smith and Carlos H. Acuña, eds., *Latin American Political Economy in the Age of Neoliberal Reform* (New Brunswick: Transaction, 1994); Catherine M. Conaghan and James M. Malloy, *Unsettling Statecraft: Democracy and Neoliberalism in the Central Andes*; Stephan Haggard and Robert R. Kaufman, *The Political Economy of Democratic Transitions*; Joan M. Nelson, "Labor and Business Roles in Dual Transitions: Building Blocks or Stumbling Blocks?" in Joan M. Nelson, ed., *Intricate Links: Democratization and Market Reforms in Latin America and Eastern Europe* (New Brunswick: Transaction Publishers, 1994); and Manuel Pastor, Jr., and Carol Wise, "The Politics of Free Trade in the Western Hemisphere," *The North-South Agenda* 20 (August 1996): 1–21.

82. Peter Evans, *State Structures, Government-Business Relations, and Economic Transformation.*

5

CAPITAL MOBILITY
AND DEMOCRATIC STABILITY

Sylvia Maxfield

Sylvia Maxfield *teaches in the department of government at Harvard University. She is the author of* Gatekeepers of Growth: The International Political Economy of Central Banking in Developing Countries *(1997) and coeditor of* The Politics of Finance in Developing Countries *(with Stephan Haggard and Chung H. Lee, 1993).*

Although the democratic governments of Latin America and Asia managed to survive the financial crises of the 1990s, there remains widespread concern that the volatility of capital flows can suddenly, even unexpectedly, force abrupt changes in economic policy and compromise political stability, especially in fledgling democracies. Over the longer term, it is feared, governments may find themselves perennially caught between socially beneficial policies preferred by voters and capital-friendly measures demanded by footloose global investors.

Doomsaying about the political consequences of capital mobility follows a venerable intellectual tradition.[1] Dependency theorists writing in the 1960s and 1970s linked international economic transactions of all kinds to democratic failures, and particularly to the rise of "bureaucratic-authoritarianism" in Latin America's Southern Cone.[2] Even earlier, John Maynard Keynes interpreted World War II as the consequence of untrammeled international capital flows under the gold standard, which forced governments to adjust their domestic policies, wreaking social havoc that led to the emergence of fascist governments. The doomsayers, however, miss important nuances in financial-market behavior and fail to appreciate the ways in which financial flows can help strengthen young democracies.

Capital flows and financial crisis are undeniably linked in developing countries. Yet it is unclear whether these crises pose a serious threat to fledgling democracies. The relationship among financial reform, capital mobility, and democracy is very complex, and the concerns about foot-loose capital and volatility are probably overblown. Moreover, after financial crises the resumption of flows can have varying effects;

some types of flows may actually have a salutary impact on democratic institution-building.

The doomsday view is wrong on several counts. First, investors do not all have the same policy interests. There is no single recipe specifying which policies investors demand of the fledgling democracies where they invest. Second, international bond investors impose what Layna Mosley calls a "strong and narrow" constraint on policy.[3] In other words, bond-market investors react strongly to government policy in some areas, but do not react at all to policy change in many other areas. The literature on the determinants of aggregate financial flows to and from emerging markets supports this hypothesis.[4] For these reasons, international investors do not constrain government policy as much as the doomsayers imply.

Furthermore, international capital mobility and the related growth of the international securities market should help strengthen democracy in at least two ways. First, securities-market growth could help prevent the concentrations of economic power so typical of emerging-market countries today. Second, capital-market development will likely bring with it a greater demand for transparency in both the private and public sectors. Not only should this limit the scope for cronyism in emerging-market countries; it should also help strengthen democratic institutions. Above all, investors seek predictability. It is easier to anticipate future economic policy in a well-functioning democracy than in a system where policies are made behind closed doors.

Financial Reform and Economic Crisis

The empirical record suggests that financial-market deregulation and financial crises are closely linked in emerging-market countries.[5] Recession often follows on the heels of financial and balance-of-payments crises. By financial-market deregulation, I mean measures that allow market-based individual or corporate borrowing from domestic and international financial institutions, that free domestic actors to purchase and sell shares of stock or bonds issued in local or international financial exchanges, that allow foreigners to purchase and sell securities freely on local exchanges, and that permit foreign corporations to purchase or establish domestic financial institutions.

But do these policies necessarily lead to financial crisis? The conventional wisdom is that the sequencing and pace of financial reform can raise or lower the likelihood of a problem, as can the type of exchange-rate regime in place and international liquidity cycles. This argument holds that increased access to international capital amplifies inefficiencies in recently liberalized local financial markets in what is known as the "trampoline effect." In the face of rising international capital flows, newly reformed local financial markets act as trampolines rather than shock absorbers.[6] Capital inflows translate into an exponential rise in lending by domestic banks.

Generally speaking, financial reform involves policies designed to replace the all-too-visible hand of the state with the invisible hand of the market in arenas such as foreign exchange and domestic credit. Most emerging-market countries have financial systems based on banks and loans (credit markets) rather than on securities exchanges and capital markets. In countries ranging from Latin America (prior to the 1990s) to Asia, government industrial policy relied on partial government control of credit and foreign-exchange markets. In the context of financial reform, particularly rapid and far-reaching reform, firms and governments must adjust to a world where market forces, not government mandates, allocate credit and capital. Yet it is highly unrealistic to expect once-controlled markets to become efficient overnight. Instead of lending as the government dictates, banks must evaluate creditworthiness on their own. If competition is opening up in the financial sector, institutions must learn market-based lending while simultaneously facing growing competition. New opportunities to borrow internationally can lead to overzealous domestic lending.

The history of many countries' experiences with financial liberalization illustrates why it is often blamed for financial crises. The stylized picture of too much money flowing through a domestic financial sector unable to allocate it efficiently applies, despite important differences across these cases, to Chile in 1974–82, Argentina and Uruguay in the same period, and Thailand, Korea, and Indonesia in the 1990s.

The Chilean experience of 1974–82 deserves particular attention because it is so similar to the Asian stories of the 1990s.[7] Chile's financial liberalization began in 1974 with the privatization of the country's commercial banks, which had been nationalized during the Allende regime. Interest rates were freed, putting an end to the system of government intervention in credit allocation, in which banks lent at preferential rates for activities and to sectors identified by the government. A second phase of liberalization began in 1977, when commercial banks were first authorized to borrow abroad. Large nonfinancial entities were also permitted to borrow abroad, but small and medium-sized companies could not. In 1979, remaining government limits on foreign borrowing by banks were abolished and a series of further measures followed, including permission for commercial banks to invest in foreign financial assets. Because Chilean interest rates (now freed from government ceilings) were high and international interest rates were low, any Chilean entity able to borrow internationally did so. The profits available through arbitrage between international and domestic interest rates spurred a large spike in foreign borrowing. Between 1975 and 1982, the differential between peso rates and devaluation-adjusted international rates averaged between 35 and 65 percent. Domestic banks became increasingly indebted.

The problem was twofold. First, foreign borrowing was heavily concentrated in Chile's largest companies; second, these companies put the funds to short-term use in the domestic market. Firms that did not have access to foreign funds struggled with very high domestic interest rates. Thus the financial sector grew, while the manufacturing and agricultural sectors shrank. The funds borrowed internationally by Chile's banks were not put to uses that would expand Chile's capacity to earn foreign exchange to repay foreign debts. In fact, they were not used in accordance with any criteria of long-term productive efficiency.

The Chilean story and the very similar Argentine, Uruguayan, and Mexican experiences between 1976 and 1981 present a stark picture of foreign funds flowing into a domestic financial system that did not "intermediate" the flows (pass them on to domestic borrowers) in a manner consistent with the long-run health of the economy.[8] Inflows tended to finance short-term speculative investment or poorly conceived productive investments. The same scenario repeated itself in Asia in the 1990s.

Thailand and Korea

The Thai case illustrates the pattern.[9] Financial reform in Thailand focused initially on development of the country's stock and bond markets. A series of measures beginning in 1975 culminated in 1992 with the Securities Exchange Act and the creation of the Bangkok International Banking Facility (BIBF). The BIBF facilitated foreign-capital inflows as part of an effort to promote Thailand as a regional financial center. That same year, the Thai government also eliminated interest-rate ceilings. Despite this liberalization, the domestic banking sector remained oligopolistic and inefficient. This inefficiency manifested itself in domestic interest rates that remained far above international rates. Thailand liberalized its financial sector more rapidly than Korea or Indonesia, especially with regard to foreign capital inflows, which boomed in response to both the high local interest rates and Thailand's promotion of its stock and bond markets.

These capital inflows financed a lending boom. The ratio of private-sector credit to GDP rose significantly in the years leading up to the summer 1997 collapse. Much of the credit boom financed investment in real estate. In essence, foreign capital was flowing into Thai financial institutions, which passed the money on in the form of loans to real-estate developers. This created a problem, because the loans were increasingly short-term and had to be repaid in dollars, while the income potential of the real-estate business accrued in Thai baht over the longer term. In 1995, the Thai government responded to this problem with several measures, including the introduction of reserve requirements on all new foreign borrowing under one year in duration. In hindsight, we know that these measures were insufficient to avert the crisis. As in the Latin American cases, the link between financial reform and economic crisis was a domestic financial system unable to pass on foreign capital to domestic users efficiently.

The Korean case also fits the "trampoline" theory.[10] Financial liberalization began in earnest in Korea in 1992, driven by capital-account liberalization requirements for membership in the Organization for Economic Cooperation and Development (OECD). In 1993, the government liberalized a wide range of domestic interest rates. This signaled a dramatic change in government economic policy. Earlier, the Korean government had intervened heavily in the financial sector, using directed and subsidized credit as the centerpiece of an active industrial policy. These directed credits were called "policy loans." Banks were considered an extension of the national Planning Board. In addition to lifting interest-rate ceilings on domestic credit, liberalization of foreign borrowing and securities issuance hastened the decline of the government-controlled, credit-market–based financial system.

After the financial market was deregulated, newly licensed Korean merchant banks and *chaebol* began to borrow internationally with all the self-restraint of children let loose in a candy shop. Korea became vulnerable to crisis, in part because its banks and *chaebol,* freed from decades of state control, gained access to international financial resources but failed to allocate them prudently and efficiently. Whereas the government previously had directed credit according to a general plan, after liberalization the system became prone to credit allocation based on cronyism.

Are such financial crises politically destabilizing? Do they threaten fledgling democracies? The Asian and Latin American cases of the 1980s and 1990s suggest that these crises are not necessarily lethal to democratic governments. In Argentina, Uruguay, and Indonesia, financial crisis was the straw that broke the back of dictatorship. Even in Mexico, financial crisis in 1982 led to an eight-year economic malaise during which pressure on Mexico's single-party hegemony mounted significantly. The Chilean and Malaysian dictatorships, however, both survived the financial crisis. In a definitive analysis of the political implications of the 1997 Asian financial crisis, Stephan Haggard argues that democratic governments in Thailand and Korea were better able to manage the crisis than authoritarian ones in Malaysia and Indonesia because in the two former countries, elections installed new governments that were able to mobilize support for reforms.[11] Haggard's account reveals surprisingly little evidence of a populist backlash against market-oriented policies in the wake of the financial crises in the two Asian democracies.

A glance at political developments in Latin America also reveals little evidence of a populist backlash. In Argentina, both leading presidential candidates on the October 1999 ballot campaigned on very similar economic-policy platforms. When Peronist candidate Eduardo Duhalde was misinterpreted as supporting a debt moratorium, and possibly capital controls as well, he hastened to clarify that he had no such intentions. In Brazil, Fernando Henrique Cardoso won reelection in 1998 on a platform of economic continuity. Over the past few years, presidential candidates in Chile, Colombia, Ecuador, Mexico, Panama, and Venezuela campaigned not on economic policy but rather on strengthening political institutions and eradicating corruption in government. Furthermore, the newly elected Chilean government of socialist Ricardo Lagos is preparing to eliminate that country's controls on international financial flows.

Two Hypotheses

The argument that unregulated capital flows pose a threat to fragile emerging democracies comes in two contemporary versions: the "efficiency" hypothesis and the "volatility" hypothesis.[12] The former contends that if the flow of capital is unregulated, governments will adopt only policies that markets deem favorable—or, in other words, efficient. Public spending will decline because markets take a dim view of big government. Tax structures will become more regressive because footloose investors will seek the most favorable tax environments. This argument assumes that the policy demands of international investors are antithetical to those of national voters. Fledgling democracies will thus be caught between the antisocial policy demands of international investors and the antimarket policy demands of their citizens.[13]

According to the second argument, as a consequence of financial liberalization, capital can leave at a moment's notice, forcing immediate changes in government policy, which, in turn, can result in political instability. In response to this volatility, the government may build structures designed to protect its constituents against the vagaries of international capital.[14]

Together, the two theories provide a bleak picture. Volatility demands social protection by government, but efficiency mandates against it. To my knowledge, only two large-scale quantitative studies have tried to shed empirical light on these arguments, and the evidence is mixed.[15] Geoffrey Garret shows a correlation between high trade and capital mobility, on the one hand, and lower public spending on the other. Dennis Quinn, however, finds that government spending and corporate taxation rise, rather than fall, with increased capital mobility. There are at least two possible explanations that could reconcile these studies. One is that they use different data. A second is that they introduce different control variables—in other words, they elaborate the theory differently and put different intervening variables into the story linking capital mobility to the government's policy choices. This suggests that the theory that capital mobility poses a threat to sustainable democracy needs further elaboration.

First we have to ask: What do international investors want? What makes them invest or divest? How do they make money on their investments, and what kinds of policies affect their returns? The "efficiency" hypothesis implies that capital mobility will hinder democratic consolidation because investors will punish expansionary fiscal polices. Yet while this may be true of bondholders who seek high interest rates, stockholders and direct investors may prefer to see growth, even if this involves an expansionary fiscal policy. In fact, investors may have differing (or even conflicting) desires regarding the economic policy choices of the governments running the countries that host their investments. To simplify, the return on an investment in stock depends on the success of the company invested in and on the growth of the sector of the economy in which it operates. Commercial-bank loan officers depend on the country to have sufficient reserves, backed by a strong balance-of-payments situation, to repay the loan when it comes due. Investors who buy bonds and plan to hold them until maturity share the loan officer's interest in policies shaping the balance of payments and reserves. If they do not plan to hold the bond to maturity, however, they will focus on the interest rate or coupon the bond pays out regularly until maturity. Research on capital flows and their political consequences should take into account the composition of capital flows, because different kinds of investors are influenced by different aspects of host-country economic policy and performance. The varying policy preferences of international investors may be more or less consistent with the kinds of policies desired by the electorates of fledgling democracies.

In recent years, the fastest-growing category of international investment has been the purchase of stocks and bonds. Bondholders' motivations fit the doomsayers' predictions: They invest or divest depending on how host-country policies are likely to shape interest rates and, through them, the coupon on the bond. The most direct policy constraint exercised by bondholders on host-country economic policy is the pressure they can put on interest rates.

A direct and strong relationship between certain types of capital flows and policies affecting interest rates is not necessarily good news. Indeed, investor responses to interest-rate differentials are pushing real interest rates up all over the developing world. Governments must raise rates to mirror perceived risk and rates in other countries in order to avoid capital outflow and devaluation, especially if exchange rates are fixed. Other things being equal, this generalized interest-rate hike could have a negative long-run impact on income distribution, because net debtors suffer while net creditors gain. How severe will the regressive impact be? The answer to this empirical question rests on the evaluation of other factors, including the extent to which higher real interest rates make credit available to those who were previously rationed out of the market and whether these borrowers can put the money to productive use.

The interest-rate constraint will be greatest when the international money supply is contracting or interest rates in the advanced economies are rising. Investors decide to invest based on the size of the premium offered by the riskier investment over that of the lower-risk investment. What this means is that when the international money supply is expanding due to events in the countries with the largest monetary bases, such as the United States and Britain, the price of money (the interest rate) will decline, even in relatively risk-free countries, and investors will be more likely to seek out the higher returns of developing-country bonds.

The Mexican peso crisis of 1994 provides a dramatic illustration of this. The U.S. Federal Reserve raised interest rates several times in early 1994, signaling a tightening in global liquidity. The Mexicans were heavily dependent on continued foreign-capital inflows at that time, but a rise in Mexican rates to mirror the U.S. increase would have been politically inconvenient. The government of President Carlos Salinas gambled that capital inflows, in the absence of a rate hike, would be sufficient to sustain the exchange rate until after the 1994 presidential elections. That gamble failed, but it might have paid off if U.S. rates had been relatively low and stable. This story illustrates that the risk of volatility is greatest for developing countries when the global supply of money is shrinking or interest rates are rising in the advanced econo-mies.

Before we rush to portray villainous bondholders champing at the bit during a global money-supply contraction to punish signs of growth in emerging-market countries because this could signal inflation, lower real interest rates, and falling central-bank reserves, we should note that all bondholders are not alike. Bondholders have different strategies for making money. Some have short time horizons and may respond nega-tively to growth-oriented policies if they involve lower interest rates. These investors tend to be the mutual-fund managers who face end-of-quarter redemptions if their yields fall below average. Investors with a hedge-fund mentality, however, do not face quarter-to-quarter redemp-tions. Typically the money under hedge-fund management is committed under contract for a longer time, a year or more. One general hedge-fund strategy is to invest when a crisis has pushed bond prices very low and everyone else is afraid to buy. As "contrarian" investors (investors who do the opposite of the average market participant), hedge-fund bond investors should help lessen volatility. The universe of emerging-market bondholders also includes a growing number of international and local pension and insurance companies who invest with a long-term horizon, seeking the benefits of country diversification or of long-term return from the bond's combined coupon (interest) and price appreciation until maturity. Their returns will correspond to the countries' overall long-term economic prospects. These bond investors will not be as quick to sell as the mutual-fund managers.

When we ask about the motivations of international investors, we learn two things: First, the policy constraint imposed by international capital flows cannot be as great as the doomsayers hypothesize, because different types of investors earn returns in different ways. Second, the most pertinent and pernicious policy constraint operating during the 1990s boom in international financial flows stemmed from short-term bondholders' focus on interest rates. Even this constraint, however, can be more or less severe, depending on international liquidity cycles. Fledgling democracies will face the worst constraints when they are popular investment havens for bondholders with short time horizons and when international liquidity is falling—that is, when U.S. interest rates are rising.

Financial Liberalization and Democratic Consolidation

Lost in the doomsayers' rhetoric are at least two ways that financial liberalization might contribute to democratic consolidation. First, liberalization that boosts corporate bond and equity markets should help nurture democracy by helping to dismantle oligopolistic corporate structures. A shift from private to public ownership places a premium on modern corporate governance involving international standards of corporate transparency and reporting. Second, a rudimentary understanding of herd behavior and contagion based on informational inefficiencies can yield insights into investors' views of democratic institution-building. If investors learn from their mistakes, they will increasingly reward democratic institution-building for the transparency it affords and its potential contribution to lowering the cost of gathering information.

The first potentially beneficial consequence of capital flows comes to light if we ask: Who in the developing country is borrowing, and how? The predominant North-South capital flows in the 1980s were commercial bank loans. In the 1990s, flows resulting from stock or bond purchases became much more important. Medium-term and long-term commercial bank loans typically involved the government of the developing country either as direct borrower or sovereign guarantor. The money flowed to the government and to large companies allied with the government. This observation led Jeffrey Frieden to argue that the commercial loans of the 1970s bolstered the semi-authoritarian governments and oligopolistic economies of Latin America during that era.[16] The portfolio flows of the 1990s, by contrast, should not have the same pernicious impact. They could help bolster democracy by spurring the growth of a vibrant entrepreneurial community in Latin America, where none had existed for decades.

Credit rationing is a universal phenomenon; financial markets will always charge more to lend to countries or companies that can least afford it. But the more that money is lent directly to private-sector borrowers and through mechanisms such as equity participation, the greater the dispersion of capital will be. Although it is still only the larger (or at least the more sophisticated) borrowers that can issue debt or equity, financing should become less of a constraint on business development as local capital markets grow in response to financial reform. One can argue about whether capital-market development has dispersed or concentrated economic power in the past, but technology should soon put an end to any doubts its impact in the future. Financial players in the United States are agog with the "democratization of capital markets" made possible by the Internet. Emerging-market countries are already rushing to reap the benefits of the electronic securities-exchange models that have been so successful in the United States. In these models, individual investors are put in direct contact with companies willing to share equity in exchange for cash, cutting out the intermediate steps that historically were controlled by a few very large international investment banks or institutional investors.

The democratization of access to capital should help to change the oligopoly structure of business typical of the recent past in many emerging-market countries. In addition, the risk sharing involved in equity participation and the more limited government guarantees behind corporate-bond issuance should help minimize the potential for government to underwrite the costs of imprudent investor and borrower actions.

Democratic governments should benefit from the corporate-governance reforms that bond and equity investors will demand. These reforms call for institutionalizing the kinds of corporate reporting to shareholders required under U.S. law. Corporate-governance reform will help limit the potential for cronyism and corruption. Similar consequences should flow from the emphasis on prudential regulation and supervision that is now *de rigueur* as part of financial reform.

Investors in emerging markets have been hurt by herd behavior or market contagion resulting from a variety of conditions, including the lack of reliable information. Without reliable information, an investor cannot distinguish among borrowers with sufficient confidence. If one borrower faces trouble, investors tend to sell all assets in the affected asset class. Gaining access to information is crucial to the investor; only the investor who sells first benefits when herd sentiment turns negative. What does this have to do with democracy? Stronger institutions and regulatory practices improve transparency and the quality of information available to investors. For example, if emerging-market countries had independent national-election surveys similar to those in the United States, it would make election outcomes easier to predict and make it easier for investors to calculate the risk to their investments.

There is, of course, a vast literature on how regime type relates to growth and investment, and, more recently, on how particular institutional components of democratic government affect economic performance. The investor preferences and behavior hypothesized here are consistent with results demonstrating a connection between "quality of government" and economic performance.[17] Anecdotal evidence also reinforces the plausibility of this hypothesis. For example, a majority of 100 New York–based money managers polled in March 1997 about the July 1997 Mexican congressional election said that they would decrease the weight of Mexican assets in their portfolios if the PRI retained its congressional majority. Why? Because they believed that this would signal the weakness of Mexican democracy. In the immediate aftermath of the elections, where the PRI did lose its majority, prices of Mexican bonds and equities soared, reflecting increased investor demand. Portfolio investors also flocked to Mexico in July 2000, buoyed by the first opposition victory in 80 years.

I do not mean to imply that financial-market deregulation, capital mobility, and democracy coexist in mutually reinforcing bliss. The relationship among them is distant at best. We should resist oversimplification. Our theories must aim to reflect the complexities of the causal chain linking these broad world-historical trends. More nuanced analysis may highlight new and different malignancies, as well as the potential political benefits flowing from financial reform and capital mobility.

NOTES

1. "Thinking . . . about the bond market and its influence on policy raises serious questions about the autonomy of democratic institutions to choose and pursue economic outcomes," writes Gregory E. McAvoy, "The Bond Market as a 'New Institution' in Macroeconomic Policymaking," paper prepared for the 1997 annual meeting of the American Political Science Association, Washington, D.C., 27–31 August 1997. See also Atilio Boron, "Faulty Democracies?" in Felipe Agüero and Jeffrey Stark, eds., *Fault Lines of Democracy in Post-Transition Latin America* (Miami: North-South Center Press, 1998); and Mary Ann Haley, "Emerging Market Makers: The Power of Institutional Investors," in Leslie Elliott Armijo, ed., *Financial Globalization and Democracy in Emerging Markets* (New York: St. Martin's, 1999).

2. Guillermo O'Donnell, *Modernization and Bureaucratic-Authoritarianism: Studies in South American Politics* (Berkeley: Institute of International Studies, 1973).

3. Layna Mosley, "International Financial Markets and Government Economic Policy," paper prepared for the annual meeting of the American Political Science Association, Washington, D.C., 27–31 August 1997.

4. See Sylvia Maxfield, "Understanding the Political Implications of Capital Flows to Developing Countries," *World Development* 26 (July 1998): 1201–20.

5. Graciela Kaminsky and Carmen Reinhart, "The Twin Crises: The Causes of Banking and Balance of Payments Problems," International Finance Discussion Paper No. 5444, Board of Governors of the Federal Reserve System, Washington, D.C., 1996.

6. Michael J. Howell, "Asia's Victorian Financial Crisis," paper prepared for the Institute of Development Studies conference on the "The East Asian Crisis," Sussex, England, 13–14 July 1998.

7. Stephan Haggard and Sylvia Maxfield, "The Political Economy of Financial Internationalization in the Developing World," *International Organization* 50 (Winter 1996): 35–68; Barry R. Johnston, Salim M. Darbar, and Claudia Echeverria, "Sequencing Capital Account Liberalization: Lessons from the Experiences in Chile, Indonesia, Korea and Thailand," IMF Working Paper, November 1997.

8. José M. Fanelli and Rohinton Medhora, *Financial Reform in Developing Countries* (New York: St. Martin's, 1998); and Sylvia Maxfield, *Governing Capital: International Finance and Mexican Politics* (Ithaca, N.Y.: Cornell University Press 1990).

9. Laurids S. Lauridsen, "The Financial Crisis in Thailand: Causes, Conduct and Consequences," *World Development* 26 (August 1998): 1575–91; Soedradjad Djiwandono, "Financial Sector Liberalization and Reform: The Experience of Asia," in Priya Basu, ed., *Creating Resilient Financial Regimes in Asia: Changes and Policy Options* (New York: Oxford University Press, 1998); and Robert Wade, "The Asian Debt-and-Development Crisis of 1997–?" *World Development* 26 (August 1998): 1535–53.

10. Ha-Joon Chang, "Korea: The Misunderstood Crisis," *World Development* 26 (August 1998): 1555–61; Ha-Joon Chang, Hong-Jae Park, and Chul Gyue Yoo, "Interpreting the Korean Crisis: Financial Liberalisation, Industrial Policy and Corporate Governance," *Cambridge Journal of Economics* 22 (November 1998): 735–46.

11. Stephan Haggard, *The Political Economy of the Asian Financial Crisis* (Washington, D.C.: Institute of International Economics, forthcoming). See also Stephan Haggard, "The Politics of Asia's Financial Crisis," *Journal of Democracy* 11 (April 2000): 130–44.

12. Geoffrey Garret, "Globalization and Government Spending Around the World," Yale University, mimeo, September 1999.

13. John R. Freeman, "Banking on Democracy: International Finance and the Possibilities for Popular Sovereignty," paper prepared for the annual meeting of the American Political Science Association, San Francisco, 29 August–2 September 1990; John R. Freeman, "The Politics of Finance: A Pilot Study," paper prepared for the annual meeting of the Midwest Political Science Association, Chicago, 10–12 April 1997; Benjamin Page,"Trouble for Workers and the Poor: Economic Globalization and the Reshaping of American Politics," paper prepared for the conference on "The Clinton Years in Perspective," University of Montreal, 6–8 October 1996.

14. Dani Rodrik, "Trade, Social Insurance, and the Limits to Globalization," National Bureau of Economic Research Working Paper 5905, 1997.

15. Dennis Quinn, "The Correlates of Change in International Financial Regulation," *American Political Science Review* 91 (September 1997): 531–52; Geoffrey Garret, "Globalization and Government Spending Around the World."

16. Jeffrey A. Frieden, "Third World Indebted Industrialization: International Finance and State Capitalism in Mexico, Brazil, Algeria and South Korea," *International Organization* 35 (Summer 1981): 407–31.

17. Alejandro Gaviria, Ugo Panizza, Jessica Seddon, and Ernesto Stein, "Political Institutions and Economic Outcomes," Office of the Chief Economist, Inter-American Development Bank, mimeo, Washington, D.C., 1999.

6

DIMENSIONS OF DEVELOPMENT

Francis Fukuyama and Sanjay Marwah

Francis Fukuyama is Bernard Schwartz Professor of International Political Economy at the Johns Hopkins University's Nitze School of Advanced International Studies and author of The End of History and the Last Man *(1992),* Trust: Social Virtues and the Creation of Prosperity *(1995), and most recently,* The Great Disruption: Human Nature and the Reconstitution of Social Order *(1999).* **Sanjay Marwah** *is a Bradley Research Fellow at George Mason University's School of Public Policy.*

It is of course very difficult to compare two regions as large, varied, and complex as East Asia and Latin America. Each region contains within it as much variation as exists between the regions as a whole; Burma and Japan are as dissimilar as Haiti and Argentina. Nonetheless, regions do matter, and it is possible to make certain broad generalizations about the patterns of economic and political development within each.

Broadly speaking, East Asia has achieved higher and more sustained rates of economic growth throughout the postwar period, while Latin America has been more democratic. These general differences narrowed somewhat during the 1990s, particularly during the Asian economic crisis, when Asia became more democratic while stumbling economically relative to Latin America.

In order to make meaningful comparisons, one must start by imposing certain limitations on the regions in question. We will concentrate on the larger and more successful societies and make some possibly arbitrary exclusions. In the case of Latin America, we will exclude communist Cuba and the other states of the Caribbean, while including the relatively poor countries of Central America. In East Asia, we will exclude communist North Korea and authoritarian Burma but will include communist China and Vietnam, which have opened their economies to market forces in recent years.

Per-capita GNP rankings in 1998 for the 12 East Asian and 17 Latin American countries considered here reveal that East Asia is ahead of Latin America (see the Table on the following page). Japan, Singapore,

TABLE—1998 PER-CAPITA GNP IN U.S. DOLLARS

EAST ASIA	NOMINAL DOLLARS	PURCHASING- POWER PARITY	LATIN AMERICA	NOMINAL DOLLARS	PURCHASING- POWER PARITY
Japan	32,380	23,180	Argentina	8,970	10,200
Singapore	30,060	28,620	Uruguay	6,180	9,480
Hong Kong	23,670	22,000	Chile	4,810	12,890
Taiwan	10,855	N/A	Brazil	4,570	6,160
Korea	7,970	12,270	Mexico	3,970	8,190
Malaysia	3,600	6,990	Venezuela	3,500	8,190
Thailand	2,200	5,840	Panama	3,080	6,940
Philippines	1,050	6,740	Costa Rica	2,780	6,620
China	750	3,220	Colombia	2,600	7,500
Indonesia	680	1,700	Peru	2,460	3,540
Vietnam	330	1,690	El Salvador	1,850	2,850
Cambodia	280	1,240	Paraguay	1,760	3,650
			Guatemala	1,640	4,070
			Ecuador	1,530	4,630
			Bolivia	1,000	2,820
			Honduras	730	2,140
			Nicaragua	420	1,790
MEAN	9,485	10,317	MEAN	3,050	5,980

Source: The World Bank, *Entering the 21st Century: World Development Report 1999/2000* (New York: Oxford University Press, 1999).

Hong Kong, and Taiwan are the clear leaders in East Asia, and Argentina, Uruguay, and Chile are the leaders in Latin America.

If income is measured in terms of purchasing-power parity rather than nominal dollars, some of the rankings at the top change dramatically: Japan, whose nominal per-capita income is distorted by wide fluctuations in the yen-dollar exchange rate, falls below Singapore, while China rises quite substantially; in Latin America, Chile moves ahead of Argentina. In purchasing-power terms, incomes in East Asia as a whole are still greater than those in Latin America, but the median per-capita GNP levels are close for the two regions. Obviously, however, the East Asian average is weighed down significantly by China.

With respect to growth rates rather than per-capita GNP, East Asia consistently outperformed Latin America. East Asia as a whole started from a much lower base, yet it has achieved much higher and more sustained levels of growth. Until 1995, annual growth rates of per-capita GNP in East Asia averaged around 5 percent. In contrast, Latin America has seen growth rates of around 1 percent. The variance in growth rates among East Asian countries, however, has generally been greater than in Latin America.

The 1997 Asian economic crisis pushed East Asia's rankings down somewhat with respect to Latin America, since East Asia experienced a decline of 3.65 percent for 1997–98, compared to positive growth of 1.9 percent for Latin America. The variance for this period was much greater in East Asia, ranging from Singapore, which saw only a minor drop in per-capita income, to Indonesia, which encountered economic disaster. In 1999, however, much of East Asia (outside of Japan) returned to positive growth, while much of Latin America fell into recession following the Brazilian devaluation of early 1999.

Indicators for 1998 and 1999 show that, overall, there is more economic freedom in East Asia than in Latin America. What is striking, however, is how close the regional averages have become. Given Latin America's history of economic nationalism, the fact that it has pulled so close is testimony to the impact of its economic reforms over the past decade. World Bank figures confirm another common perception: There is more economic inequality in Latin America than in East Asia. Data on the share of national income of the top 10 percent of the income distribution in each country show that it is 33 percent higher in Latin America than in East Asia (41 versus 32 percent). Gini-index numbers show a similar difference.[1]

Political Differences

We now turn to measures of democracy and political freedom. Freedom House's latest indices for political rights and civil liberties show that, in both categories, Latin America does considerably better than East Asia. All of the countries in Latin America except for Peru and Mexico were reasonably classified as democracies, while half the countries in East Asia were rightly considered authoritarian (Singapore, Hong Kong, Malaysia, China, Vietnam, and Cambodia).[2]

Static rankings do not give a good sense of the dynamic character of political change over time. Democracy came to Asia much later than to Latin America. At the beginning of the postwar period, only Japan and the Philippines could be considered democracies, in both cases as a direct result of American pressure and influence. While Japanese democracy remained fairly stable, democracy in the Philippines did not, as the country went through various periods of martial law and dictatorship. Though democratic elections were held in Thailand and South Vietnam, interrupted by military coups or communist takeover, the next important East Asian democratizations did not occur until the 1980s.

Latin America, by contrast, has had democracy for much longer. Many Latin American countries were established as democracies after independence in the nineteenth century. Costa Rica, Colombia, and Venezuela have had functioning democratic polities over the entire postwar period, while Chile's democracy survived from the nineteenth century until the 1970s. Latin American democracy, however, has been relatively fragile. During the 1960s, many Latin American democracies were overthrown in military coups and replaced by bureaucratic-authoritarian regimes. Since the onset of the "third wave," there has been an upsurge in democracy in both regions, though the trend is stronger in Latin America than in Asia.[3]

The nature of authoritarian governments in the two regions has also been somewhat different. Asian dictatorships have tended to take the form of ruling parties rather than military dictatorships, which may explain why they have been more successful in staying in power.[4] There are also in Asia what Fareed Zakaria would label "liberal non-democracies" (including Singapore and Hong Kong prior to reversion to China), countries that inherited a British rule of law but do not permit significant popular participation. There is more federalism in Latin America than there is in East Asia: Brazil, Argentina, Mexico, Venezuela, and Colombia have federal systems, while East Asia does not boast a single case.[5]

A final issue concerns what is today called "institutional effectiveness," which refers not to the democratic orientation of a political system but to how well it delivers government services. *The International Country Risk Guide* is a privately produced assessment of different aspects of governance, including levels of corruption, prevalence of rule of law, and quality of government bureaucracies. Regional averages from September 1999 show that Latin America does better than East Asia on corruption, but worse on rule of law and bureaucratic quality. (The corruption numbers for Asia are higher in 1999 than for earlier years, perhaps reflecting greater sensitivity to this issue since the Asian economic crisis.) These averages, of course, are very much affected by which countries are included and are not weighted by either population or GNP.[6]

An alternative measure of the corruption component of institutional effectiveness—the 1999 Transparency International Corruption Perception Index—indicates that, overall, the level of corruption in East Asia is lower than in Latin America when taking a simple average of countries. If weighted by population, East Asia's level would be higher because of the impact of China, but if weighted by size of economy, it would probably be lower. It is also interesting that the variance in levels of corruption is greater in East Asia than in Latin America, ranging from squeaky-clean Singapore to highly corrupt Indonesia and China.

Explaining Economic Performance

Three major factors explain differences in long-term growth rates: first, starting endowments of capital, labor, and natural resources; second, quality of economic policies; and third, quality of institutions. East Asia on the whole has no particular advantages over Latin America with regard to the first category. On the other hand, the quality of economic policies has been higher over much of the past four decades in East Asia than in Latin America, though this advantage has diminished significantly in the past ten years. Perhaps most important has been the superior quality of institutions in East Asia, at least with regard to the region's fastest-growing economies.

Economic policies. There have been very clear differences in economic policies between the two regions that are correlated with differences in growth. The high-growth, high-income countries in East Asia achieved this status by maintaining stable macroeconomic fundamentals (indeed, Taiwan's public sector actually ran surpluses and thus added to national savings over the course of several decades). Latin America, on the other hand, stressed economic nationalism over sustainable policies for much of the period up to the 1980s. In the middle decades of the century, Lázaro Cárdenas in Mexico, Juan Perón in Argentina, and Getulio Vargas in Brazil sought to build strong national industrial bases through the protection of domestic industries. They consolidated their political power through populist labor-market policies that greatly expanded each country's public sector and granted workers a variety of privileges and protections usually reserved for citizens of much more developed countries. Bloated public sectors led in turn to fiscal deficits that during the oil crisis of the 1970s were financed by external borrowing, laying the groundwork for the debt crisis of the 1980s.

This pattern was broken first by Augusto Pinochet's Chile, whose adoption of economic orthodoxy with the help of the "Chicago boys" is by now a familiar story. During the late 1980s and early 1990s, there was a cascading effect as Bolivia, Mexico, Argentina, Peru, and eventually Venezuela and Brazil all sought macroeconomic stabilization by cutting their public sectors, reducing levels of protection and subsidy, privatizing loss-making state-owned industries, and weakening the power of pubic-sector unions. The success of these so-called "neoliberal" reforms varied widely across the continent. Nonetheless, the change that occurred between the 1980s and the 1990s throughout the continent was remarkable and has led to Latin America today being nearly as economically free as East Asia.

While this account of the differences in economic policies between the two regions has become conventional wisdom, it is possible to overstate their importance. The countries of East Asia (except Hong Kong) hardly pursued anything resembling orthodox liberal strategies of economic development. In Northeast Asia, in particular, governments were as interventionist as in Latin America, if not more so. Japan, Korea, and Taiwan all put in place comprehensive industrial policies, in which the government used its control over credit allocation and licensing to guide broad sectoral transitions. Indeed, intervention was often microeconomic, with planning agencies picking individual companies as national champions. As in Latin America, many Asian countries employed capital controls of various sorts, including sharp limits on foreign direct investment (FDI). Although Japan lifted most formal controls on FDI in the late 1960s, it instituted a complex system of cross-shareholding within its *keiretsu* networks in order to discourage foreign equity buyers, while South Korea kept stringent formal controls in place through the 1990s.

Many East Asian countries, like their Latin American counterparts, protected infant industries and discouraged their consumers from buying imported goods. Alice Amsden points out that South Korea's average level of protection during the 1980s was actually *higher* than that of Argentina—and that is Argentina prior to Domingo Cavallo's tenure as finance minister.[7] Nor is it possible to argue that East Asian countries historically had smaller state sectors or less public ownership of productive assets. In the 1950s, as much as 30 percent of Taiwan's GDP was produced by state-owned companies, a percentage that has shrunk dramatically, not so much as a result of privatization, but because the private sector grew at a much faster rate. In South Korea, the state retained ownership of much of the banking sector and still has huge influence over credit allocation.

There has, of course, been a great deal of controversy over how to interpret the impact of industrial policy in Asia, particularly after the publication of the World Bank's 1993 World Development Report, *The East Asian Miracle*.[8] Some defenders of economic orthodoxy argued that East Asia grew in spite of government intervention, a view that seems implausible in view of the fact that these very countries achieved historically unprecedented rates of economic growth. Other scholars, including the authors of *The East Asian Miracle,* note that apparently similar interventionist policies were carried out in better ways in East Asia than in other parts of the world. The fact that South Korean and Brazilian policies both violated the rules of economic orthodoxy, but that South Korea did not suffer for it in terms of economic performance while Brazil did, suggests that there was something deeper at work than the specific policies followed.[9] What is notable about East Asia is that during the region's high-growth period there was little correlation between the degree of state intervention (communist countries like Vietnam and North Korea excepted) and long-term economic performance.

In Latin America, by contrast, there has been a higher degree of correlation between economic policy and performance. Chile and Argentina, which have pursued sounder economic policies since the 1980s, have by and large been rewarded with better performance. Furthermore, it is hard to think of a single Latin American country that pursued a highly interventionist industrial policy and actually succeeded in achieving sustained growth. Brazil did achieve some success with industrial policy in the 1960s but quickly ran into trouble financing oil deficits during the 1970s and ended up in a severe debt crisis.

The differences between East Asia and Latin America with regard to economic policy had narrowed substantially by the late 1990s, and Latin America did a much better job of weathering the financial crises of 1997–98. However successful industrial policy was during East Asia's high-growth period, it became an increasing liability for countries like Japan and South Korea in the 1990s. State control over credit allocation created moral hazard and over time led to the development of highly inefficient banking sectors that failed to evaluate risk properly. Economic planning made sense when East Asian economies were well behind the world's technological leaders and the next stage of development was clear; it makes much less sense when countries like Japan, Korea, and Taiwan are at the global technological horizon.

Quality of institutions. This brings us to the third major factor underlying economic growth: institutional effectiveness. It is now widely recognized within the development community that countries need not only correct economic policies but also competent institutions to administer them. It may even be the case that, in certain circumstances, a wrong-headed policy administered by a strong institution will lead to better results than a good policy administered by a weak institution.[10]

There is no question that, historically, there has been a huge gap between East Asia and Latin America in terms of institutional effectiveness, despite the lack of a firm consensus on exactly what constitutes institutional effectiveness or how to measure it. An institution can be labeled effective if it is able to set clear-cut goals for itself and achieve them. In economic policy making, particularly with regard to complex policies like managing a sectoral transition through directed credits, it is absolutely critical that the government agency in charge focus on long-term economic growth and be protected from pressures to divert resources toward the many rent-seeking claims that exist in the larger society. Needless to say, the bureaucrats administering such a policy need to have a high degree of professional competence and be free of any personal corruption.

Many countries in East Asia have succeeded in creating effective institutions. The Finance Ministry and the Ministry of International Trade and Industry (MITI) in Japan, the Economic Planning Agency (EPA) in Korea, and the Central Bank and the Council for Economic Development and Planning in Taiwan are all built around small cadres of highly trained professional bureaucrats. These officials tend to be recruited from the most prestigious universities and are trained as cohorts (the so-called "mandarin" system), with few opportunities for lateral entry. The *esprit de corps* that results is similar to that of French bureaucrats who have survived the pyramidal French administrative education system that culminates in the Ecole Nationale d'Administration. This type of elite education, coupled with competitive wage levels and the prestige associated with governmental jobs, has served to protect these bureaucrats from many of the personal and political temptations that plague government bureaucracies in Latin America. Hong Kong, Singapore, and to a lesser extent Malaysia also have governments with a high degree of institutional effectiveness; in these cases, it stems not so much from indigenous bureaucratic traditions as from British administration.

Most of the countries in Latin America, by contrast, have had strong states and weak institutions. That is, they inherited a tradition of strong bureaucratic centralization and economic *dirigisme* from Spain and Portugal but did not inherit (or invent for themselves, with the possible exception of Chile) institutions that promoted effective administration. Having a relatively low degree of institutional effectiveness is not necessarily an insurmountable obstacle to development if countries are able to match their governmental ambitions to their real capabilities. The focus on provision of public goods—such as education, infrastructure, and rule of law—should complement long-term economic planning rather than result in politicized bureaucracies concerned with their own prosperity. East Asia differs from Latin America insofar as this matching of institutions to capabilities has been carried out more effectively across the region. But not every East Asian country has been able to create a MITI or EPA—some, such as Indonesia, the Philippines, and China, have been plagued by high levels of official corruption.

Culture and Institutions

Why have certain countries in East Asia been able to develop more effective institutions? It is hard at this point to avoid falling back on cultural and historical explanations. Japan, for example, had a long tradition of bureaucratic professionalism going back not just to the imperial bureaucracy but, more importantly, to the Han or provincial bureaucracies of the Tokugawa period (1600–1867). The mandarinate constituted the core of the Imperial Chinese administrative system, one that had evolved over a period of nearly 3,000 years with its own distinctive rituals, exams, training, and meritocracy, so it is perhaps not surprising that contemporary Chinese societies know something about how to build a good bureaucracy. Many Latin American states, by contrast, evolved out of patrimonial regimes where bureaucratic office was seen primarily as a means of enriching one's family or faction. Modern administration had few indigenous roots and had to be imported from abroad.

The training of mandarins is only one part of Confucian ideology. Respect for well-trained bureaucrats spills over in most Confucian countries into a respect for learning as such, and many of the most successful countries in East Asia have spent a great deal of effort putting into place high-quality universal public-education systems. The East Asian emphasis on education was evident in Japan's 60 percent rate of male literacy during the Tokugawa period, prior even to the large-scale educational reforms that took place after the Meiji Restoration.

There is perhaps another cultural aspect to East Asia's institutional performance. The Confucian tradition not only gives guidance in the selection and training of bureaucrats; it also teaches common people to respect their authority. East Asia differs from Latin America not just in the quality of its bureaucrats but also in the willingness of its people to defer to their wishes. In the 1950s, for example, Japanese economic planners decided to encourage the sectoral transition out of primary materials and labor-intensive manufactures and into heavy manufacturing. As part of this process, the Japanese government oversaw the shutting down of the Japanese coal and mining industries and the loss of several hundred thousand jobs in these sectors.[11] The fact that this did not lead to strikes, protests, or violence is testimony both to the paternalism of the bureaucracy, which sought new forms of employment for these workers, and to what can only be called the pliability of Japanese workers. It is very difficult to imagine a Latin American government (or a North American or European one, for that matter) being able to carry out such a transition without creating a major political crisis.

Good administration is in part a question of institutional design, but it is also a political matter. East Asian countries were more successful in keeping their economic bureaucracies insulated from societal forces not only because there was cultural support for deference to authority but also because they were, on the whole, less democratic than their Latin American counterparts. South Korea was able to be competitive under Park Chung Hee by maintaining a minimal welfare state and forcibly suppressing worker demands, which exploded during the country's democratization after 1987. Rent seeking is, after all, a perfectly legitimate (if often unhealthy) activity in a liberal democracy. Hence we need to turn to the question of political development in the two regions.

The Democratic Divide

Why has there been more democracy in Latin America than in East Asia? There are a number of possible explanations, none of which is entirely satisfactory. We will look at four: 1) foreign threats and domestic instability; 2) level of development; 3) external demonstration effects and influence; and 4) political culture.

1) Foreign threats and domestic instability. Authoritarian rule is often justified by the need to mobilize a society against external enemies or internal subversion, and East Asia has been more subject to these than Latin America. Foreign threats have abounded in East Asia: The governments of South Korea, Taiwan, and South Vietnam were formed at mid-century in the crucible of civil war, and all faced enemies dedicated to overthrowing them (successfully, in the final case).

In terms of foreign wars, Latin America's violent nineteenth century was followed by a relatively peaceful twentieth. While there have been a number of border conflicts, almost all of the instability experienced by Latin American states in this century has been domestic. In general, Latin America has been prone to high levels of political violence and crime, which is consistent with the tradition of *caudillos* (military and political strongmen) firmly ingrained in its history.

Foreign and internal threats, however, do not go very far in explaining broad patterns of democracy and authoritarianism in either region. Most of East Asia started out authoritarian; external threats may have delayed the advent of democracy, but in the end they only reinforced a trend that was already present. Similarly in Latin America, the kinds of subversive threats faced by governments in the 1960s seemed to be manifestations of existing economic and regional disparities and ethnic and linguistic heterogeneity, deepening the already high levels of internal instability that existed in the region. Foreign defense and security assistance and intervention have been greater in East Asia than in Latin America for much of the second half of the twentieth century, but neither region was lacking in external and internal threats that could be used to justify authoritarian rule.

2) Level of development. The level of economic development goes some way in explaining why Latin America was more democratic than East Asia, but it is an imperfect explanatory variable. The relative lack of democracy in East Asia could be explained by the fact that the region as a whole was much poorer than Latin America at the end of the Second World War. At the end of the century, when much of East Asia had pulled ahead of Latin America economically, there were indeed more democracies among the region's wealthier countries. In between, however, the correlation was very loose: Democratic regimes were overthrown in the 1960s not in Latin America's least-developed countries, as a linear correlation between development and democracy would suggest, but rather in the region's most advanced nations. Moreover, there are some high-income countries in East Asia, such as Singapore and Hong Kong, that are not democratic; indeed, the former has stood out for its sometimes belligerent advocacy of its own brand of soft authoritarianism under the rubric of "Asian values."

There have been a number of attempts to amend or refine the correlation between democracy and development by defining various nonlinear relationships. For example, there is the theory that the correlation is N-shaped: positive for low-income countries, then negative for middle-income ones, and then positive once again for high-income nations. While this works for Latin America, it does not help explain East Asia's political development, since, with the exception of the Philippines, there have been relatively few low-income East Asian democracies. Adam Przeworski and his colleagues have a different version of the theory, arguing that states may flip over from authoritarian to democratic at any level of per-capita GNP but that they are sure to remain democracies only past a level of some $6,000 in 1992 purchasing-power-parity terms.[12] That is to say, the correlation is step-functional rather than linear: There is a certain absolute level of wealth that more or less guarantees democratic stability. This theory is consistent with the political trajectories experienced in both East Asia and Latin America, but it does not account for why there were relatively fewer "flips" to democracy at lower income levels in the former region.

The instability of democracy in Latin America may also reflect the fact that economic growth has been distributed less equally there than in East Asia. Countries like Brazil, Peru, and Mexico, as well as the small states of Central America, are famous for their highly skewed income distribution, which has created a narrow, well-educated elite at the top of the society but has left a large majority of the population either as impoverished rural peasants or as an urban underclass.

It is widely assumed that one of the reasons that development tends to lead to democracy is that it promotes the emergence of a broad middle class. Unlike many of their Latin American counterparts, Japan, South Korea, and Taiwan all went through extensive land-reform programs in the early postwar period. In a way, these countries benefited from the extreme political instability they experienced at mid-century: War, revolution, or foreign occupation succeeded in undermining the traditional landowning classes and elites, replacing them with new elites that were more meritocratic. Mancur Olson has suggested that Britain suffered economically from its relative greater political stability, since it left intact a long accumulation of rent-seeking interest groups.[13] Something similar may have happened in twentieth-century Latin America, where land tenure in certain societies remains quasi-feudal. In addition, the emphasis placed on education by many East Asian countries probably also had an impact in reducing economic inequalities and creating a broader middle class in countries like Japan, South Korea, and Taiwan.

3) *External demonstration effects and influence.* External demonstration effects are the positive counterpart to security threats: Rather than being driven into authoritarianism by national-security concerns, states are encouraged to become democratic by the example of other democracies around the world. Alternatively, countries can find it in their interest to democratize given the nature of their alliances and the external threats they face. These were obviously major factors promoting democracy in both East Asia and Latin America, as the United States exerted substantial influence over the political development of its friends and allies.

In East Asia, it is certainly no accident that four of the region's most prominent democracies at present—Japan, Taiwan, Korea, and the Philippines—have had security relationships with the United States. The United States, of course, wrote Japan's postwar constitution, and Taiwanese leaders knew full well that their country's democratization would help to burnish its credentials among its supporters in the U.S. Congress. The United States has also been accused of supporting authoritarianism in Asia by backing dictators during the Cold War. In the long run, however, there is no question that American influence has helped democracy. This is not to say that these countries would never have become democratic without American pressure and support, but in their absence it is unlikely that democracy would have taken root as early as it did in Japan and, more recently, in South Korea and the Philippines.

The same is broadly true in Latin America. Not only were most Latin American countries democracies after independence in the nineteenth century; many deliberately based their constitutions on the U.S. presidential system (which was perhaps not the best model for some). As in East Asia, the United States has been accused of supporting authoritarian dictators in the Cold War struggle against communism and, in the case of Chile, has been blamed for toppling the democratically elected regime of Salvador Allende. The real story is somewhat more complicated, since the United States was also broadly supportive of the shift on the continent toward democracy during the third wave.

4) Political culture. The final explanation is political culture, disdained by many social scientists as a residual to which one turns when other explanations fail. Some combination of the factors listed above— external and internal threats, level of development, external demonstration effects, and U.S. influence—together explain various aspects of political development in the two regions. What none of these factors satisfactorily explains, however, is why Latin America was more democratic than East Asia at a relatively low level of economic development. Here, political culture is as good a candidate as any for giving an account of broad regional differences.

The simplest explanation for the greater incidence of democracy in Latin America is that Latin America has always perceived itself to be part of the Christian West, while East Asia has not. There is an intimate connection between Christianity and modern democracy, as thinkers as varied as Tocqueville, Hegel, and Nietzsche have noted. Indeed, as Samuel Huntington has shown, there is an extraordinarily strong correlation today between Western Christianity and democracy.[14]

Latin America's Christian inheritance is Catholic rather than Protestant, a factor that delayed democracy's arrival there considerably, just as it did in Latin Europe. The Catholic Church, being hierarchical and authoritarian internally, found a natural ally in the centralized, hierarchical state common in Latin Europe; Church and State were transplanted as a package to countries in the New World. Indeed, what many Latin American countries received was not the latitudinarian Catholicism of the late medieval Church but the militant and intolerant Catholicism of the Counter-Reformation. As Huntington points out, the Church did not make its political peace with democracy until after the Second Vatican Council in the 1960s (and, in some sense, did not make its peace with modern capitalism until Pope John Paul II). As a result, the third wave, when it finally came in the 1970s and 1980s, was a largely Catholic affair, from Spain and Portugal in Southern Europe to the countries in Latin America to Poland and Hungary in Eastern Europe.

The single most important unifying cultural system in East Asia, by contrast, was Confucianism, which in the political sphere mandated a high degree of hierarchy and authority. We believe that Confucianism ultimately poses no decisive barriers to the development of modern democracy and, in certain respects, supports it (for example, through cultural support for education and meritocracy and in the private space allotted to the family).[15] On the other hand, there is no natural "fit" between Asian culture and democracy, as there is in the case of Christianity: The universality of right and the transcendence of law are foreign concepts in Asia, as is the Western notion of the individual. Thus it should not be surprising that, unlike Latin America, Asia's default starting state was not one of democracy.

Continuing Convergence?

There is reason to think that there will be continuing convergence between East Asia and Latin America in both the economic and political realms—that is, Latin America will catch up with East Asia to some degree in economic performance, while East Asia will become more democratic. A gap is likely to remain between the regions in both areas, however.

In terms of economic performance, countries in Latin America that have undertaken difficult liberalizing reforms in the 1990s, such as Mexico, Argentina, and Chile, in many respects have better growth prospects than certain former star performers in East Asia. However good the past institutional capabilities of state planning agencies in countries like Japan, Korea, and Taiwan, these organizations have by now become clear-cut liabilities. Institutional reform is no less difficult to undertake in East Asia than anywhere else: Institutions develop constituencies and entrenched clients over time and, in the absence of a powerful political consensus, can be extremely difficult to change or dismantle. Japan's prolonged recession in the 1990s appears to have laid the basis for financial-market deregulation, but the process has been an uphill struggle and it is still not clear whether the veto power of entrenched economic actors has been overcome. The severity of Korea's financial crisis created the political basis for that country to undertake more ambitious structural reforms than Japan; once again, however, Korea's quick economic recovery may mask continuing problems with moral hazard and state interference in credit markets. While there are still important institutional reforms to be made in Latin America, many of the painful decisions to take on entrenched political interests were made in the past decade.

In Asia, no less than in other parts of the world, democracy appears to be the only reliable source of legitimacy in bad times as well as good ones.

With regard to future political development, the only reason one can predict future convergence is the impact of economic development and economic crisis on political life. If economic development does in fact create the conditions for stable democracy, then the return of East Asia to sustained growth should over time lay the basis for democratic polities.

But economic crises and setbacks are also at times helpful to the cause of democracy. Although authoritarian regimes in Singapore and Malaysia have weathered the Asian crisis, it did expose the fragile roots of Asian authoritarianism. For all their talk about Asian values, most authoritarian states in East Asia have ultimately fallen back on economic growth to legitimate their continued tenure. This works as long as such regimes can reliably produce growth, but when, as in the case of Indonesia, they fall into severe economic hardship, they find their legitimacy vanishing. Without economic legitimacy, democracy becomes the only consensual basis for establishing a new political order. Indonesia's new experiment with democracy will doubtless face severe trials in the coming years, but it is revealing that there was no alternative source of authoritarian legitimacy coming out of the crisis. The South Korean regime, experiencing a similar setback, faced no systemic opposition and in fact elected as president long-time human-rights campaigner Kim Dae Jung in the midst of the crisis. In Asia, no less than in other parts of the world, democracy appears to be the only reliable source of legitimacy in bad times as well as good ones.

NOTES

1. Gerald P. O'Driscoll, Jr., Kim R. Holmes, and Melanie Kirkpatrick, *2000 Index of Economic Freedom* (Washington, D.C.: The Heritage Foundation and Dow Jones & Company, 2000); James Gwartney, Robert Lawson, and Dexter Samadi, *Economic Freedom of the World 2000* (Vancouver: The Fraser Institute, 2000); and The World Bank, *World Development Report 1999/2000.*

2. Freedom House, *Freedom in the World* (New York: Freedom House Press, 1999); Keith Jaggers and Ted Robert Gurr, *Polity III: Regime Type and Political Authority* (Ann Arbor, Mich.: Inter-university Consortium for Political and Social Research 6995,

1996); and Johann Graf Lambsdorff, *The Transparency International Corruption Perception Index 1999—Framework Document* (Berlin: Transparency International, 1999). Past research has found three groups of indicators to be prominent in distinguishing the two regions: political rights/civil liberties, executive recruitment/competition, and bureaucratic efficiency/quality. See Nauro F. Campos and Jeffrey B. Nugent, "Development Performance and the Institutions of Governance: Evidence from East Asia and Latin America," *World Development* 27 (March 1999): 439–52.

3. Keith Jaggers and Ted Robert Gurr, "Tracking Democracy's Third Wave with the Polity III Data," *Journal of Peace Research* 32 (November 1995): 469–82.

4. Stephan Haggard and Robert R. Kaufman, *The Political Economy of Democratic Transitions* (Princeton, N.J.: Princeton University Press, 1995).

5. See Shahid J. Burki, Guillermo E. Perry, and William R. Dillinger, *Beyond the Center: Decentralizing the State* (Washington, D.C.: World Bank Latin American and Caribbean Studies, 1999), 9–15.

6. The PRS Group, *International Country Risk Guide* (East Syracuse, N.Y.: The PRS Group, 1999). Countries included in the East Asian average include China, Hong Kong, Indonesia, Japan, Korea, Malaysia, Papua New Guinea, Philippines, Taiwan, Thailand, Singapore, and Vietnam. Countries included in the Latin American average include Argentina, Bolivia, Brazil, Chile, Colombia, Costa Rica, Ecuador, El Salvador, Guatemala, Guyana, Honduras, Mexico, Nicaragua, Panama, Paraguay, Peru, Suriname, Uruguay, and Venezuela. We are grateful to Steve Knack for supplying these figures.

7. Alice H. Amsden, "Why Isn't the Whole World Experimenting with the East Asian Model to Develop? Review of The East Asian Miracle," *World Development* 22 (April 1994): 627–33.

8. World Bank, *The East Asian Miracle: Economic Growth and Public Policy* (Oxford: Oxford University Press, 1993).

9. The argument can be made that Korea and other Asian countries were in fact punished for their violations of economic orthodoxy during the Asian financial crisis. See Werner Baer, William R. Miles, and Allen B. Moran, "The End of the Asian Myth: Why Were the Experts Fooled?" *World Development* 27 (October 1999): 1735–47.

10. J. Edgardo Campos and Sanjay Pradhan, *Building Blocks Toward a More Effective Public Sector* (Washington, D.C.: World Bank Institute Working Papers, 1998), 6. This point is also supported by Peter Evans and James E. Rauch, "Bureaucracy and Growth: A Cross-National Analysis of the Effects of 'Weberian' State Structures on Economic Growth," *American Sociological Review* 64 (October 1999): 748–65.

11. See James C. Abegglen and George Jr. Stalk, *Kaisha: The Japanese Corporation* (New York: Basic Books, 1985).

12. Adam Przeworski, Michael Alvarez, José Antonio Cheibub, and Fernando Limongi, "What Makes Democracies Endure?" *Journal of Democracy* 7 (January 1996): 39–55.

13. Mancur Olson, *The Rise and Decline of Nations* (New Haven, Conn.: Yale University Press, 1982).

14. Samuel P. Huntington, *The Third Wave: Democratization in the Late Twentieth Century* (Norman: University of Oklahoma Press, 1991).

15. See Francis Fukuyama, "Confucianism and Democracy," *Journal of Democracy* 6 (April 1995): 20–33.

7

ALTERNATIVE SYSTEMS OF CAPITALISM

Gordon Redding

Gordon Redding *is Senior Affiliate Professor of Asian Business at INSEAD and professor emeritus at the University of Hong Kong, where he was based for 24 years, and where he founded and directed its business school. He earlier spent over a decade as an executive in the United Kingdom before researching for a doctorate at Manchester Business School. His main field of interest and research is comparative systems of capitalism, in particular the variations within Asia, and he is author of* The Spirit of Chinese Capitalism *(1993).*

The role of the state in an alliance with business has been crucial in East Asian development. This is inadequately acknowledged by many development economists, who are diverted by a concern with policies as such and not with their formulation and implementation.[1] Recent concern to prevent economic analysis from being so undersocialized, evident in the emergence of socioeconomics and visible in the work of such reviewers of societal progress as Landes, Huntington, and Fukuyama, has brought us to a point where more all-encompassing models of development may be seen as justified.[2] The discipline-obsessed nature of academic research is rarely conducive to interdisciplinary integration on more than a modest scale, but the practitioner of international business has always known enough of the complexity he is up against to have multifold models in his head to guide him. This chapter attempts to do some bridging between those two worlds.

The background to these considerations is the return of the convergence debate. Ten years of globalization, seen superficially, would perhaps indicate widespread global standardization. Global markets appear to impose global logics. Increasingly significant volumes of international capital, emerging mainly in the United States and channeled largely through the financial intermediaries of Wall Street, London, and Zurich, are carrying with them Western rules for their use.

There appears to be convergence in certain international liberal values, such as democracy, environmentalism, and human rights protection.

Modernization may carry with it inevitable requirements for states to behave more similarly to each other. Against these assumptions stands the conclusion from the first major set of studies on convergence in the 1960s.[3] Albeit from a world prior to the apparently integrated one of today, these studies concluded that in the world of earning a living and spending there was convergence, but in the world of the mind there was not. This latter carries implications for the organization of economic action. The conclusion was of a perpetuation of industrial pluralism.

Revisiting this question today, and with the specific concern of placing the role of the state in context, an overall framework is presented as a stimulant to multidisciplinary thinking on the question. Behind it lie the following assumptions, which this chapter will attempt to defend in the context of East Asia:

- The role of the state in shaping the context of business is so significant that distinct business systems may be identified within political boundaries.
- These business systems are societally embedded and have emerged by a process of historical evolution.
- If their workings are to be understood they are best analyzed as functioning wholes to be compared with each other.

One of the strong implications of this viewpoint is that the imposition of change by outside forces will meet resistance if the related internal connections in a business system are resistant to change. Change will then be more muted, take longer, and may end as hybridization rather than straight incorporation of the structures the outsider attempts to impose. Slow and partial institutional change in the aftermath of the Asian crisis of 1997–98 is instructive here.

It is necessary to add that such discrete business systems as those of, say, the United States, Japan, and South Korea are always changing, as will any healthy system as it evolves. It is useful, however, to disaggregate the change into three categories: 1) that resulting from internal evolution and adjustment, some of which may rest on the conscious borrowing of specifics from elsewhere and their adaptation, as in post-Meiji Japan or postwar Taiwan; 2) that resulting from impositions from outside by institutions, such as the World Bank, IMF, WTO, UN, and so on; and 3) that sought in a collaborative process of hybridization and visible in one way in foreign direct investment, training, and technology transfer, and in another way in the selling of goods to another country.

For this chapter, the central question arising from the Asian trauma is whether it has forced a change in state-business relations. A related question is whether such a change is visible more widely in industrialized democracies. These cannot be separated from whole clusters of other ques-

FIGURE 1—THE EMERGENCE OF ALTERNATIVE BUSINESS SYSTEMS

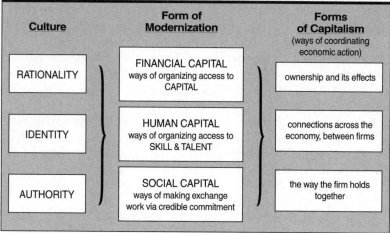

Culture	Form of Modernization	Forms of Capitalism (ways of coordinating economic action)
RATIONALITY	FINANCIAL CAPITAL ways of organizing access to CAPITAL	ownership and its effects
IDENTITY	HUMAN CAPITAL ways of organizing access to SKILL & TALENT	connections across the economy, between firms
AUTHORITY	SOCIAL CAPITAL ways of making exchange work via credible commitment	the way the firm holds together

tions and issues not addressed directly here but worthy of acknowledgement. Among these would at least be such forces as globalization, technological advance and the new internet economy, growth itself, and the pressures for social change coming from the spread of liberal values.

There is no single academic discipline capable of handling all these questions. Even so, progress may be proposed toward an integrating explanatory framework in which the specific issues can be seen in context. With this it may be possible to encourage interdisciplinary analysis and more nuanced and more complete proposals for explanation. This may help to reduce the tendency toward monocausal reasoning and the reliance on single-discipline explanation, both of which are capable of producing heat without light.

The essence of the explanatory dilemma is how to incorporate the rational logics of economics, the contextual forces of sociology, the social psychology of culture, the realities of specific political domains, and the behavior of those running organizations. At the same time, any explanation needs to allow for historical shifts and the evolution of societies and has to deal with the modern-day manifestation of such forces and the question of convergence or divergence. Above all, the unit of analysis has to be one that fosters both understanding and comparison.

Business Systems and the Role of Government

The conceptual framework proposed here is one in which the role of government may be seen in context and also analyzed for the mechanisms of its influence. The framework is given in Figure 1 above. It draws in large measure on the work of Richard Whitley and business-systems theory, but it has been extended from this to place heavier

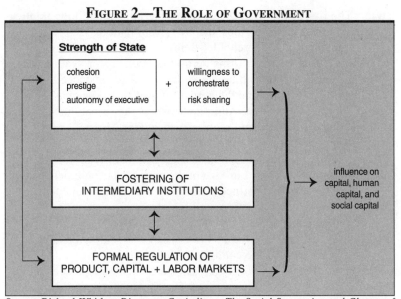

FIGURE 2—THE ROLE OF GOVERNMENT

Source: Richard Whitley, *Divergent Capitalisms: The Social Structuring and Change of Business Systems* (Oxford: Oxford University Press, 2000).

emphasis on the mechanisms of cultural conditioning, thus taking account of work such as that of Fukuyama on trust, Huntington on "civilization"-based influence, and critics of convergence using different perspectives, such as Gray with his attack on the assumedly necessary ascendance of shareholder value, or Sennett on the negative personal consequences of work in the new American capitalism.[4]

The unit of analysis in this model is the "business system," an ideal type used as a convenience around which to gather together an explanation of the functioning of an economy seen from a management or organizational perspective. The boundary of the society in question is essentially political because of the strong flow of influence from state government, but it is also feasible to analyze a business system across states if there is some political homogeneity across the units, as might arguably be the case for the ethnic Chinese in ASEAN. The use of such a large unit of analysis is justified under the principal constraint that, in social science, understanding is best fostered by coming to terms with complex interdependencies among multiple determinants. Thus how the whole system of business functions in Japan (assuming a shorthand means of encapsulating that) may be compared usefully with how the equivalent functions in South Korea or Germany. This is seen as more valuable than the comparison across systems of parts that are inevitably deracinated and that lose meaning out of context.

In this framework, the business system to be explained is seen in terms of three aspects of the coordination and control of economic behavior. The first is the structure of firm ownership and all the implications that carries along various spectra—from nationalized to private, from entrepreneurial to shareholder-dominated. The second mode of coordination is that between firms across an economy, a feature which allows a clear distinction to be drawn between, for instance, the horizontal ties seen in Japan and the vertical ties of South Korea. The third type of coordination is that within the firms as they meet the challenge of achieving predictable and motivated behavior by employees based on willing cooperation toward preferably shared purpose.

These forms of coordination have emerged historically and display sufficient homogeneity within each of the advanced economies to allow for an ideal type to be constructed from the combined components. The realm of daily economic action, and the structures that support it, are seen as embedded in society on two levels. More immediate as a set of conditioning features are the institutions of the society, and these in turn are conditioned by the culture.

The institutional fabric of society, as it affects the shape of economic behavior, is analyzed in three aspects. The first is that set of institutions which governs access to and distribution of capital. The second is the set governing the creation and dissemination of skill and talent, or human capital. The third is that governing social capital, the facilitating or inhibiting processes which stem from the availability of trust and its instruments in, for instance, civil society. In all three fields the role of government is often crucial but not necessarily the dominant feature of the institutional landscape.

The flow of capital in South Korea, for instance, is shaped essentially by government, but this is not the case in the United States, the United Kingdom, or Hong Kong, where private-sector markets are the main vehicle. The creation and dissemination of human skill and talent is strongly influenced by systems of education and by employment and union legislation and institutions, and much of this is a function of government policy. There are at work, however, influences other than the governmental that affect human capital, one example of which would be the senses of duty to family and of personal discipline that influence the way in which the education provided comes to be used—a feature arguably visible in the striking success of Asian students in the California education system.

Social capital is the capacity of a society to engender trust in economic transactions and to release the efficiency of credible commitment in business exchanges. It is strongly but not entirely associated with civil society, which is by definition not governmental. But government does provide the legal frameworks of institutionalized trust and some of the supporting fabric of standardization, such as weights and measures, reliable coinage, and so on. It may also act negatively, as for instance in Singapore, to stifle the freedom of association upon which civil society depends.[5]

The institutional fabric of society has many origins. Some features may spring suddenly from influential redesigns such as the Napoleonic Code. Others may be in constant incremental evolution as with case law or education. Some might stem from foreign borrowing, as in the current restructuring by China of its stock market systems.[6] But the majority are likely to reflect an accretion over centuries of a society's means of producing order at the micro level. Progress from the premodern to the modern is essentially progress through the barrier of learning to conduct reliable transactions with strangers so that the density and extent of economic exchange can increase. The institutional fabric supports this traffic, but having grown in the main incrementally, it does so in the light of, and conditioned by, the society's means of legitimizing some structures rather than others.

The way societies produce order for their daily workings is a response worked out over time through trial and error, which is itself based in collective understandings about how social life should be best shaped. Two sets of design principles came to be worked out to cover horizontal and vertical order—that is, rules for whom you are connected with and how—and these stabilize relationships and make orderly social functioning possible. The remaining culturally determined feature is rationality, not seen here (as in economics) as a universal assumption, but instead seen (as in socioeconomics) as something that takes shape variously society by society. The key aspects of its variation are two: the purposes for which economic behavior is established, and the orderliness and intensity with which those purposes come to be pursued. For example, from the 1960s on, South Korea knew exactly what it wanted—national development based on export industry—and organized itself in a very focused way to get it. Many Latin American states adopted unclear and changing agendas and organized less well to achieve them. They were less rational in these senses.

It is possible to argue, then, that the role of the state may be seen in terms of four propositions: 1) The role itself is to provide support for the growth in quantity and quality and of access to capital, human capital, and social capital. 2) This role will be exercised by mechanisms of commitment; by the encouragement of facilitating intermediaries; and by the regulation of product, capital, and labor markets. 3) As the choices of method and core purpose will vary, so too will the end result, that is, the business system. 4) The variation in choices will be conditioned by historical experience, by borrowing, and by cultural predispositions, especially in the domains of rationality and of vertical and horizontal order.

The Role of the State in Wider Context

The evolution of market-based capitalism has been described by Dunning as having three phases: entrepreneurial capitalism from 1770 to 1875, hierarchical capitalism from 1875 to 1980, and alliance or flexible capitalism from 1980 onwards.[7] In describing the current emergence of alliance capitalism he points out two distinctive features: firstly, an increasing emphasis on partnership between the various organizational modes of resource allocation and, secondly, an increase in the role of government as overseer and arbitrator of the functions undertaken by private and public institutions. Arguing that as a society becomes more prosperous and as the tradeoffs between further economic growth and other goals change, Dunning sees the function of government as becoming more rather than less critical, although changing in nature. Instead of participating directly in the economy, the new government roles will be 1) creating and sustaining the institutional, legal, and commercial infrastructure; 2) fashioning value systems and ideologies; and 3) providing a consensus for allocation decisions. He notes that the growing integration of the world economy has led to an increase in government involvement in cross-border alliances plus a higher level of intergovernmental cooperation via supranational regulatory or facilitating bodies.

In a rejoinder to Dunning, Richard Lipsey points out that the fertile relations between government and the private sector that are seen as necessary in conditions of globalization are closer to East Asian structures than to North American or European ones.[8] But he cautions against the advocacy of a standardized approach, saying that adjustments will differ dramatically across nations and will depend heavily on country-specific factors. These will vary by historical context (for example, catch-up as opposed to leading-edge), and also by government capacity, as for instance when government power is restricted constitutionally or when the brokerage of regional interests is involved. Civil-service quality and sectional interests will also be influential. In brief, he sees a plurality of formulae for state-business relations and argues for the necessity of this. Minimalist government may be right for the United States, while activist government may be right for Asia.

Susan Strange has considered the challenges of globalization for governments, as well as what she sees as a retreat of the state.[9] She sees the main forces at work as three: the accelerated internationalization of production, the sharply increased mobility of capital, and the greater mobility of information. These forces interact with each other and cause governments to pay attention to six challenging outcomes: 1) countercyclical economic management; 2) financial stability; 3) financing state budgets; 4) industrial and competition policy; 5) managing labor relations; and 6) crime prevention. The main point of Strange's argument is captured in the following quote:

> The shift from state to markets has actually made political players of the TNCs [transnational corporations]. The argument is not that they influence the foreign policies of states or are, in any general and important sense, the "powers behind the throne," even though in special circum-

stances they may be so. Rather it is that they themselves are political institutions, having political relations with civil society. These political relations are even more important than their political involvement with other firms or with specific governments.[10]

The way in which the workings of corporations invade the traditional territory of governments lies in their exercise of parallel authority over questions of the location of industry and investment, the direction of technological innovation, the management of labor relations, and the fiscal extraction of surplus value. An example of these forces flowing together is the decline of union power. Previously protected by legislation within a country, unions can no longer insist on certain negotiating positions when firms can move work elsewhere.

There are two directions of movement in the current diffusion of state power. One is upwards and outwards as governments get civil society to accept international rules (the IMF, international accounting standards, EU standardization, ISO factory gradings, and so on). The other is downwards to the local level. Strange argues that, after several centuries of increasing centralization of economic decision making within the state, we see an unusual recent shift toward the diffusion of such powers.[11] It is unusual in two senses: Firstly, it has occurred at a very high speed in historical terms; secondly, it has affected a very large number of states in the last two decades.

The difficulty of presenting a clear picture of this widespread trend lies in the variety of responses within the overall pattern. As pointed out by Vivien Schmidt,[12] the ways in which states will respond to the new pressures of globalization vary in accordance with the following influences (among others):
- the particular state-society relationship embodied in the policy-making process: corporatist, statist, pluralist;
- country size and thus the penetrability of policy in practice;
- culture and history;
- governmental structure: federal or unitary;
- governmental capacity: to reform or not;
- labor history: conflictual or consensual;
- labor organization: cohesive or fragmented;
- business size: large or small;
- business organization: cohesive or fragmented;
- business orientation: domestic or international.

It is clear in the light of this that national adjustments to the forces of globalization—even if the direction of movement is consistent—are still likely to follow many pathways and to display many deviations. Before considering the adjustments, it is necessary to consider more closely the nature of the transformation being faced.

Stephen Kobrin has offered a valuable explanation of the current

TABLE 1—INDUSTRIAL ADJUSTMENT STRATEGIES OF EAST ASIAN NICs

NIC	INDUSTRIAL ADJUSTMENT STRATEGY	INTENSITY OF STATE INTERVENTION	PATTERN OF PREFERENCE IN OWNERSHIP	LINKAGE BETWEEN MACROECONOMIC MANAGEMENT AND INDUSTRIAL POLICY
Hong Kong	Marketeer strategy	Minimal intervention to allow market to reign	Minimal state ownership; no predilection for national control	Macroeconomic management only; no linkage
Singapore	International-ist strategy	Discretionary control of structural incentives to supplement market signals	Predilection for joint venture and foreign participation	Macroeconomic management has priority over industrial restructuring
Taiwan	Statist strategy	Discretionary control of structural incentives to supplement market signals	Predilection for state ownership and joint venture	Macroeconomic management has priority over industrial restructuring
South Korea	Nationalist strategy	Detail-oriented intervention to alter or replace market signals	Predilection for national control	Macroeconomic management policy complements industrial restructuring objectives

Source: Yun-han Chu, "State Structure and Economic Adjustment of the East Asian Newly Industrialized Countries," International Organization 43 (Autumn 1989): 647–72.

qualitative transformation of the world economy.[13] Arguing that globalization does have substantive meaning, he sees its effects as three major changes. Firstly, increases in the scale, cost, and risk of the technology used in many industries have made even the largest national markets inadequate to sustain the investment. As a result national markets are no longer the principal units in business action and are not even simply linked across borders; instead they have become "fused" transnationally. Secondly, there has been a fundamental shift in the mode of organization in use, away from markets or hierarchies with their focus on trade and multinational enterprises, toward postmodern global networks, for example dealing simultaneously with subnational, national, regional, international, and supranational authorities. This influence makes increasingly redundant the modern, territorially defined international political system. Thirdly, the new network structures are coordinated more and more by information systems and less and less by hierarchical organizational structures.

In this new context, the capacity of a state to make its own autonomous decisions is clearly compromised by the fusion of both markets and information. This may well have implications for state sovereignty itself—in other words for the ability of the state to govern its own internal affairs and come to its own policies for external relations. Pointing out the paradox that there is nothing in the nature of markets that necessarily defines them spatially, but everything in the nature of a state that does, Kobrin is clearly anticipating that sovereignty as a central component of the modern world may not survive intact the transition to the postmodern. This echoes the "end of geography" scenario for the new world of financial integration depicted by Stopford and Strange and by O'Brian.[14]

TABLE 2—STATE STRUCTURES AND CORRESPONDING INDUSTRIAL
ADJUSTMENT STRATEGIES OF THE EAST ASIAN NICS

NIC	STATE STRUCTURE			INDUSTRIAL ADJUSTMENT STRATEGY
	ORGANIZATION OF STATE ECONOMIC BUREAUCRACY	POLICY NETWORKS	RELATIONSHIP BETWEEN THE STATE AND SOCIETY	
Hong Kong	Dominant fiscal authority; limited economic bureaucracy	Few channels of access to private sector except for major banks	Colonial state insulated from society; alliance between the colonial administrative elite and the dominant banking and commercial interests	Marketeer strategy: minimal intervention; reliance on market mechanisms
Singapore	Autonomous fiscal and monetary authority and decentralized planning authority; extensive control of production resources	Effective channels of access to organized labor	Inclusionary party-based authoritarian regime; technocrat-dominated multi-class alliance with corporatist inclusion of the urban popular sector	Internationalist strategy: anticipatory adjustment and solicitation of TNC participation
Taiwan	Dominant fiscal and monetary authority with checks on the activities of planning technocrats; extensive state involvement in production activities	Limited channels of access to private sector	Preemptive party-based authoritarian regime; alliance between the national minority elite and the local dominant class	Statist strategy: selective promotion and strategic positioning of the state
South Korea	Dominant planning authority; compliant fiscal and monetary authority; centralized, resourceful bureaucracy	Multifaceted channels of access to private sector	Exclusionary, military-based authoritarian regime; alliance between the military, big business, and state technocrats	Nationalist strategy: strong, multifaceted support for large domestic firms

Source: Yun-han Chu, "State Structure and Economic Adjustment of the East Asian Newly
Industrialized Countries," *International Organization* 43 (Autumn 1989): 647–72.

The argument of this chapter so far may be summarized as follows:

- The complexity of the issues involved is such that only a multi-disciplinary and historically grounded model will be able to en compass the explanatory factors.
- A model is proposed using the notion of a national business system as *explanandum,* and tracing its trajectory and its embeddedness.
- The role of the state is changing at a high speed under pressure from the forces of globalization.
- In this, the manner whereby governments influence economic behavior has adjusted to accommodate the new forms of alliance or network capitalism.
- In this the large corporation has become a political player.
- The variety of national responses within this pattern is great.

Two things are impossible to reach conclusions about in the present
state of knowledge. One is whether the total quantum of government
influence is in decline, or whether its newly diffused structure has simply reallocated its power and refocused its energy for the future. For
instance, there has been a steady increase in government spending as a
percentage of GDP over several decades to date in most industrialized
countries.[15] The second area of cloudy understanding is the pattern of

FIGURE 3—INTERDEPENDENCES BETWEEN INSTITUTIONS AND THE
POSTWAR TAIWANESE BUSINESS SYSTEM

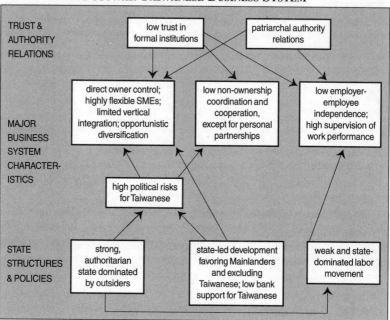

Source: Richard Whitley, *Divergent Capitalisms: The Social Structuring and Change of Business Systems* (Oxford: Oxford University Press, 2000).

government reaction to the global pressures of marketization, something in itself connected with the variety of national structures governing relations with the economy. Until the variety is illuminated it will not be possible to attempt any meaningful estimates about general tendencies, and so some attention will now be paid to depicting the diversity of the structures in which government plays a part.

A Proliferation of Formulae for State-Business Relations

In a study of state structures and economic adjustment in the East Asian NICs, Chu depicts the variety of adjustment strategies and government policies and modes of intervention across Hong Kong, Singapore, Taiwan, and South Korea.[16] (See Table 1 on page 138.) He also summarizes the relevant characteristics of the state structure in terms of three variables: 1) the organization of the state economic bureaucracy; 2) policy networks; and 3) the relationship between the state and society. These are given in Table 2 on page 139, and they provide clear evidence for the conclusion that no two countries, even within a category, are alike—including the Asian NICs commonly treated as relatively homogeneous.

In her review of national responses to international pressures, Schmidt

FIGURE 4—INTERDEPENDENCES BETWEEN INSTITUTIONS AND THE POSTWAR KOREAN BUSINESS SYSTEM

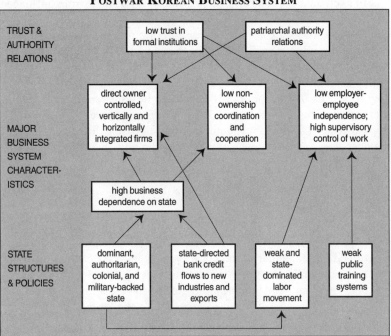

Source: Richard Whitley, *Divergent Capitalisms: The Social Structuring and Change of Business Systems* (Oxford: Oxford University Press, 2000).

equally provides evidence of this plurality in her thumbnail depictions: the unbalancing of corporatism in smaller European countries, corporatism under siege in Germany, the statist end of the old-style statism in France, liberal statism with a difference in the United Kingdom, statist resistance to the pressures of internationalism in Japan, and in the United States the recreation of a quasi-statist pattern in a pluralist polity. Clearly there are few grounds here for finding common formulae.[17]

In his wider and deeper analysis, Whitley illustrates for the cases of South Korea and Taiwan (see Figures 3 and 4 above) the way in which state structures and approaches interact with certain prior cultural givens to produce coherent, stable, and self-replicating patterns within their distinct business systems. Here the historical origins of present-day structures are made explicit. Also the grounds for resistance to radical change are clarified, and so too the tendency for evolutionary, incremental adjustment and the maintenance of long-term consistency of core characteristics within each national boundary.[18]

The variety of East Asian business systems includes variety in one of their prime components, namely the role of the state. In South Korea the state has dominated the workings of the economy and has shared risk in exchange for control. In Japan the state has had strong influence but has not taken direct control. Instead, it has fostered a high level of cooperation with state aims by major corporations and also a high level of cooperation between firms across the economy in the interest of national purposes. In Taiwan a strong state entered directly into ownership of key economic sectors and by influencing firm strategies there it was able to see its overall policies filter down into the small and medium sector that occupies so much of Taiwan's energy and explains so much of its success. In Singapore another strong state took direct command of major sectors and filled much of the remainder with guest transnationals. In Hong Kong the state stood back and let business find its own pattern of strategy but still kept monopoly control on the key resource of property and intervened heavily in fields of utilities, to influence cost structures.

The governments of Indonesia, Malaysia, the Philippines, and Thailand, speaking broadly, could not match the "Confucian" governments mentioned above, either in the clarity and specificity of their development visions or in the great legitimacy accorded societally to policy makers. This latter was important in getting the aims implemented and adhered to. This ASEAN group came late to the "miracle" and to its core policies of labor-intensive, export-orientated industrialization and, though growing, have continued to be in a lower table of wealth.

The Asian success cases, although differing in approach from each other, have thus been built upon strong state influence. In assessing the role of these governments, Dunning has pointed to the key features of strength and efficiency, while Haggard has similarly identified decisiveness and credibility as crucial. In a similar vein both Fukuyama and Wade have argued that having the right policies is less important than the quality of the institutions that will carry them.

Against these achievements there now arrive the forces of individualist capitalism based on the perceived sacred dominance of the market and the relative retirement of government from the scene. How will this challenge be met and why?

The core of the issue is the insistence by Western possessors of capital that the Asian business systems convert to the Wall Street formula for handling capital. This includes 1) openness and disclosure in the financial system; 2) the pursuit of shareholder value as the central rationale behind the allocation of capital; and 3) mobility of capital between firms, sectors, and countries in pursuit of rationally calculated yield.

There can be little doubt that the daunting productive health of such individualist capitalism in the United States requires that its logics be taken seriously. That is not at issue. The issue is whether you can uproot a component of a total system and inject it elsewhere where it does not fit with the context. No matter how good it is back home, the question of its right to colonize everywhere else is at base a moral one about a society's core design principles. Only an imperial mindset can conceive its own core design principles as universal. There is in addition the practical question of absorption and change. Let us now consider, for the cases of Japan and Korea, the impact of free-market global financial capital, American-style.

Japan. In Japan capital is accessed through long, close alliances between firms and banks, and much bank risk has been ultimately underwritten by the Bank of Japan. This means that the state has taken part in the acceptance of risk, and its recent behavior in the bailing out of companies in difficulty has illustrated the logical consequences of this understood position. In cases where the state has stood out against further subsidy in the light of perceived managerial incompetence by some corporations, the decision has apparently been made with great difficulty.

The structure of the Japanese business system is essentially one of a large and complex alliance between government and major manufacturers. The logics of it are that Japan saw its postwar reconstruction as being based on export-led industrialization and thus on international competitiveness in manufacturing. At the same time, the acceptance of a high social overhead was seen as culturally appropriate, and to resolve the discrepancy between manufacturing competitiveness and high social costs it was necessary to provide a constant supply of low-cost capital. This basic design was supplemented by an intricate series of alliances between politics and industry, which included the barter of contributions in exchange for favors. In consequence. political stability was maintained. As described by Park:

> Japan's politics is on the side of the capital users, not the suppliers who happened to be highly inefficient and hapless financial intermediaries. The system totally abused and neglected Japanese savers. The present form of Japan's democracy is built on cheap interest rates and a powerful industrial-political alliance.[19]

Capital is also sourced by firms internally out of retained earnings, and usually ploughed back into productivity-enhancing investment. Yield on the Tokyo stock exchange is extremely low by international standards, and the right of shareholders to take precedence in the distribution of surplus remains weak. The result of this constant reinvesting of surplus back into companies has two direct effects: Firstly, it gives a steady flow of investment in such assets as new machinery, training, and research; secondly, and perhaps more significantly in the larger scheme of things, it leaves the decisions about investment in the hands of the managers of companies, and not in the hands of investment analysts observing a very wide spectrum of investment opportunities. The battle of the short term versus the long term is stalled here, with the managerial long-termists ascendant over the finance-market short-termists.

Japanese industry has benefited from the resulting long-term managerial decisions in the past and has been able to build powerful competences in certain kinds of industry where the embedding of such competences in capital-intensive production systems has paid off in competitive terms. On the other hand, the overall economy has suffered from the absence of the discipline of close comparative scrutiny of performance data beyond market share and across sectors. This scrutiny is now coming but only to the limited extent that Japan needs external capital. Otherwise the Japanese will predictably adjust their familiar system and not abandon it. Key employees then remain employable in the long term, which is arguably the central tenet in the substructure of ideals.

High savings rates in the population at large have traditionally underpinned this structure, providing huge volumes of capital for eventual use by industry through the intermediation of the government and the banking sector. The banking sector in turn has been at the core of the set of alliances that make up this distinct system of capitalism, and has served to bridge the industry-government connection.[20] Share ownership is dispersed across industry broadly and public shareholding has not been a source of much influence.

This is what Whitley characterizes as "highly coordinated" capitalism, it being arguably more knitted together than other systems. Its ties bind it across all three of the elements of the system. Ownership of firms is shared across an industrial arena and pulls together a set of institutions such as banks, suppliers, members of business groups, providers of key services such as insurance, and sources of key information. In addition to such ownership coordination, visible in a typical Japanese boardroom of 30 or 40 directors, is the second form of coordination: the active networking involved in production, sourcing, subcontracting, and marketing. Such cooperative behavior is normally based on stable alliances of long duration. The third form of coordination in which Japan's system is distinctly "tight" is that with employees, especially the key employees with skills. Here the levels of two-way commitment between firm and employee, and the long-term reliability, utility, and quality of the contribution that results, have been objects of much international interest and attempts to emulate. This is not to say that the system is faultless, but there is little doubt that it served to revolutionize globally the notions of productivity and its sources in recent years.

The imposition of shareholder-value-based free-market capitalism and full international exposure would be likely to have the following effects in Japan:

1) Investment decisions previously made by industrial managers over the use of their firm's surplus would be transferred to market analysts

along with the money. These analysts would make quite different decisions, shorter in commitment time, independent of firms and sectors, and often offshore in their application.

2) Japanese industry would have to adjust radically to the loss of access to long-term, low-cost, stable capital, and instead switch emphasis to different performance criteria. The firm would exist primarily for its shareholders and not its employees. This goes to the moral core of the Japanese system and is unthinkable.

3) The basis for industry alliances via cross-shareholdings and mutual interests would be destroyed. With that would go the coalitions nurtured by government to foster the national program. The whole edifice of vertical and horizontal partnerships would collapse. Again, this is unthinkable.

4) New forms of performance-driven management would replace the long-established paternalist professionalism, thus destroying the moral basis of vertical order in organizations. This would cause massive disruption to the social psychology of firms, affecting morale, motivation, commitment, and productivity.

5) Corporate welfarism would diminish, throwing a new burden onto the state.

6) New patterns of labor mobility would destroy the established system of training and skilling within firms, and would in turn have negative effects on social capital and on the labor flexibility within the firm that comes from multi-skilling.

7) The high level of trust, and thus of social capital, was built up in Japan on the basis of complex strands of mutual obligation exchanged between individuals and firms over decades. Competition based on specific narrow aims would place this form of trust under severe strain, potentially destroying a powerfully efficient social asset only replaceable with an army of lawyers, the latter of course only being available after many years of building a new legal system and training its operators.

South Korea. The case of South Korea is very different (usefully so given the basic premise of this paper). The state, in this case, played a cardinal role in shaping and then directing the economy, especially during the crucial years of growth from 1960 to 1990. In Whitley's terms, this is "state organized" capitalism, and he points out that the key distinguishing feature separating it from Japan lies in the structure adopted for the coordination of its economic behavior. In Japan, coordination, as just argued, was widespread and highly developed throughout the business system. In South Korea, coordination is high in the field of ownership, but low in the field of business networking between firms and in the area of worker cooperation. In the field of ownership, it also takes on a quite different form from that of Japan.

The Korean miracle was built in circumstances where entrepreneurial talent was in short supply, infrastructure devastated by war, and societal wealth unavailable. Development loans were available from sympathetic countries to rebuild the economy. The prior industrial tradition was of subjection to Japanese colonial rule and the acceptance of Japanese industrial control. In 1939, 94 percent of Korean industry was Japanese-owned. This left two psychological residues: firstly never to let it happen again, which meant in turn being both defensive against, and competitive with, the outsider; secondly a familiarity with the pre-war *zaibatsu* and the industrial power that they could display.

There was also a strong tradition of patrimonialism in Korean social history, based on a Confucian ideology similar in its interpretation to that of China, leading to the idea of the strong state and the acceptance of vertical authority legitimized by nationalism.[21] This is in marked contrast to the Japanese heritage of feudalism and the decentralization of power in society.

What came to be known as "Korea Inc." was characterized by certain distinct government actions: managing the market to foster chosen industries by deliberate distortion of the price mechanism and by administrative support and protection; forming hierarchical relationships with *chaebol* and their leaders, using the latter's dependence on government capital support to influence the achievement of a series of national plans; justifying dominance by government over society by stressing public good; and insulating policy decision making from social influences in an authoritarian manner. The development policy essentially was the pursuit of export-oriented industrialization by giving special benefits to family-controlled groups whose cooperation could be assumed.

The political reality was that the government controlled industry in the patrimonial tradition, as opposed to the Japanese solution of making an alliance with it. In order for this control to work, the flow of capital was monopolized by the government, the cost of it was kept high, its availability was scarce, and the dependence of industry was maintained.

This worked through to the end of the 1980s, when it began to come under the stress of externally driven ideals, such as union influence and democracy. Since then it has been in transition to a form that is not yet clear. The current democratic government has challenged the supremacy and overall efficiency of the *chaebol* system, which in turn is under pressure to find new bases for its legitimacy. The key question, in the context of this paper, is: Will the result still be distinctly Korean?

The reforms introduced in 1998 and 1999 injected market discipline and flexibility into the economy, but these met with resistance, especially in three areas. In the labor market the rapid rise in unemployment made radical reform difficult. In the reform of state-owned businesses, there was severe resistance from the bureaucracy.[22] Thirdly, the reforms to the corporate sector were taken from the Western textbook: breaking up the *chaebol* into legally independent companies, managed professionally and much less tightly bound into one network; public accountability for performance; and the intended (but not yet accomplished) separation of ownership and control. In strategy there have been attacks on high leverage and on the pursuit of growth at the expense of profit. The duplication brought about in the economy by each group indulging in irrational proliferation has also been attacked. Workforces have been reduced. Mergers, alliances, and asset swaps have realigned some of the industrial structure, usually by the use of heavy government pressure. The cross-subsidization that protected the weak within a *chaebol* and the cross-shareholding that protected ownership have come under severe scrutiny.

Yet the reforms have not produced a carbon copy of the Western model, and there is much resistance to them, as the following headlines show: "*Chaebol* turn increasingly defiant of reform measures" (*Financial Times Information*, 17 May 2000); "Two years into reform drive, *chaebol* remain unchanged" (*Financial Times Information*, 20 July 2000); "The crawl of reform" (*Business Week*, 4 Sept 2000); "The *chaebol* spurn change" (*The Economist*, 22 July 2000). In a report titled "South Korea's *chaebol*: Unregenerate," *EIU Business Asia* commented:

> Gone are the days . . . when the state which created the *chaebol* could boss them about. In Seoul as elsewhere, government's power to bend big business to its will has eroded. If the *chaebol* choose not to change, no one can make them now.[23]

What we see happening in Korea is a coming to terms with the embeddedness of its business system. Radical change of the kind advocated would have the following effects:

1) It would de-link the government from control of the economy and require the construction of a new form of business-government relationship. In this the government would need to give up its monopoly control of capital access and allow capital to flow instead through a rational, open financial market. This suggests great struggle for two reasons: firstly, the tradition of very strong government is not likely to prove changeable except over a long period of societal development, during which more pluralism grows; secondly, Korea needs strong government to survive the period of change it has now begun.

2) The destructuring of the *chaebol* would undermine many of the internal efficiencies they have built in the fields of supply-chain management, internal labor markets for both workers and management, research and development, raw-material sourcing, and brand-name building.

3) The large elite bureaucracy that has designed and managed the country's economy for decades would be disenfranchised, as the mar-

ket would take over as the determinant of strategy. This would rob the government of much of its capacity to control matters and would be deeply destabilizing.

4) There would be a rise in the significance and power of the small and medium enterprise sector, as it flooded into the opportunity spaces created by the rationalization of the *chaebol*. This would give rise to new forces of influence on the structure of the economy as they competed for capital with the traditionally capital-intensive *chaebol,* and in turn this might well lead to a weakening of Korea's ability to handle its traditional heavy industries competitively.

5) Pluralism in the society would rise as bodies such as unions, the new bourgeoisie, new political parties, and professions would begin to create new components in the power balance alongside the traditional "iron triangle" of the government elite, the bureaucracy, and big business. This would also be threatening to the traditional order and potentially destabilizing at a time when central power may still be needed.

The Korean position is different from that of Japan in one main respect: the severity and urgency of its crisis. It cannot afford the decade of adjustment (or relative nonadjustment as many would argue) that Japan has just had. The legitimacy of Korea's changes is therefore widely accepted within the society. A second feature that makes the two cases different is that the Korean government was authoritarian, and the Japanese was not. Many of the reforms being advocated for South Korea are as much political as economic, especially the dismantling of the state's control over business and the acceptance of pluralism. These political reforms are perhaps an inevitable part of the longer development process itself, now that the initial stage of industrial development via societal sacrifice is over.

If South Korea does accept the inevitably of a decentralized state and a market-driven economy, and if democracy takes hold more fully, what business system might one expect to see emerging from the current extremely unclear situation? The survival of the *chaebol* in their old form is unlikely, but the transition within them is likely to be toward professional management and business rationalization, both of which will logically be conducive to efficiency. The problem for them will be the source of discipline, for the simple reason that a still-immature financial market, including a financial press, may not be up to the job of driving them with the intensity previously provided by 1) government control of competitive capital allocation; and 2) the drive and vision of a dominant owner. The pressure of shareholder interests to drive firms requires an institutional structure to make it work, and that does not grow overnight. The system might well lose much of its momentum.

The growth of the small and medium enterprise sector is predictable and may well produce new large firms, given the freer access to capital. But these are unlikely to be professionally managed public companies, given the Korean tendency to see paternalism as the most legitimate source of authority. New large family businesses will emerge, unprotected and efficient, and they will learn much from the *chaebol* experience about technology management and international marketing.

Networks of collaboration across industry in the economy, even with new players proliferating, are unlikely to develop as they in Japan or Germany because of the weakness of horizontal associations in South Korea and the vertical nature of most forms of identity. This means that South Korea may take on some of the "compartmentalized" nature of the U.S./U.K. business system, in Whitley's terminology. This means that firms remain separate and competitive with each other rather than collaborative. Whether they can accumulate adequate scale, given their personalistic power structures, and do so without the kind of protection the *chaebol* received, is probably the greatest test of the system, unless the system gravitates more toward the Chinese capitalist model, in which personally run small firms dominate the structure and deal with the scale problem by limited personalistic networking. This would mean a shift in the industries South Korea manages efficiently and would bring them into direct competition with China, a contest they might well lose on labor costs, unless (as in Taiwan) the state helps with raising technological competence and allows industry to move into fields where the costs of labor can be absorbed in the margins available on higher technology products.

However one looks at it, the impression that grows is that the state in South Korea cannot walk away from the economy. Nor, in the context of East Asia, would it be expected to. These are generally strong-state societies, and their being so is a function of a moral structure that leaves government with the duty to govern and provide order. This is impossible to reconcile with the full adoption of Western free-market capitalism, and a hybrid form can be predicted.

Conclusion

There is enough here, without adding more, to convey the systemic nature of any mature economy. It is clear that a radical switch in the institutional fabric handling capital will reverberate all over the society and cause destabilizing side effects in the three components of the business system itself: the structures flowing from ownership; vertical and horizontal alliances across the economy; and the psychological glue holding firms together as human systems.

So too will the other main institutional fields (human capital and social capital) be threatened with transformation. The deeper cultural norms will change at their own pace—that is, slowly—but will act as subliminal sources of deep resistance and conservatism.

In Taiwan a similar account could be made, but different in detail. The key distinguishing feature is that the moral basis, the core purpose, of Korean economic behavior remains the national economic achievement; for Taiwan it is essentially the accumulation of family wealth, and for Japan it is the maintenance of employment. These might be expected to remain salient and not to give way easily to shareholder value as a design principle. In each case there would also be a series of ricochet-like side effects to damage and destabilize the currently balanced system. Whatever the eventual formula for settlement, it would evolve under the strong but hidden influences of the basic cultural predispositions to order society according to certain fundamental and non-negotiable principles.

The Japanese, the Koreans, and others in Asia will not allow these external impositions to run their course. The embeddedness of their business systems will not allow them to. The "right" of free-market capitalism to spread everywhere will hit the barrier of morality and the debate over what business is for. Materialism is not guaranteed to prevail in that debate, despite having had, in recent decades, a good run.

NOTES

This chapter has benefited greatly from the advice of Laurence Whitehead, and also from the discussions at the November 1999 conference in Santiago, Chile. The assistance at INSEAD of the Euro-Asia Centre library and the Research Committee is also gratefully acknowledged.

1. See Robert Wade, "East Asia's Economic Success: Conflicting Perspectives, Partial Insights, Shaky Evidence," *World Politics* 44 (January 1992): 270–320.

2. David S. Landes, *The Wealth and Poverty of Nations* (New York: Norton, 1998); Samuel P. Huntington, *The Clash of Civilizations and the Remaking of World Order* (New York: Simon and Schuster, 1996); and Francis Fukuyama, *Trust: The Social Virtues and the Creation of Prosperity* (New York: Free Press, 1995).

3. Clark Kerr, *The Future of Industrial Societies,* (Cambridge: Harvard University Press, 1983).

4. Richard Whitley, *Divergent Capitalisms: The Social Structuring and Change of Business Systems* (Oxford: Oxford University Press, 1999); Francis Fukuyama, *Trust*; Samuel P. Huntington, *The Clash of Civilizations and the Remaking of World Order*; John Gray, *False Dawn: The Delusions of Global Capitalism* (London: Granta, 1998); and Richard Sennett, *The Corrosion of Character* (New York: Norton, 1998).

5. Christopher Tremewan, *The Political Economy of Social Control in Singapore* (New York: St. Martin's, 1994).

6. Gordon Redding, "The impact of multi-nationals on the Thickening of Civil Society: Current Developments in the Economy of China," in Ann Bernstein and Peter L. Berger, eds., *Business and Democracy* (London: Pinter, 1998).

7. John H. Dunning, "Governments and the Macro-organization of Economic Activity: A Historical and Spatial Perspective," in John H. Dunning, ed., *Governments, Globalization, and International Business* (Oxford: Oxford University Press, 1997).

8. Richard G. Lipsey, "Globalization and National Government Policies: An Economist's View," in John H. Dunning, ed., *Governments, Globalization, and International Business*.

9. Susan Strange, *The Retreat of the State* (Cambridge, Cambridge University Press, 1996). See also Susan Strange "An International Political Economy Perspective," in John H. Dunning, ed., *Governments, Globalization, and International Business*.

10. Susan Strange, *The Retreat of the State*, 44.

11. Susan Strange, *The Retreat of the State*, 86.

12. Vivien Schmidt, "The New World Order Incorporated: The Rise of Business and the Decline of the Nation-state," *Daedalus Conference on the Twentieth Century State*. (Cambridge, Mass: American Academy of Arts and Sciences, September 1995).

13. Stephen Kobrin, The architecture of globalization: state sovereignty in a networked global economy," in John H. Dunning, ed., *Governments, Globalization, and International Business*.

14. John M. Stopford and Susan Strange, *Rival States, Rival Firms: Competition for World Market Shares* (Cambridge: Cambridge University Press, 1991); and R. O'Brian, *Global Financial Integration: The End of Geography,* (London: Pinter, 1992).

15. *The Economist*, 31 July 1999, 8.

16. Yun-han Chu, "State structure and economic adjustment of the East Asian newly industrialized countries," *International Organization* 43 (Autumn 1989): 647–72.

17. Vivien Schmidt, "The New World Order Incorporated."

18. Richard Whitley, *Divergent Capitalisms*.

19. Ungsuh K. Park, *Balancing Between Panic and Mania: The East Asian Economic Crises and Challenges to the International Financing* (Seoul: Samsung Economic Research Institute, 2000), 400.

20. Kent E. Calder, *Strategic Capitalism* (Princeton: Princeton University Press, 1993).

21. Norman Jacobs, *The Korean Road to Modernization and Development* (Urbana: University of Illinois Press, 1985).

22. Ku-Hyun Jung, "National Governance in South Korea and Developing New State-Business Relations in the Post-Crisis Era," *Global Economic Review* 28 (1999): 30–49.

23. *EIU Business Asia,* 4 September 2000, 5.

8

DOES EDUCATION PROMOTE GROWTH AND DEMOCRACY?

Ananya Basu and Elizabeth M. King

Ananya Basu is an economist with the World Bank's South Asia Poverty Reduction and Economic Management Unit. Elizabeth M. King is the lead economist for the Development Research Group of the World Bank and author (with A. Mason) of Engendering Development—Through Gender Equality in Rights, Resources, and Voice *(2001).*

Over the past half-century, vast progress was made in many aspects of human welfare. The expansion of mass education that enabled widespread gains in literacy and educational levels is regarded as key to that progress. Education is seen as having contributed to a better quality of life. The benefits to individuals and households have been well documented. More schooling is associated with greater individual productivity and earning capacity, and with greater capacity to cope with economic hardships. In addition, these salutary effects on individuals are supposed to sum up to macroeconomic evidence of direct benefits to economic growth, a healthier society, and better governance.

Countries in Latin America and East Asia have led the progress in education in the developing world. This progress is solidly grounded in very high enrollment rates in primary education, in rising secondary enrollments, and in low illiteracy rates. How have the two regions' countries benefited from their educational progress? And have the gains from this progress been shared widely in their populations, whether in terms of faster economic growth or in better political institutions? This chapter attempts to answer these questions.

After we review the empirical evidence regarding educational progress in Latin American and East Asian countries in the next section, we discuss the benefits of this educational progress. We focus on three key areas of benefit, all of which are interrelated—economic growth, human development, and democracy. The economic literature on human capital supports the expectation that educational progress leads to greater productivity of the labor force, to more technological change, and thus to faster economic growth. Yet higher average education levels are no guarantee of faster growth, as some countries in both regions have shown.[1] Results suggest that the quality and distribution of education—as well as a country's general policy environment—can affect the impact of education on economic growth. And whether the institutional environment stifles or promotes entrepreneurial activity, production, and concerns about equity determines both the speed and character of economic development. In the two regions, similar education levels have not led to similar economic payoffs.

Educational progress is also supposed to lead to better lives through channels other than labor productivity and economic growth. Literacy and knowledge are also expected to contribute to nation-building, social cohesion, and the development of a stable and democratic society. The schooling of a child is a means by which society transmits codes of conduct and social norms and values. If schooling is an effective transmitter of desirable behaviors and values, then one might conclude that societies which have achieved higher education levels are also likely to prove more cohesive and better functioning. In this chapter we examine the link between education and political institutions. In particular, we estimate the relationship between education and measures of democracy, given the hypothesis that populations with more schooling may be better able to nurture a society in which a larger proportion of the population participates in important decision making. We recognize that the linkage between education levels and democracy can go both ways, however, and that causality is an issue requiring better information and analysis than we can provide at this time.

Lastly, we review findings on how the manner in which education is delivered—for example, whether public education is the norm, to what extent households and students are given a choice of schools or school systems, and whether beneficiaries have a voice in defining the educational process—affects the content and effectiveness of the delivery itself. In other words, shared decision making, a hallmark of greater democracy, can itself improve education outcomes, thus producing a feedback loop. East Asian countries have generally followed a centralized approach to the provision and management of basic education, though with substantial contributions from parents and communities for the finance of schools. In contrast, several Latin American countries have experimented the most with decentralizing the management and finance of schools in order to improve school performance. What then are the lessons about how the openness of the society itself and the level of community participation that it engenders feed back into educational progress, thus completing a circle?

Educational Progress

East Asia and Latin America have made considerable strides in educational attainment. At the primary level, both regions have had higher

FIGURE 1—TRENDS IN EDUCATIONAL ACHIEVEMENT IN EAST ASIA &
LATIN AMERICA, 1970–95

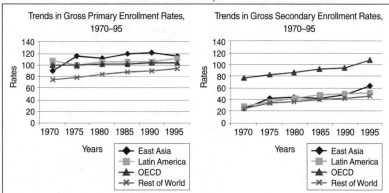

Note: Averages are population weighted.
Source: World Development Indicators 2001 (regional averages). Washington, D.C.: The
World Bank, 2001.

enrollment rates than even OECD countries since the early 1980s (see
Figure 1 above). This reflects the regions' relatively sustained investments in basic education. Enrollment rates at the secondary level have
also risen by more than 20 percent, especially in East Asia. Secondary
enrollment rates in Latin America and East Asia are lower than the mean
for OECD countries, but both regions do better compared with the rest
of the developing world. At the tertiary level, both regions also exceed
the average for the developing world, with Latin America's enrollment
rate being higher than East Asia's.

Sustained increases in school enrollment rates in the two regions have
raised their average completed years of schooling. In 1990, average years
of schooling were more than one year higher than the developing-country
average of around 4.5, though substantially lower than the averages for
OECD countries and for the transition economies of Eastern Europe
(over 9 years).[2] The sustained commitment of the two regions to basic
education is also reflected in the rapid decline in their adult illiteracy
rates, even as life expectancy rose, thus dampening this effect,
arithmetically speaking. In the mid-1990s the adult illiteracy rate was
slightly higher in East Asia than in Latin America. Furthermore, though
not shown here, gender disparities are relatively smaller in East Asia
and Latin America than in other world regions, with female-male
enrollment and literacy-rate ratios being close to unity.[3]

At the tertiary level, there is large variation within each region. In
East Asia, countries like Japan and Korea have achieved impressive levels of tertiary enrollment in excess of 40 percent, while China and
Vietnam lagged behind at about 5 percent. In Latin America, countries
like Argentina, Chile, Panama, Peru, and Costa Rica have significantly

higher rates than Paraguay, Colombia, and Nicaragua.[4] In addition, there are differences between the two regions with respect to specialization. In East Asia, students display a relative bias toward science and engineering degrees. In 1995, 42 percent of tertiary-level students in East Asia were enrolled in science and engineering programs, while the comparable percentage for Latin America was 30 percent.[5]

Inequality in the distribution of education. In assessing educational progress, it is important to consider not only average levels but also the distribution of educational advances within the population, especially with respect to our interest in democracy. Average education levels can increase in several ways: by raising the education levels of a small segment of the population considerably while keeping everyone else's schooling constant, by raising the education levels of those with the least schooling, or by increasing everyone's schooling such as to leave the distribution of education levels unchanged. How the increase is achieved affects its impact on society and the economy. One hypothesis is that the wider the spread of educational progress (especially among those with the least education) the higher are the returns in terms of social development, economic growth, and democracy.

A recent study has examined the effect of education inequality on economic growth. While standard production-function estimates for middle-income countries suggest an insignificant effect of average schooling on per capita output, if the distribution of human capital is also taken into account, then average education levels show a significant positive impact on output, while inequality (as measured by the standard deviation) has a negative influence.[6]

When one looks at the distribution of students by income group in Latin American countries, the story that emerges is one of declining inequality in rates of enrollment. The gap in completed years of schooling between 25-year-olds in the poorest decile and those in the richest decile ranges from ten years in Mexico and Panama to about six years in Uruguay, Venezuela, and Nicaragua.[7] Among children ages 6 through 14, as Table 1 on the following page indicates, there is relative equality in the enrollment rates of the richest 20 percent and the poorest 40 percent in Brazil and Peru, but large inequalities in Guatemala and the Dominican Republic.[8] Moreover, the wealth gap is more severe at higher levels of education. In Ecuador, Nicaragua, and Panama, the percentage of primary-school students from the poorest expenditure quintile actually exceeds that from the richest quintile, a result partly of the higher fertility rates among the poor.[9] In higher education, fewer than 10 percent of all secondary-school students belong to the poorest 20 percent of the population, while about 30 percent belong to the richest 20 percent. At tertiary and university education levels, depending on the country, between 40 and 70 percent of students are from the richest 20

TABLE 1—WEALTH GAPS IN ENROLLMENT
RATES AMONG 6 TO 14-YEAR-OLDS

Country, Year	Poor	Rich-Poor Gap	Rich/Poor Ratio
Latin America			
Bolivia, 1993–94	81.0	14.9	1.18
Bolivia, 1997	87.8	10.0	1.11
Brazil, 1996	89.0	9.2	1.10
Colombia, 1990	68.3	21.2	1.31
Colombia, 1995	80.9	16.7	1.21
Dominican Republic, 1991	50.3	39.3	1.78
Dominican Republic, 1995	88.7	9.1	1.10
Guatemala, 1995	46.4	44.4	1.96
Haiti, 1994–95	55.2	34.5	1.62
Nicaragua, 1998	63.9	29.1	1.45
Peru, 1991–92	83.9	6.5	1.08
Peru, 1996	85.8	8.8	1.10
Unweighted Mean	*73.4*	*20.31*	*1.33*
East Asia & Pacific			
Indonesia, 1991	66.6	23.1	1.35
Indonesia, 1994	75.5	19.6	1.26
Indonesia, 1997	80.5	14.5	1.18
Philippines, 1993	70.0	16.3	1.23
Philippines, 1998	78.9	15.9	1.20
Unweighted Mean	*74.3*	*17.88*	*1.24*

Source: Deon Filmer, "The Structures of Social Disparities in Education" (2000). (See endnote 8 for full citation.)

percent. This indicates a much higher degree of inequality at the tertiary level.

A similar pattern holds for countries in East Asia. Table 1 includes data from Indonesia and the Philippines showing that wealth gaps exist even for primary-school-age students. This wealth gap has decreased over time but is still about 20 percent according to the latest data available.[10] Information from past studies on older age groups indicates larger wealth gaps. In Indonesia, the enrollment rates at the lower secondary and upper secondary levels for the richest decile were 9 and 37 times larger, respectively, than those for the poorest decile in 1989. At the tertiary level, the net enrollment rate for the top decile was 27 percent, contrasted to less than 1 percent for the bottom six deciles combined.[11] In Vietnam in 1996, almost 70 percent of university students were from the richest 20 percent of the population, while less than 1 percent were from the poorest 20 percent.[12]

Turning to another measure of inequality, Lopez, Thomas, and Wang provide patterns in the Gini coefficients of the distribution of education in selected countries (see Table 2 on the facing page).[13] South Korea achieved a steep decline in its education Gini between 1970 and 1995. Whereas it had one of the highest Gini in both regions in 1970, by 1995 its Gini had fallen to a level comparable to, if not even better than, those in industrial countries. In other countries in East Asia, the decline in the Gini was less impressive. In Latin America, the average education Gini coefficient started off slightly lower than in East Asia in 1970, primarily because of Chile, but it does not show as large a decline as in East Asia. Education inequality dropped in Brazil, Mexico, Peru, and Venezuela during the period, but there was a slight worsening of inequality in Colombia and no change in Chile. The most impressive decrease occurred in Brazil.

The (unweighted) averages of the education Gini declined by 19 per-

TABLE 2—GINI
COEFFICIENT OF THE
DISTRIBUTION OF
EDUCATION, 1970 & 1995

COUNTRY	1970	1995
Latin America		
Brazil	.41	.26
Chile	.28	.27
Colombia	.41	.42
Mexico	.42	.32
Peru	.43	.37
Venezuela	.42	.34
Unweighted Mean	*.39*	*.33*
East Asia & Pacific		
China	.45	.38
South Korea	.44	.19
Malaysia	.44	.38
Philippines	.37	.30
Thailand	.38	.37
Unweighted Mean	*.42*	*.32*

Sources: Ramon E. Lopez, Vinod Thomas, and Yan Wang, "Addressing the Education Puzzle" (1998). (See endnote 1 for full citation.)

cent and 28 percent from 1970 in Latin America and East Asia, respectively. While the average Gini coefficient is about the same in both regions, the marginally lower Gini in East Asia is driven by South Korea's much lower inequality, and the marginally higher average Gini in Latin America is due largely to Colombia. In general, inequality in education remains an issue in both regions.

Quality of education. Given that on average East Asia and Latin America have already achieved high enrollment rates, at least in basic education, the quality of education, rather than enrollment, may be the more critical issue for enhancing educational development in the future in these two regions. Admittedly, education quality is difficult to define and measure—partly because education is a process that inherently occurs behind classroom walls and partly because its outputs are multidimensional and not always quantifiable—and many indicators used are obviously flawed.

The pupil-teacher ratio, a commonly used indicator of quality given the dearth of measures comparable across countries, does not differ significantly between the two regions.[14] In Latin America, the ratio of pupils to teacher averaged just over 26 in primary education, while in East Asia it was around 23 in the mid-1990s. Interestingly, South Korea, with its superior growth performance, has a substantially higher pupil-teacher ratio compared to, say, Argentina, which grew much more slowly over the same period.

Repetition and dropout rates are also sometimes regarded as other measures of quality—though they really confound demand factors and the effect of school quality. These rates are much lower in East Asian countries than in other countries of similar income levels, and lower than in Latin American countries in particular.[15] Primary-school dropout rates and repetition rates averaged about 10 percent and 42 percent, respectively, in Latin America, while comparable figures were only 6 percent and 14 percent in East Asia in 1980–90. Thus completion rates in most Latin American countries are below East Asian levels. For example, Brazil's primary completion rate was higher than South Korea's in the 1950s—60 percent compared to 36 percent. By the 1980s, Brazil's primary completion rate had declined instead of risen, while South Korea's completion rate had increased to about 90 percent.[16]

COUNTRY	MATHEMATICS	SCIENCE
Singapore	625	547
South Korea	611	597
Japan	597	574
Hong Kong	587	533
Thailand	490	473
International Average	*529*	*524*

Source: Data from United States Department of Education (1997). (See endnote 18 for full citation.)

If the principal goal is to achieve mastery of a specific academic curriculum, then how students perform on a test that is based on that curriculum would be the most appropriate indicator of quality. Scores on internationally comparable tests give clearer indications of quality across countries. Where comparable student test scores are widely available, they appear to be positively related to growth rates in per capita GDP, suggesting that quality, rather than quantity, is the key issue.[17]

Results from the Third International Mathematics and Science Study (TIMSS), undertaken in 1995 for fourth-graders, indicate stellar performances for students from East Asian countries.[18] In mathematics, the four top-ranking nations were Singapore, South Korea, Japan, and Hong Kong, though Thailand scored below the international average. In science, South Korea and Japan occupied the top two slots, while Singapore and Hong Kong placed above the international average as well (see Table 3 above). In contrast, evidence from other cognitive achievement tests shows students in Latin America to be performing poorly. In a 1992 assessment of mathematics and science skills for 13-year-olds, for example, students from China, South Korea, and Taiwan outperformed Brazilian students. In a similar reading test for nine-year-olds, Venezuela was outranked by all countries in the sample, including Indonesia, Singapore, and Hong Kong.[19] In science and mathematics tests administered to students in the eighth grade, Colombian students ranked well behind their counterparts from Singapore and South Korea.[20] Because many countries in the two regions did not participate in the study, it is not wise to make blanket statements from the results for the few that did. Yet these provide provisional conclusions that, despite similar enrollment rates at the primary and secondary education levels in the two regions, education quality appears to be dissimilar.

The distribution of the quality of education also matters in assessing educational progress. Low-quality public education generally harms low-income students more than it harms richer students. This is because low-income students have fewer options; they are less able to transfer to better non-government schools. There is evidence that quality differs between private schools and government or public schools. Controlling for student background and selection bias, Jimenez and Lockheed find that in Colombia, the Dominican Republic, Thailand, and the Philippines, students in private schools outperform their counterparts in public schools in a variety of tests.[21] The reasons? One is that private schools invest more in instructional material and teacher training than do public schools. Another is that most students from poorer backgrounds in Latin America attend public schools that are less efficient, while higher-income families choose private schools that provide better quality education.

Benefits of Educational Progress

As suggested by the evidence presented above, East Asia and Latin America have broadly similar education profiles, especially with respect to levels and distribution of student enrollment. How has education progress in these two regions translated into economic growth? How far does education help to cope with the effects of several economic crises? And how does education affect individual and family well-being? In this section we examine the evidence on the benefits from education. We focus first on standard types and measures of benefits: the effect of education levels on economic growth and human development indicators. We then discuss the effect of educational development on democracy and political institutions. Before beginning our discussion of the benefits, we note that while the following subsections focus on aspects of benefits for which we can find comparable measures—and thus may seem "bloodless"—we recognize the far-ranging gains that education confers on individuals and societies, and agree with Sen that "an illiterate person is . . . much less equipped to defend herself in court, to obtain a bank loan, to enforce her inheritance rights, to take advantage of new technology, to compete for secure employment, to get on the right bus, to take part in political activity, in short, to participate successfully in the modern economy and society."[22]

Economic growth and coping with crises. It is commonly accepted that a person's educational attainment enhances his or her employability and earning capacity in the labor market. Estimates of individual wage equations for a number of countries suggest that private returns on education are high. On average, Psacharapoulous estimates them to be 29.1, 18.1, and 20.3 percent, respectively, for primary, secondary, and tertiary education.[23] But the benefits of education are said to extend beyond the individual. According to Lucas, for example, a worker's schooling also enhances the productivity of coworkers, thereby giving rise to classical externalities or spillover effects.[24] In turn, the general level of education in the workforce expands production possibilities, by facilitating the discovery, adaptation, and use of more economically rewarding, albeit technologically more demanding and knowledge-intensive, production processes. Thus educational progress ultimately can be expected to benefit macroeconomic performance. Barro, using cross-country data for 1960–85, shows that countries with higher levels

FIGURE 2—RELATIONSHIP BETWEEN INITIAL ENROLLMENT LEVEL
& ECONOMIC GROWTH

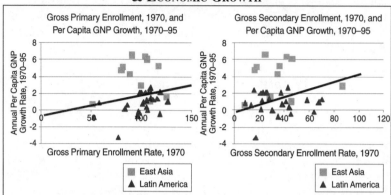

Note: The regression lines are derived from multiple regression estimates for about 100 countries around the world, while the scatter plots show only the points for Latin American and East Asian countries. See Appendix Table A1 for the list of Latin American and East Asian countries. The regressions for primary and secondary education are based on cross-country data, controlling for initial GDP per capita in 1970. The coefficients on initial enrollment rates and GNP per capita are significant in both cases. The estimated equations are as follows:

Growth Rate$_i$ = -.4349392 -.0000528 (Initial Per Capita GNP$_i$) + .02412 (Initial Primary Enrollment Rate$_i$), R^2 = .12, N = 105.

Growth Rate$_i$ = .3793284 -.0001172 (Initial Per Capita GNP$_i$) + .0453176 (Initial Secondary Enrollment Rate$_i$), R^2 = .21, N = 101.

Source: World Development Indicators 1999. Washington, D.C.: The World Bank, 1999.

of primary and secondary enrollment rates are more likely to have higher growth rates in real per capita incomes, controlling for other factors like initial income.[25] He estimates that a 1-percentage-point increase in initial primary and secondary enrollment rates would have raised average annual per capita GDP growth rates across countries during 1960–85 by 1.13 percent and 1.38 percent at the mean, respectively.[26]

While Latin America and East Asia have broadly similar achievements in education, their economic performances over the last few decades have been strikingly different. The Latin American economies experienced slow or negative growth rates in per capita incomes, whereas many East Asian countries achieved annual growth rates beyond 5 percent. Part of this difference in growth performance can be traced to inter-regional differences in education levels. For example, based on Barro-type growth regressions, had South Korea's enrollment rates in 1960 been at Brazilian levels, the average annual growth rate in per capita GDP would have been 5.6 percent instead of 6.1 percent.[27] Even on this basis, however, the differences in education levels between the two regions are not large enough to explain all, or indeed most, of the difference in their income growth.

Updating these studies to cover 1970–95, we also found a positive

FIGURE 3—PER CAPITA GNP GROWTH & GROWTH IN EDUCATIONAL ATTAINMENT, 1970–95

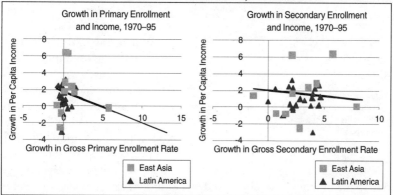

Note: The regression lines are derived from multiple regression estimates for about 100 countries around the world, while the scatter plots show only the points for Latin American and East Asian countries. The regressions for growth in primary and secondary enrollment are based on cross-country data. The coefficients on growth rates in GNP per capita are insignificant in both cases. The estimated equations are as follows:

Primary Enrollment Growth Rate$_i$ = 1.069673 - .09515 (Growth in Per Capita GNP$_i$), R^2 = .02, N = 90.

Secondary Enrollment Growth Rate$_i$ = 3.150332 - .05224 (Growth in Per Capita GNP$_i$), R^2 = .02, N = 90.

Source: World Development Indicators 1999. Washington, D.C.: The World Bank, 1999.

relationship between growth rates in GNP per capita and initial levels of educational attainment, controlling for initial per capita GNP. As with previous studies, education in Latin American countries did not lead to higher growth rates as effectively as it did in East Asian countries. World regression lines derived from this analysis have been drawn in Figure 2 on the facing page, in order to provide a comparison for the scatter plots representing the two regions. The plots show that most countries in East Asia achieved growth rates that exceeded what could be expected on the basis of their initial educational attainment and thus mostly lie above the "world" regression lines, while most countries in Latin America had growth rates that fell below the regression line. In fact, from about 1960 to the pre-crisis period of the late 1990s, the "four tigers"—Hong Kong, South Korea, Singapore, and Taiwan—and the newly industrializing economies of Indonesia, Malaysia, and Thailand grew about three times as fast as Latin American countries, on average.

The positively sloping world regression lines become negatively sloping when the growth in enrollment rates is substituted for initial education levels, indicating a negative, rather than a positive, relationship between the change in enrollment rates and growth rates in per capita income (see Figure 3 above). The two regions show different results, however, at least for primary education. In general, there does not seem to be any

TABLE 4—EDUCATION, GROWTH &
OPENNESS, 1970–95

	EAST ASIA	LATIN AMERICA
Growth in Per Capita GNP	5.65	1.22
Growth in Primary Enrollment	.99	.17
Growth in Secondary Enrollment	3.86	2.54
Growth in Exports	10.70	5.89
Growth in Imports	10.75	5.39

Note: All numbers are annual compound averages calculated using World Development Indicators (1999) with regional averages in 1970 and 1995 as end-points.

relationship between growth rates in primary enrollment and income growth, as there was hardly any growth in primary enrollment rates in the two regions, with the exception of one country in East Asia.[28] This result is hardly surprising since enrollment rates were already high at the beginning of the period in the two regions. In fact, for the developing world as a whole, gross enrollment rates, which can take a value greater than one due to the number of overage students enrolled, can fall back to a value of one despite, or because of, education progress. When students enter school at the right age such that the number of overage students falls, gross enrollment rates can show a negative growth rate. If this quirky nature of gross enrollment rates is not accounted for, then education growth rates in countries with already high enrollment rates are a misleading indicator of progress.

Gross enrollment rates at the secondary level are a different matter, since they are usually far below 100 percent. The two regions had positive growth rates in secondary education (except for one East Asian country). The regression results show no pattern for East Asia, but reveal a pattern for Latin America that appears to follow the world regression line with a slight negative relationship.[29]

It has been suggested that the policy framework is a key factor that allows economies to reap higher benefits from education. A 5 percent increase in average years of schooling for the labor force yields a 0.85 percent gain in the annual growth rate of per capita income in a liberal economic environment.[30] Table 4 above shows that the East Asian economies have had much higher growth rates in openness indicators, as well as higher growth rates in per capita income, than did the average Latin American economies. The import-substituting, capital-intensive strategies adopted by Latin American countries did not generate high demand for skilled labor. Moreover, the 1980s were an especially difficult period of hyperinflation and stagnation in Latin America.

How about when, for many reasons, economies experience stagnation or even negative growth—does education make a difference then? Both East Asia and Latin America have experienced economic crises and policy changes over the last few decades. In the early 1980s, a number of Latin American countries undertook structural-adjustment policy measures in an attempt to stabilize their economies in the face of hyperinflation and stagnation and put them back on the trajectory of long-run economic growth. In most cases, this was accompanied by measures to

TABLE 5—DEVELOPMENT INDICATORS, EAST ASIA & LATIN
AMERICA AVERAGES

REGION	LIFE EXPECTANCY, 1997	TOTAL FERTILITY RATE, 1997	INFANT MORTALITY RATE PER 1,000 LIVE BIRTHS, 1995
East Asia	68.72	2.16	39.84
Latin America	69.61	2.72	40.91
World	66.73	2.76	60.46

Source: World Development Indicators 2001 (Washington, D.C.: The World Bank, 2001).

reduce the fiscal deficit.[31] There is limited evidence that education may have helped individuals to cope better with the policy changes and austerity measures of the period. For instance, comparing average salaries before and after severance for displaced employees of the Central Bank of Ecuador during downsizing measures in the early 1990s, Rama and MacIssac find that the earnings loss for employees is roughly 3 percent less for every additional year of schooling, controlling for other characteristics like past experience and seniority.[32]

As for East Asia, the impressive growth trend was interrupted in the late 1990s. The currency and financial crisis that emerged in Thailand spread through the region, bringing economic hardships and adjustments both in the labor market and in the home. After decades of growth of 4 percent per annum in the region, per capita income levels fell in economies like South Korea's, Indonesia's, and Malaysia's.[33] There is reason to believe that higher education levels may have helped to mitigate somewhat the impact of the crisis. For example, one study on Indonesia concludes that additional years of education may have offered both men and women some protection against losing a job in 1998, and that postprimary education of the household head was associated with significantly higher labor income in both rural and urban areas after the crisis hit.[34]

Longer lives and smaller populations. The benefits of more education show up in development indicators together with income growth and economic progress. For example, higher education is associated with better health and nutritional status. Various findings relate to the benefits of female education. A study of 63 countries concludes that mothers' education accounts for 43 percent of the total decline in child malnutrition over the period 1970–95.[35] Another study estimates that a 10 percent increase in female primary and secondary enrollment lowers the infant mortality rate by 4.1 and 5.6 deaths per 1,000 live births, respectively.[36] Female education is also associated with lower fertility rates. Using data from more than 100 countries in 1990, Klasen estimates that every additional year of female schooling reduces the total fertility rate by 0.23 births per woman.[37] Reducing fertility and population growth is desirable in contexts where high fertility imperils the lives of both children and mothers, and where rapid population growth poses a serious threat

TABLE 6—REGRESSION RESULTS FOR HUMAN DEVELOPMENT
INDICATORS, EAST ASIA & LATIN AMERICA

Dependent Variable	Per Capita GDP (LOG)	Gross Primary Enroll-ment	Gross Secondary Enroll ment	Gross Tertiary Enroll-ment	Literacy Rate	Region Is East Asia	Region Is Latin America & Caribbean
Life Expectancy	4.787 (42.728)	.098 (14.973)				3.083 (5.968)	3.051 (8.064)
Life Expectancy	3.118 (23.642)		.160 (22.764)			4.264 (8.931)	4.732 (13.637)
Life Expectancy	4.844 (37.185)			.065 (4.766)		4.163 (7.246)	3.789 (8.852)
Life Expectancy	3.460 (27.300)				.203 (27.274)	1.973 (4.156)	1.257 (3.748)
Total Fertility Rate	-.698 (-35.072)	-.017 (-12.583)				-.646 (-6.350)	.074 (.974)
Total Fertility Rate	-.273 (-11.495)		-.036 (-29.037)			-.917 (-10.566)	-.333 (-5.135)
Total Fertility Rate	-.659 (-25.813)			-.023 (-8.954)		-.872 (-7.760)	-.125 (-1.467)
Total Fertility Rate	-.273 (-11.206)				-.047 (-32.577)	-.532 (-6.050)	.359 (5.644)

Notes: T-statistics given in parentheses. Regressions include constant term which is not reported. All regressions include time dummies. Data pertain to the period 1960–2000.

to the environment. The available evidence on East Asia and Latin America confirms the association between education and other human development outcomes at a regional level (see Table 5 on the previous page). Both regions have lower fertility rates and infant mortality rates, and higher life expectancy at birth, on average, than the world as a whole.

Regression analyses that control for other factors affecting human development also confirm that education exerts an influence on development indicators independent of per capita income (see Table 6 above). Data on life expectancy at birth in years and total fertility rate over 1960–2000 are combined with data on per capita income and education to examine these effects for countries in the two regions.[38] While the two regions have comparable life expectancies that are higher than world averages, Latin America has a higher fertility rate than East Asia. Controlling for per capita income, higher school-enrollment rates and literacy rates make for longer lives and smaller families.

Democracy and social cohesion. Education has long been associated with other community-level benefits besides its direct impact on economic production. These effects include improving civic behaviors and social equity, engendering broad political participation, strengthening national cohesiveness, reducing crime rates and corruption, and so on. It has been argued that the early years of education are a particularly effective means for instilling social norms, common values, and conformity. There is also a growing body of research that links education to attitudes toward democracy, as well as the effectiveness of governments and institutions. Studies have used these notions to regard

FIGURE 4—MEASURES PERTAINING TO CHIEF EXECUTIVE'S OFFICE

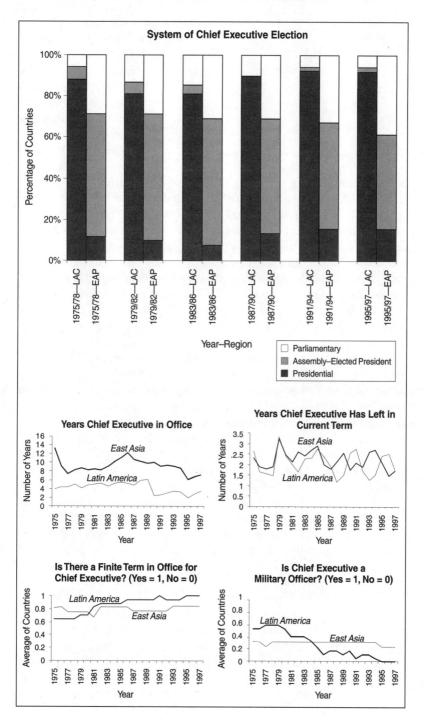

FIGURE 5—CONTROL OVER RELEVANT HOUSES

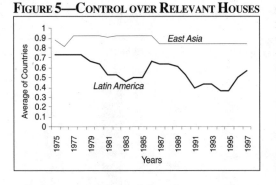

Years

education as a communal responsibility and to support public involvement in both its financing and its substance. This is largely why the state provides at least ten years of compulsory education in industrialized countries and why the state is also the main source of finance of primary schooling in many other countries.

In this section, we consider only a limited aspect of this broad topic: specifically, whether educational progress in the two regions has led to more prodemocratic political institutions. The question implies two propositions—first, that democratic political institutions are desirable, and second, that educational progress somehow leads to more democratic institutions. We address the second proposition largely in a positive sense—through econometric inquiry—rather than in a normative sense.

While the state of political institutions is difficult to characterize fully—or satisfactorily—in a quantitative way, for the purpose of undertaking a statistical analysis, we limit the analysis to quantifiable measures for which time-series, cross-country data are available. Since we estimate statistical relationships, we prefer to use measures of institutional quality that are derived from objective evaluations which could support comparisons across countries and over time. The data employed are from the Database of Political Institutions.[39] From this database we have selected several variables that describe the type of executive and legislative branches of government, the degree and quality of shared decision making within the country, and whether there was serious vote fraud or voter intimidation in the last election.[40]

Figure 4 on the previous page displays clear differences between the two regions with respect to several of the measures pertaining to the executive office. For example, in Latin America, the predominant system for the executive branch of government is a nationally elected president, with more than four-fifths of countries following this system, while in East Asia the prevalent system is a president elected by a national assembly. Moreover, in East Asia, there has been a trend away from a presidential system and toward a parliamentary form.

There are also regional differences with respect to the number of years a chief executive is in office. The average number of years a chief executive has been in office in any given year during 1975–97 was 4.5 years in Latin America and 9.7 years in East Asia—a large difference. The incumbent is expected to stay an average of 2 more years in either

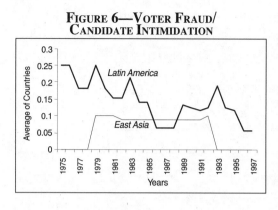

FIGURE 6—VOTER FRAUD/
CANDIDATE INTIMIDATION

region. These numbers indicate that turnovers in the executive branch have been less frequent in East Asia than in Latin America, but that the two regions do not differ greatly with respect to whether there is a term limit to the chief executive's office. The corresponding numbers are 90 percent of the countries in Latin America as compared with 83 percent in East Asia, indicating that the regional pattern in average tenure is not necessarily due to a difference in the system. Lastly, the two regions differ with respect to whether or not the chief executive is a member of the military. This military presence was more pronounced in Latin America in the 1970s and the early 1980s but had disappeared by the mid-1990s. In East Asia, the military presence in the executive office was lower than in Latin America at the beginning of the period but has remained at about one-third of the countries throughout the period.

As Figure 5 on the facing page shows, there is also a regional pattern regarding political parties. In East Asia, more than in Latin America, the political party of the chief executive also controls the legislative houses. This is the case in approximately 90 percent of East Asian countries—and the pattern has been quite stable over the past 30 years. In Latin America, there has been much greater fluctuation in this variable over time, but all in all, about one-half of the countries follow this pattern. One might conclude from this regional difference that there is more sharing of political power in Latin America than in East Asia.

Finally, there is also a regional difference regarding the quality of political elections. Data indicate that electoral fraud and intimidation of candidates have been reported in a larger number of countries in Latin America than in East Asia, although this number admittedly has declined over time, and that the fraud and intimidation were serious enough to have influenced the election results (see Figure 6 above). To the extent that a freer and cleaner election means that the contest is a more democratic process, one might conclude that, by this measure, Latin America's political institutions are less democratic on average than East Asia's. Since the information depends on reports, however, it is quite possible to have false negatives; that is, fraud and intimidation are more likely to go unreported in less democratic countries than in more democratic ones.

The different measures of the state of political institutions do not

TABLE 7—EDUCATION & POLITICAL INSTITUTIONS: REGRESSION RESULTS

	LITERACY	PRIMARY ENROLLMENT	SECONDARY ENROLLMENT	TERTIARY ENROLLMENT	LAC	EAP	R²	N
CE's tenure	-.010 (-1.04)				-4.143 (-8.97)	2.524 (3.67)	0.06	2220
CE's tenure		-.001 (-0.06)			-3.517 (-7.47)	2.257 (3.31)	0.03	2134
CE's tenure			-.042 (-5.48)		-3.433 (-7.34)	2.645 (3.88)	0.06	2075
CE's tenure				-.120 (-7.37)	-2.858 (-5.65)	3.999 (5.57)	0.08	1820
Finite term	.003 (6.72)				.184 (7.07)	.089 (2.40)	0.12	2182
Finite term		.002 (4.72)			.172 (7.25)	.103 (3.08)	0.14	2104
Finite term			.001 (4.64)		.184 (8.01)	.117 (3.63)	0.14	2044
Finite term				.006 (5.82)	.165 (6.68)	.103 (3.00)	0.15	1791
Military CE	-.005 (-9.60)				.131 (4.59)	.265 (6.45)	0.15	2217
Military CE		-.003 (-9.21)			.049 (2.13)	.208 (5.76)	0.20	2133
Military CE			-.004 (-9.94)		.022 (1.07)	.190 (5.49)	0.21	2074
Military CE				-.005 (-5.33)	.037 (1.20)	.188 (5.02)	0.19	1807
CE controls legislature	-.007 (-10.88)				-.039 (-1.59)	.220 (6.85)	0.11	1759
CE controls legislature		-.001 (-1.71)			-.083 (-2.74)	.149 (3.43)	0.09	1785
CE controls legislature			-.005 (-10.88)		-.104 (-3.39)	.177 (4.19)	0.14	1733
CE controls legislature				-.014 (-11.73)	-.031 (-0.92)	.243 (5.46)	0.18	1542
Voting fraud	-.001 (-2.91)				.090 (4.40)	.007 (0.25)	0.06	1680
Voting fraud		-.001 (-2.05)			.066 (3.61)	-.001 (-0.03)	0.05	1722
Voting fraud			-.001 (-4.07)		.065 (3.70)	-.001 (-0.02)	0.06	1677
Voting fraud				-.003 (-4.64)	.084 (4.46)	.031 (1.21)	0.08	1484

Note: T-statistics given in parentheses. CE refers to Chief Executive's office. Regressions for Chief Executive's tenure include a constant term that is not reported. All other dependent variables are binomial, with 1 denoting 'Yes' and 0 denoting 'No'. The first derivatives from probit estimates are reported in order to indicate partial or marginal effects. All estimations include year dummies and the country's level of GDP per capita.

point definitively to one region or the other as being more or less democratic. In terms of basic freedoms, data would indicate that the two regions are at par with each other. Consider what is perhaps a more sensitive measure of freedoms—an index of women's social and economic rights, using as standard a set of United Nations conventions.

Can we discern statistically significant relationships between these aspects of the political system and educational progress in the two regions? Once again, we are faced with the question about the direction of causality of the estimated relationship. On the one hand, a positive relationship could mean that higher education levels lead to more open and transparent political processes; on the other hand, a political system that is more open and where power is shared would be better disposed, and able, to provide public mass education. Given the sparseness of the data that are available and comparable across countries and across several points in time, the following analysis is limited in its ability to sort out this relationship, and should be regarded as exploratory. We use alternative measures of educational progress—a country's illiteracy rate as well as enrollment rates at the primary, secondary, and tertiary levels— and the different political variables discussed above. Since political institutions are likely to be affected also by the level of economic progress in a country and by other unmeasured characteristics specific to each region, we include in the equations per capita income level, a regional dummy variable that is meant to reflect unmeasured regional fixed effects, and year dummy variables that capture period effects (see Table 7 on the facing page).

The results from our multivariate analyses show clear and often statistically significant patterns in the relationships between political institutions and education. The chief executive's tenure is shorter the higher the literacy in the country or the higher the school enrollment rates at the different education levels, with the magnitude of the relationship being larger and more significant for the higher levels of secondary and tertiary education. By itself, tenure may indicate either political stability or monopoly of power. It has to be looked at in the context of institutions regarding the transfer of power. In this vein, the results show that the probability of the chief executive's term having a finite duration is positively related to literacy and enrollment rates, although the size of the relationship is quite small. More educated societies are less likely than less educated societies to have a military person in the executive office or to have a chief executive who also has control over the legislature, relationships that are statistically significant, though small. Lastly, national elections are less likely to be fraudulent in more educated societies, also a statistically significant result.

In sum, our regression results suggest that democratic political institutions—that is, whether power is shared and whether elections are relatively clean—are more likely to exist in countries that have higher literacy rates and higher education levels. Since the regressions also have accounted for the level of per capita income, and have included dummy variables for world regions and time trends, the fact that the education-related results are statistically significant means that even stronger conclusions can be made regarding the relationship between democracy and educational progress.

A word about the dummy variables for the two regions: there are interesting patterns in the relative position of the two regions vis-à-vis the rest of the world in the nature of their political institutions, after accounting for the education effects. Holding income and education levels constant, chief executives in the East Asian countries are more likely to have longer tenure, and those in Latin American countries to have shorter tenure, than the rest of the world, although chief executives in *both* regions are more likely than elsewhere to have a finite term. Juxtaposing the results about tenure and about term limits indicates greater political stability in East Asia than in Latin America. The chief executives in East Asia are also more likely to control their legislatures, and those in Latin America are less likely to do so, compared with other countries. The East Asian result can be interpreted in a positive light—for example, parliamentary (or legislative) support for the chief executive might enhance political stability and effectiveness—or in a negative light—there is less power-sharing and fewer checks and balances in the system. Countries in both regions are more likely to have a military officer as chief executive compared with other world regions. Finally, electoral fraud is more likely in Latin American countries and less likely in East Asian countries, relative to the rest of the world, although the results for East Asia are not statistically significant.

Public and Private Roles in Education

Thus far we have addressed the question of whether educational development engenders more economic growth, more human development, and a more democratic system of governance. In this section, we turn to the question of whether the way educational development has been achieved also enhances these benefits. In asking this question, we refer again to the literature which argues that the public provision of education is justified if the state wants to influence not only the level of education achieved but also its content. This literature recognizes that whether the state finances and/or delivers education will determine its ability to affect educational content. Specifically, the premise is that through public education the state will be able to define an education curriculum, as well as establish incentives to affect the behavior of direct providers, such as teachers, head teachers, and school supervisors.[41] In addition, who uses public education determines how widely education's content is spread. The more elitist and regressive is its reach, the less its direct impact on society as a whole.

Focus and incidence of public spending. Both regions have invested substantial resources in education—and with a signature focus on how to use public resources. The allocation of a larger share of public expenditures to the basic level of education has ensured maximum leverage for fiscal resources since basic education lays a solid foundation for higher levels of schooling. Overall public spending on education as a percentage of GNP has ranged from about 1 percent in Indonesia to 5 percent in Malaysia in about 1995, but all the East Asian countries showed a marked bias toward primary education. Primary education accounted for between 40 and 60 percent of the education budget while the share of tertiary education was only between 10 and 20 percent in the late 1980s.[42] Latin American countries also display this bias toward basic education. The percentage share of public spending on education in total GNP is not dissimilar to East Asian averages—ranging between 2 and 5 percent for most countries.[43] In the mid-1980s, over 50 percent of public spending on education in Latin American countries went to primary education, while 25 percent went to tertiary education.

Despite similar budget shares, per-child expenditures on basic education tended to be higher in East Asian countries compared to Latin American countries.[44] Average annual expenditure per primary-school pupil in Latin America fell from $164 to $118 between 1980 and 1989, while it rose in East Asia. In South Korea, for example, expenditure on basic education per eligible child rose from $95 to $433 over 1970–89, while it rose from $68 to only about $112 in Mexico over the same period. This cannot be attributed to government commitment, since public expenditure on basic education as a share of GNP actually rose in Mexico and fell in South Korea over the same period—but since GNP in South Korea increased so much faster over the period, the absolute expenditure levels rose faster as well.

Part of the inequality in access to education can be traced to the distribution of public subsidies. Where households bear a larger share of the costs of education, inequities between rich and poor households are likely to show up more starkly. In most countries, despite strong government commitment to universal basic education, primary education is not free, even to the poor. Even without official fees, there are a multitude of other costs that households need to bear to send their children to school—including registration, mandatory contributions, cost of uniforms and supplies, and so on. Of the total expenditure in public primary education, governments bear about 80 percent in China, Indonesia, Thailand, and the Philippines, but only about 50 percent in Vietnam and 25 percent in Cambodia.[45] In Latin America, public spending is 48, 66, and 76 percent of overall expenditures for primary education in Brazil, Colombia, and Chile, respectively.[46]

So who is reached by public subsidies on education? An important policy question to raise is whether this incidence of public expenditure for education is consistent with the government's objectives with respect to public mass education. Available data for several countries during the 1990s indicate that the poorest income (expenditure) quintile in the population generally receives the lowest share of public spending in education. On average, in Latin America, the poorest quintile receives less than 15 percent of government education subsidies, while

TABLE 8—PROPORTION OF PUBLIC SUB-
SIDY RECEIVED BY THE POOREST INCOME
QUINTILE BY EDUCATION LEVEL

COUNTRY, YEAR	PRIMARY	SECONDARY	TERTIARY
Columbia, 1992	39	21	5
Ecuador, 1994	26	11	6
Jamaica, 1992	23	20	9
Nicaragua, 1993	18	4	0
Peru, 1993, 1994	21	8	3
Malaysia, 1989	36	32	10
Indonesia, 1989	33	11[a]	0[b]
Vietnam, 1991	23	11	0[b]

Notes: [a] For junior secondary education; for senior secondary education, the proportion is 5 percent.
[b] Because the number of students from the poorest quintile who attend tertiary education is very small, this proportion is negligible.
Source: Guo Li, Diane Steele, and Paul Glewwe, "Distribution of Government Education Subsidies in Developing Countries" (2000). (See endnote 9 for full citation.)

the top quintile receives 27 percent. While comparable data for East Asian countries is not available, there is inequality in the distribution of subsidies in Vietnam, with the richest quintile of households receiving more than 35 percent of government education subsidies and the poorer four quintiles receiving the remaining 65 percent. Disaggregating by level of education provides a clearer picture of the incidence of public spending (see Table 8 to the left). Except Nicaragua, the poorest 20 percent of the population gets more than their proportionate share of public spending for primary education. This is because public education is the predominant schooling at this level, enrollment rates are very high, and there are likely to be more children in the poorest households. At the secondary level, Malaysia stands out as being particularly pro-poor. Colombia and Jamaica also allocate the proportionate share of public resources to the poorest quintile. Some countries have worked toward the specific purpose of addressing inequalities in access to education. In China, targeted bursaries are given to schools specifically for the educational needs of the poor and minorities. In Mexico, bursaries are meant to help indigenous students pay for textbooks and other learning materials.

Moving away from standard state provision. In addition to using fiscal resources to achieve high basic enrollment rates, governments in Latin America and East Asia also developed and used partnerships with the private sector to meet education needs that government resources alone could not satisfy effectively. Private schools enroll a large number of students, often with the assistance of government subsidies. Governments have stimulated additional private-school capacity in various ways—by providing the cost of construction, but relying on private groups to build and manage schools (the Philippines), subsidizing part of the construction and maintenance costs of private schools and assigning some public-school teachers to teach in private schools (Bangladesh, Indonesia), providing tax incentives to private schools (many countries), introducing matching grants schemes (Brazil), providing resources to parents for private school tuition (Chile, Colombia, Pakistan), and assisting private schools serving poor children through the provision of school supplies, nutrition programs, and technical assistance (the Dominican Republic).

Besides supplementing inadequate public supply, government support for private education has other uses. For one, encouraging competition between public and private schools can force schools to offer higher-quality education. Several countries have been experimenting with voucher programs that transfer resources directly to parents for use on private-school tuition. The pro-voucher literature argues that since school resources are tied to parental demand, which, presumably, responds to school quality, voucher programs force schools to provide higher-quality education efficiently—or face bankruptcy. Voucher opponents have disputed the efficiency and quality claims, suggesting that vouchers will only further segregate access to schools by wealth. To date, however, limited empirical evidence fuels the debate about which view is correct. In Chile, the introduction of a voucher scheme coincided with a doubling of enrollment in private schools participating in the program, while enrollment in private non-program schools declined marginally during 1980–86.[47] Math and language test scores suggest that students in private schools participating in the program outperformed students in public schools. There is some evidence that the voucher scheme may have contributed to increased overall efficiency in the schooling system, as private schools were more cost-effective than public schools.[48] Yet test scores of students in non-program private schools were higher than that of program schools. In Colombia, the national (PACES) voucher program in operation during the period 1992–97 was targeted to poorer children. Only children from low-income neighborhoods who had previously attended public schools were eligible to receive vouchers. Even here, voucher school students did at least as well as public-school students on math and language tests, while students in private non-program schools did significantly better.[49]

Lastly, several countries are modifying the provision of public education by increasing the powers and responsibilities of local governments and school communities. The hope is that bringing decision making and accountability closer to those who teach and manage schools will make schools more directly accountable to students, parents, and communities, and by doing so, will make schools more effective.[50] Latin American countries have been leading the charge with respect to this type of reform, with some evidence that broader participation in the education process leads to more and better education.[51] For example, El Salvador's EDUCO has been expanding education in rural areas by enlisting and financing community management teams, composed of elected parents, to operate schools, with the requirement that they follow a centrally mandated curriculum and have at least a minimum student enrollment. These teams have the power to hire and fire teachers and to equip and maintain the schools. Jimenez and Sawada examine the impact of this program on several education outcomes.[52] They find that, compared with traditionally managed schools, EDUCO schools have lower teacher and student absenteeism and comparable student achievement, holding constant the characteristics of students.

Conclusion

The developing world has made huge strides in expanding basic education in the past generation, and many countries, including the those of East Asia and Latin America, have achieved what may be regarded as universal primary education. Public support for education has been a key factor behind this achievement. Overall, the accumulation of human capital appears to have been a key dimension in the development strategy in East Asia. Along with a marked improvement in the *quantity* of education, the *quality* of education has also improved and is comparable or superior to that in many developed countries. Educational attainment in Latin America has improved over time as well, although the quality of education has been less impressive. Inequality in access to education is also evident in both regions among the rich and poor—though this appears to be more of an issue in Latin America.

Partly because of their relatively high levels of education, several countries in East Asia and Latin America have been key players in the global economy—and are poised to continue to do so. Yet education policy alone cannot explain most of the differences in economic development patterns between the two regions. Undoubtedly, the macroeconomic policy environment also determines how education has benefited these regions' economic growth. In addition to its effect on the economy, educational development also appears linked to the nature of political institutions in both regions. Though exploratory, the results of multivariate analysis of cross-country data indicate that higher educational development is associated with greater power-sharing in political institutions.

As a last point, how educational progress is attained is likely to be relevant to whether the progress delivers the objectives of mass education. The extent and nature of public-sector involvement are salient considerations in assessing the impact of educational development on key societal goals. Decentralization and devolution to lower levels of government, meaningful partnerships with the private sector, and the introduction and diffusion of new technology in the delivery of education offer promise for expanding access to basic education and raising the quality of that education in the world's poorest countries. The trade-off may be that public education will be less effective in imparting the desired content of education.

Appendix

TABLE A1—HIGHER EDUCATION IN SELECTED EAST ASIAN & LATIN AMERICAN COUNTRIES

COUNTRY	GROSS TERTIARY ENROLL- MENT RATE	% OF ALL STUDENTS IN SCIENCE & ENGIN- EERING
Latin America		
Argentina	39.3	28.3
Chile	28.2	38.0
Colombia	15.0	27.8
Costa Rica	32.6	20.2
Mexico	15.3	34.2
Nicaragua	11.0	n/a
Panama	30.0	28.2
Paraguay	10.0	n/a
Peru	31.1	n/a
Uruguay	28.4	n/a
Venezuela	26.0	n/a
Unweighted Mean	*24.3*	*29.5*
East Asia & Pacific		
China	5.3	42.5
Hong Kong	25.7	n/a
Indonesia	11.3	39.0
Japan	41.4	20.7
Korea	52.0	57.8
Malaysia	12.0	n/a
Papua New Guinea	3.2	n/a
Philippines	29.0	22.3
Singapore	33.7	n/a
Thailand	20.1	57.5
Vietnam	4.1	n/a
Unweighted Mean	*21.6*	*39.9*

Source: World Development Indicators 1999 (Washington, D.C.: The World Bank, 1999).

TABLE A2—GROWTH IN ENROLLMENT RATES & PER CAPITA GNP IN SELECTED EAST ASIAN & LATIN AMERICAN COUNTRIES

COUNTRY	GROWTH IN PRIMARY ENROLLMENT	GROWTH IN SECONDARY ENROLLMENT	GROWTH IN PER CAPITA GNP
Latin America			
Argentina	0.27	1.97	0.33
Brazil	-0.05	2.30*	2.14
Chile	-0.22	2.48	2.07
Colombia	0.31	3.94	2.06
Cost Rica	-0.27	2.14	1.37
Ecuador	0.85	2.69*	2.06
El Salvador	0.15	1.87	0.12
Guatemala	1.62	4.55	0.85
Guyana	-0.14	0.63	-0.21
Mexico	0.32	4.00	1.12
Nicaragua	1.12	4.18	-3.28
Panama	0.09	2.24	0.72
Paraguay	0.05	3.80	2.35
Peru	0.57	3.28	-0.02
Trinidad& Tobago	-0.42	2.17	2.65
Uruguay	-0.15	1.35	1.22
Venezuela	-0.32	0.01	-0.75
Unweighted Mean	*0.22*	*2.56*	*0.87*
East Asia & Pacific			
China	1.03	3.98	6.62
Hong Kong, China	-0.86	2.85	5.34
Indonesia	1.40	4.65	4.81
Japan	0.12	0.71	2.91
Korea, Rep.	-0.33	3.54	6.43
Malaysia	0.61	2.16	4.33
Philippines	0.21	2.10	1.07
Singapore	-0.41	1.87	6.14
Thailand	0.24	4.54	5.16
Unweighted Mean	*0.22*	*2.93*	*4.76*

Note: All growth rates are annual averages over 1970–95, except the entries marked with *, which are for 1970–94.

Source: World Development Indicators 1999 (Washington, D.C.: The World Bank, 1999).

TABLE A3—GROWTH, OPENNESS & EDUCATION IN SELECTED EAST ASIAN & LATIN AMERICAN COUNTRIES

COUNTRY	EXPORT GROWTH	IMPORT GROWTH	PER CAPITA GNP GROWTH	GROSS PRIMARY ENROLLMENT	GROSS SECONDARY ENROLLMENT
Latin America					
Argentina	5.25	5.78	0.33	112.8	72.7
Brazil	7.79	6.08	2.14	117.6	45.0*
Chile	8.26	5.66	2.07	98.8	69.5
Colombia	6.04	6.65	2.12	108.9	61.3
Ecuador	8.72	4.34	2.06	122.6	50.0*
El Salvador	2.32	4.85	0.12	87.5	34.3
Guatemala	2.78	2.83	0.85	87.5	26.2
Mexico	8.63	6.29	1.07	114.7	61.2
Nicaragua	1.47	2.30	-3.28	102.6	43.9
Paraguay	8.75	11.34	2.18	110.7	40.3
Peru	2.02	2.80	-0.02	122.9	69.7
Trinidad & Tobago	3.01	4.05	2.58	98.2	73.7
Uruguay	5.92	4.50	1.22	108.1	82.4
Unweighted Mean	*5.46*	*5.19*	*1.03*	*107.15*	*56.17*
East Asia & Pacific					
China	12.21	12.50	6.52	118.0	67.0
Hong Kong, China	11.10	11.80	5.34	94.0	73.0
Indonesia	5.99	10.30	4.81	113.4	51.0
Japan	6.49	5.15	2.90	103.0	103.0
Korea, Rep.	14.29	12.39	6.43	95.0	101.0
Malaysia	9.97	10.93	4.33	104.0	59.0
Philippines	6.89	6.70	1.08	114.0	78.0
Thailand	11.49	9.40	5.16	87.0	54.0
Unweighted Mean	*9.80*	*9.90*	*4.57*	*103.55*	*73.25*

Note: Growth rates are annual averages over 1970–95. All enrollment data are for 1995 except the entries marked with *, which are from 1994.

Source: World Development Indicators 1999 (Washington, D.C.: The World Bank, 1999).

TABLE A4— SHARE OF PUBLIC SPENDING BY LEVEL OF EDUCATION IN SELECTED EAST ASIAN COUNTRIES, LATE 1980S

	PRIMARY	SECONDARY	TERTIARY	OTHER
China, 1985	40.6	41.8	17.6	0.0
Indonesia, 1985	61.8	27.1	9.2	2.0
Korea, 1985	57.1	33.5	9.4	0.0
Malaysia, 1988	36.3	34.2	25.7	3.8
Philippines, 1988	61.0	23.0	17.0	0.0
Thailand, 1985	58.1	23.6	12.4	5.9

Source: Jee-Peng Tan and Alain Mingat, *Education in Asia: A Comparative Study of Cost and Financing* (1992). (See endnote 42 for full citation.)

TABLE A5—PUPIL-TEACHER RATIO IN PRIMARY SCHOOL, 1994–95

COUNTRY	PUPILS PER TEACHER
Latin America	
Argentina	17.53
Brazil	22.66
Chile	26.38
Colombia	24.81
Costa Rica	30.61
Ecuador	25.83
El Salvador	28.02
Guatemala	33.63
Guyana	29.97
Mexico	28.34
Nicaragua	38.01
Paraguay	24.15
Peru	28.25
Trinidad & Tobago	25.49
Uruguay	20.08
Venezuela	20.79
Unweighted Mean	*26.53*
East Asia & Pacific	
China	23.30
Hong Kong, China	23.73
Indonesia	22.34
Japan	18.54
Korea	31.82
Malaysia	19.70
Singapore	21.60
Unweighted Mean	*23.00*

Source: Data is for 1994–95 from *World Development Indicators 1999* (Washington, D.C.: The World Bank, 1999).

TABLE A6—TABLE OF MEAN & STANDARD DEVIATIONS

	LATIN AMERICA & CARIBBEAN	EAST ASIA & PACIFIC
System of Government	.2225	1.2101
Parliamentary (2), Assembly-elected President (1), Presidential (0)	(.6026)	(.6545)
How many years has the Chief Executive been in office?	4.2608	9.4710
	(5.4747)	(10.3875)
Is there a finite term in office?	.8644	.7794
Yes (1), No (0)	(.3427)	(.4153)
Is Chief Executive a Military Officer?	.2736	.3200
Yes (1), No (0)	(.4464)	(.4673)
Years Chief Executive has left in current term	2.0591	2.1574
	(1.4645)	(1.4316)
Does party of Chief Executive control all relevant houses	.5512	.8679
Yes (1), No (0)	(.4981)	(.3392)
Were vote fraud or candidate intimidation serious enough to affect	.1398	.0648
the outcome of last election? Yes (1), No (0)	(.3473)	(.2467)

Note: Standard deviations in parentheses.

NOTES

1. See the following studies: Jess Benhabib and Mark M. Spiegel, "Role of Human Capital in Economic Development: Evidence from Aggregate Cross-Country Data," *Journal of Monetary Economics* (Netherlands) 34 (October 1994): 143–73; Lant Prtichett, "Where Has All the Education Gone?" *World Bank Economic Review* 15 (September 2001): 367–91; Ramon E. Lopez, Vinod Thomas, and Yan Wang, "Addressing the Education Puzzle: The Distribution of Economic and Education Reforms," Policy Research Working Paper 2031 (Washington, D.C.: The World Bank, 1998).

2. Robert J. Barro and Jong Wha Lee, "International Measures of Schooling Years and Schooling Quality," *American Economic Review, Papers and Proceedings* 86 (May 1996): 218–23.

3. World Bank, *Engendering Development—Through Gender Equality in Rights, Resources, and Voice* (New York: Oxford University Press, 2001), Chapter 1.

4. See Appendix Table A1 for data on some of the better-performing countries.

5. Source of data is The World Bank, *World Development Indicators 1999* (Washington, D.C.: The World Bank, 1999).

6. Ramon E. Lopez, Vinod Thomas, and Yan Wang, "Addressing the Education Puzzle."

7. Ramon E. Lopez, Vinod Thomas, and Yan Wang, "Addressing the Education Puzzle."

8. Deon Filmer, "The Structures of Social Disparities in Education: Gender and Wealth," Policy Research Working Paper 2268 (Washington, D.C.: The World Bank, 2000).

9. Guo Li, Diane Steele, and Paul Glewwe, "Distribution of Government Education Subsidies in Developing Countries: Preliminary Estimates" (Washington, D.C.: The World Bank, 2000).

10. Deon Filmer, "The Structures of Social Disparities in Education."

11. Elizabeth M. King, "Who Pays for Education in Indonesia? The Roles of Government and Families in Indonesia," in Christopher Colclough, ed., *Marketizing Education and Health in Developing Countries: Miracle or Mirage?* (Oxford: Clarendon Press, 1997), 165–82.

12. Guo Li, Diane Steele, and Paul Glewwe, "Distribution of Government Education Subsidies in Developing Countries."

13. This education Gini coefficient is calculated in two ways: First, an education Lorenz curve is constructed based on the proportions of populations with various levels of schooling and length of each level of schooling, which shows the cumulative years of schooling with respect to the proportion of population; second, the coefficient is calculated as the ratio of the area between the Lorenz curve and the 45-degree line of perfect equality to the area of the triangle (Ramon E. Lopez, Vinod Thomas, and Yan Wang, "Addressing the Education Puzzle").

14. See Appendix Table A5 for results from individual countries.

15. Vinod Thomas, Mansoor Dailami, Ashok Dhareshwar, Daniel Kaufmann, Nalin Kishor, Ramon Lopez, and Yan Wang, *The Quality of Growth* (New York: Oxford University Press for the World Bank, 2000), 54.

16. Nancy Birdsall, David Ross, and Richard Sabot, "Education, Growth and Inequality," in Nancy Birdsall and Frederick Jaspersen, eds., *Pathways to Growth: Comparing East Asia and Latin America* (Washington, D.C.: Inter-American Development Bank, 1997).

17. Eric A. Hanushek and Dongwook Kim, "Schooling, Labor Force Quality, and Economic Growth," Research Working Paper No. 5399 (Cambridge, Mass.: National Bureau of Economic Research, 1995).

18. See United States Department of Education, *Pursuing Excellence: A Study of U. S. Fourth-Grade Mathematics and Science Achievement in International Context*, National Center for Education Statistics 97-255 (Washington, D. C.: U.S. Government Printing Office, 1997). Other countries in the study included Australia, Austria, Canada, Czech Republic, Cyprus, England, Greece, Hungary, Iceland, Iran, Ireland, Israel, Kuwait, Latvia, Netherlands, New Zealand, Norway, Portugal, Scotland, Slovenia, and the United States.

19. Lawrence Wolff, Ernesto Schiefelbein, and Jorge Valenzuela, "Improving the Quality of Primary Education in Latin America: Towards the 21st Century," Latin America and Caribbean Technical Department, Regional Studies Program Paper No. 28 (Washington, D.C.: The World Bank, 1993).

20. Albert E. Beaton, Ina V.S. Mullis, Michael O. Martin, Eugenio J. Gonzales, Dana L. Kelly, and Teresa A. Smith, *Mathematics Achievement in the Middle School Years: IEA's Third International Mathematics and Science Study (TIMSS)* (Chestnut Hill, Mass.: International Association for the Evaluation of Educational Achievement, 1996).

21. Emmanuel Jimenez and Marlaine Lockheed, "Public and Private Secondary Education in Developing Countries: A Comparative Study," World Bank Discussion Paper 309 (Washington, D.C.: The World Bank, 1995).

22. Amartya Sen, *Development as Freedom* (New York: Alfred A. Knopf, 1999), 109.

23. George Psacharopoulos, "Returns to Investment in Education: A Global Update," *World Development* 22 (September 1994): 1325–43.

24. Robert E. Lucas, Jr., "On the Mechanics of Economic Growth," *Journal of Monetary Economics* 22 (July 1988): 3–42.

25. While higher education levels reasonably can be expected to aid economic growth, the linkage between growth and education runs both ways, with rapid growth also contributing to expansions in educational attainment. Economic growth expands the demand for education by creating more jobs requiring higher skills, increasing real wages, and raising private returns to education. On the supply side, higher incomes enable governments to allocate more resources to educational progress.

26. Robert J. Barro, "Economic Growth in a Cross Section of Countries," *Quarterly Journal of Economics* 106 (May 1991): 407–43.

27. Nancy Birdsall, David Ross, and Richard Sabot, "Education, Growth and Inequality."

28. See Appendix Table A2 for results from individual countries.

29. The correlation coefficient between growth rates in secondary enrollment and per capita GNP is 0.5 in East Asia, but it is only 0.06 in Latin America.

30. Ramon E. Lopez, Vinod Thomas, and Yan Wang, "Addressing the Education

Puzzle." Similar results are suggested for a cross-section of 60 developing countries in the World Bank's *World Development Report 1991: Challenge of Development* (Washington, D.C.: The World Bank, 1991).

31. These economic crises also have implications for educational attainments. Figure 1 on page 154 indicates stagnation in the trend for primary enrollment in Latin America in the 1980s and a slowdown in the growth rate of secondary enrollment coincident with the crisis and adjustment period, but for reasons discussed above, gross enrollment rates can be misleading. Average years of schooling completed are a better measure. Indeed, they show a slowdown for children born between 1960 and 1970, who would be making schooling decisions during 1975–85, the early years of the crisis. (See Jere R. Behrman, Suzanne Duryea, and Miguel Szekely, "Schooling Investments and Aggregate Conditions: A Household Survey-Based Approach for Latin America and the Caribbean," Inter-American Development Bank Working Paper Series 407 [Washington, D.C.: Inter-American Development Bank, 1999].) The slowdown was reflected particularly strongly in completion rates rather than in enrollment rates. Econometric analyses confirms that macroeconomic instability—measured by unfavorable international terms of trade movements and income volatility—was an important element contributing to the slowdown.

32. Martin Rama and Donna MacIssac, "Earnings and Welfare after Downsizing: Central Bank Employees in Ecuador," *World Bank Economic Review* 13 (January 1999): 89–116.

33. Reduced public funding for education, higher prices of schooling, and lower incomes had the potential to set back past gains in education. Studies of the impact of the crisis in Indonesia and the Philippines indicate that children were pulled out of schools in response to the crisis. Estimates from the Government of Indonesia point to 890,000 and 640,000 students dropping out of primary and junior secondary schools, respectively, in just a single year (World Bank, *East Asia: The Road to Recovery* [Washington, D.C.: The World Bank, 1998]). Panel data estimates from Indonesia indicate that the expenditure share of education in household budgets fell 8 percent among urban households and 24 percent among rural households (Duncan Thomas, Elizabeth Frankenberg, Kathleen Beegle, and Graciela Teruel, "Household Budgets, Household Composition and the Crisis in Indonesia: Evidence from Longitudinal Household Survey Data," RAND Working Paper [Santa Monica, Calif.: RAND Corporation, 1999]). As of now, it is too soon to predict the full impact of the crisis on education and economic growth in the long run, but preliminary evidence suggests that the impact will be felt among future generations.

34. Kathleen Beegle, Elizabeth Frankenberg, and Duncan Thomas, "Economy in Crisis: Labor Market Outcomes and Human Capital Investments in Indonesia" (Santa Monica, Calif.: RAND Corporation, 1999).

35. Lisa C. Smith and Lawrence Haddad, "Explaining Child Malnutrition in Developing Countries: A Cross-Country Analysis," Food Consumption and Nutrition Division Discussion Paper 60 (Washington, D.C.: International Food Policy Research Institute, 1999).

36. M. Anne Hill and Elizabeth M. King, "Women's Education and Economic Well-Being," *Feminist Economics* 1 (Summer 1995): 1–26

37. Stephan Klasen, "Does Gender Inequality Reduce Growth and Development? Evidence from Cross-Country Regressions," Policy Research Report on Gender and Development Working Paper 7 (Washington, D.C.: The World Bank, 1999).

38. All data are from World Development Indicators (2001). Regressions are based on 1270 to 1773 observations. They display a relationship over time as they include time dummies.

39. We are grateful to Phil Kiefer for making his database (Version 3.0, May 2001) available to us.

40. For the executive branch, we examine differences across countries in whether the executive office is direct presidential, parliamentary, or assembly-elected presidential; how many years the chief executive has been in office; and whether there is a constitutional limit to the number of years the executive can serve before new elections must be called. For the legislative branch, we examine an index of electoral competitiveness in the legislature and an index of political cohesion that is a measure of the extent to which the executive and legislative branches of government are controlled by the same party or by different parties.

41. Mark Gradstein and Moshe Justman, "Human capital, social capital, and public schooling," *European Economic Review* 44 (May 2000): 879–90; Estelle James, "Why is there proportionally more enrollment in private schools in some countries?" Policy Research Working Paper No. 1069 (Washington, D.C.: The World Bank, 1993); and Michael R. Kremer, "Research on schooling: What we know and what we don't: A comment on Hanushek," *World Bank Research Observer* 10 (August 1995): 247–54.

42. Jee-Peng Tan and Alain Mingat, *Education in Asia: A Comparative Study of Cost and Financing* (Washington, D.C.: The World Bank, 1992). See Appendix Table A4 for data on individual countries.

43. Source of the information for Latin America is the World Bank's Edstats data base.

44. Nancy Birdsall, David Ross, and Richard Sabot, "Education, Growth and Inequality."

45. Mark M. Bray, *Counting the Full Cost: Parental and Community Financing of Education in East Asia* (Washington, D.C.: The World Bank, 1996).

46. Mun C. Tsang, "Private and Public Costs of Schooling in Developing Countries," *International Encyclopedia of Education*, 2nd ed. (Oxford: Pergamon Press, 1994), vol. viii: 4702–8.

47. Tarsicio Castaneda, *Combating Poverty: Innovative Social Reforms in Chile During the 1980s* (San Francisco: International Center for Economic Growth, 1992).

48. Donald A. Winkler and Taryn Rounds, "Municipal and Private Sector Response to Decentralization and School Choice," HRO Working Paper 8 (Washington, D.C.: The World Bank, 1993).

49. Elizabeth M. King, Peter Orazem, and Darin Wohlgemuth, "Central Mandates and Local Incentives: Colombia's Targeted Voucher Program," *World Bank Economic Review* 13 (September 1999): 467–91.

50. Jane Hannaway and Martin Carnoy, eds., *Decentralization and School Improvement: Can We Fulfill the Promise?* (San Francisco: Jossey-Bass Publisher, 1993); and Jon Lauglo, "Forms of decentralization and the implications for education," *Comparative Education* 31 (March 1995): 5–29.

51. Edward Fiske, *Decentralization of Education: Politics and Consensus*, Directions in Development Series (Washington, D.C.: The World Bank, 1996); and E. Mark Hanson, *Educational Reform and Administrative Development: The Cases of Colombia and Venezuela* (Stanford, Calif.: Hoover Institution Press, 1986).

52. Emmanuel Jimenez and Yasuyuki Sawada, "Do Community-Managed Schools Work? An Evaluation of El Salvador's EDUCO Program," *World Bank Economic Review* 13 (September 1999): 415–41.

9

THE HAZARDS
OF CONVERGENCE

Laurence Whitehead

Laurence Whitehead is an Official Fellow in Politics at Nuffield College, and series editor for Oxford Studies in Democratization. He is author of Democratization: Theory and Experience *(Oxford University Press, 2002), the most recent volume in that series, and editor of* International Dimensions of Democratization *for the same series (2001 updated edition). He is also coeditor (with Guillermo O'Donnell and Philippe Schmitter) of* Transitions from Authoritarian Rule *(1986), and lead contributor to John Crabtree and Laurence Whitehead (eds.),* Toward Democratic Viability: The Bolivian Experience *(2001).*

Economic and political liberalization have both proceeded apace since the 1980s. Much of the time these two processes have seemed to advance in tandem. By the end of the 1990s, at the time of the conference in Santiago on which this volume is based, it had become conventional to assume that they were both mutually reinforcing, and that such trends could be extrapolated well into the future. The driving force of economic liberalization was the cumulative success of the U.S. economic model and its transmission to the rest of the world through such institutions as the International Monetary Fund (IMF), the World Bank, and the World Trade Organization (WTO). Washington's lead was reinforced not only by the other OECD countries but also by an array of other economies, including those of East Asia and Latin America. This agenda was matched by the international drive toward political democratization, also evident in these two regions.

Of course there were also countercurrents and setbacks. The financial crisis that swept East Asia in 1997 and the "contagion" that climaxed with the forced Brazilian devaluation of January 1999 showed that not everything would run smoothly at all times and in all places. The resilience of communist rule in mainland China, as well as the weakening of democracy in Colombia and Venezuela, indicated that such convergence was likely to encounter opposition or resistance. Street protests against the WTO in Seattle also underscored that it was not only in the "peripheral" economies that such objections could arise. Still, the prevailing assumptions about liberal internationalism remained intact. The East Asian economies recovered speedily after 1997 and democratic institutions held firm. In some instances, there were democratic advances: the fall of the dictatorship in Indonesia and the ejection by voters in Taiwan of the Kuomintang. In Latin America, Brazil also emerged from its exchange-rate crisis with its democratic institutions in place, and Mexico proceeded toward a truly competitive multiparty system while reaffirming its commitment to NAFTA. The foregoing chapters of this book reflected the assumption that further cumulative progress toward a liberalized world system could more or less be taken for granted and that the rewards for economic and political liberalization would continue. Latin America and East Asia thus seemed to be on convergent paths toward this end.

How firm do such assumptions seem in the wake of subsequent developments, in particular the devastating terrorist assaults on New York and Washington in September 2001? Some shocking events are so momentous that they can shift even the most basic assumptions, especially when they compound other changes taking place.

When world trade and private international investment flows are rapidly expanding and national income is rising in the core democratic market economies, the impetus toward liberalization and convergence may be hard to resist. Yet liberalized markets can be cyclical and unstable, with periods of fast growth inducing speculation, overconfidence, and over-investment, whether in a mature market economy or in a poorly managed enclave at the periphery of the system. Indeed, the more internationalized and interdependent the system, the quicker the speed at which the effects of contagion spread outwards from the center. The problems facing Argentina and Turkey are illustrative of this potential. Similarly, in a world system where democratic expectations and entitlements have been more widely diffused, the scope for "shock treatment" or radical authoritarian responses is limited. In imposing austerity, governments face a public that is more questioning about the sacrifices it is expected to bear. Essential reforms have to be negotiated, bargained over, legislated upon, and even modified by governments that need to submit themselves to periodic elections. The ability to attract foreign investment or to secure the approval of the international financial institutions may no longer be an electorally winning formula. Venezuela's Hugo Chávez seemed an untypical throwback when he won the presidency at the end of 1998, but three years later the political and economic benefits of an unquestioning endorsement of a liberalized world system seem more doubtful. Such doubts were in evidence in East Asia as well as Latin America. In Thailand, the victory in January 2001 of the Thai Rak Thai party over the Democrats can be seen as a partial rejection of liberal reformist orthodoxies. "Mutual recognition" between Latin

America and East Asia might therefore be seen as having a rather different meaning.

This chapter takes up the issues raised in the Santiago conference, and attempts to provide an updated synthesis in the light of subsequent international developments. In so doing, there is a risk of "presentism." If the prevailing assumptions of the end of the 1990s seemed misleading in late 2001, then presumably the same could be said of the revised interpretation. Up until September 2001, Western policy still rested basically on assumptions similar to those of a few years earlier. It was possible to argue that the world economy had suffered a larger setback than previously anticipated, that social protest against "globalization" had been unexpectedly virulent, and that liberalizing experiments had been derailed (as in Argentina), without questioning that economic and political liberalization were still the most desirable and inevitable ways forward. It was also possible to argue that the leaders of peripheral countries that had embraced this reality were most likely to benefit, whereas those that resisted would take longer and pay a higher price to eventually reach the same conclusion.

So, this chapter will proceed on the basis that such assumptions will continue to guide Western policy makers. Nevertheless, it is impossible to discount the alternative possibility that the international commitment to further liberalization was weakening before the destruction of the World Trade Center, and that the attacks could precipitate a major shift away from liberalization toward a new concern about international security and subversion. Even before this, doubts about the prospects for a liberal world system were growing in Latin America and East Asia alike. With the downturn in the business cycle, the reversal of economic and financial expectations was proving just as severe as in earlier cycles. The optimism surrounding the role of the "new economy" as well as liberalization as motors of growth had been dashed. All the leading economies seemed to be facing a synchronized downturn. The worst excesses of the financial "bubble" were concentrated in the telecom, media, and technology sectors, while there were growing doubts over whether technical change had really raised the underlying rate of productivity growth. The East Asian export economies were especially exposed to this cyclical downturn—reinforced by intensified competition from China, newly admitted to the WTO—although other leading practitioners of internationally approved economic reforms (such as Argentina) also found themselves on the rack. Both Chile and Taiwan, previously among the most dynamic of the new export economies, were obliged to adjust downwards their short-to-medium-term growth expectations. Even though the leading countries in both regions were both strongly committed to "market opening" and internationalization, the liberal world system in which they were aiming to immerse themselves no longer seemed so fixed or assured.

Governments and opinion-formers in these peripheral regions have therefore become more aware of the "hazards" of the convergence path on which they are embarked. Here, we seek to abstract from short-term volatility in moods and perceptions and to view such hazards in a longer-term perspective. This chapter seeks to do this in four sections: a consideration of the major consequences likely to follow from the establishment of a more integrated international market economy, a review of the alternative possible domestic responses to such "globalizing" tendencies, a discussion of cross-regional comparisons and contrasts between East Asia and Latin America within this framework, and finally a consideration of the implications of liberal-democratic market convergence in both regions and in the periphery more generally.

The Impact of Market Opening

To start with, a distinction needs to be drawn between three key aspects of heightened economic integration as these impact on what have been classified as the newly industrializing countries (NICs).[1] Firstly, a more integrated international market imposes firmer discipline on those who participate in it. Secondly, it involves a redistribution of power and resources, not just between enterprises or between nations, but between larger world regions. Thirdly, if the market system is stable, then heightened integration transmits that stability. If it is unstable, however, it can destabilize those enmeshed within it. Each of these can be considered in isolation, but in practice all three coexist and together can exert powerful effects over all the countries and economies they impinge on. Emerging markets and NICs are likely to be more affected by such firmer market disciplines, by the redistributive power of markets that tend to have most impact on newcomers, and by the potential for market instability, which can affect the periphery more directly than the core.

Although all three aspects may coexist, they do not all operate on the same time scale. The internationalization of new international market disciplines—such as demands for heightened efficiency, more uniform product standards, increased legal security, more uniform accounting practices, and perhaps even more sustainable labor and environmental standards—should be thought of as a cumulative, long-term process. Advances may be jerky and uneven, but the pressures of international competition and standardization—including institutional pressures through such agencies as the WTO and market pressure through privatization and outsourcing—are likely to persist and intensify. The redistributive dimension is also long-term and potentially cumulative, although here factors like the volatility of commodity prices may introduce a cyclical dimension. For instance, variations in oil prices will redistribute resources back and forth between oil exporters and importers. Where there is global transmission of instability, by contrast, the

impact is likely to be intense, short-term, and sometimes quickly re-
versible, although in severe cases (such as Argentina and Indonesia), a
burst of instability may precipitate a steep change to a higher level of
chronic difficulties.

Thus far we have outlined the potential consequences of economic
globalization for NICs in general, abstract terms. Yet if we are to analyze the variations between large world regions (East Asia and Latin
America), or within these regions, considerable disaggregation is required. The notion of heightened international economic integration is
extremely broad and requires refinement. Since the 1980s, the major
shift toward a more "globalized" world system has taken place in manufacturing, trade, and private financial and investment flows. The lead
has been taken by a limited number of large multinational enterprises
and financial institutions. Sectors such as telecommunications, information technology, vehicle manufacture, utilities, and banking have been
central to this. Others have remained at the margin, or even off-limits,
like educational, postal, and retailing services. Small and medium enterprises have also been at a competitive disadvantage in international
markets. Agriculture is another crucial branch of economic activity where
globalization has lagged. Also, while there has been heightened international integration in key product and financial markets, this is
emphatically not the situation with labor markets. What is loosely referred to as "globalization" has often involved intensified forms of
economic integration that are regional in focus, but which discriminate
against transactions with the wider world. Consider, for example, Mexico
in NAFTA, East-Central Europe and the EU, Hong Kong and Taiwan's
links to mainland China, and so on.

Disaggregating the present liberalized world system in this way, it
becomes apparent that any "convergence" is bound to be incomplete,
partial, and asymmetrical. Although there may be powerful economic
forces at work pushing all emerging markets and NICs toward greater
uniformity in their economic behavior and enhanced "mutual recognition," the various states and regions involved have diverse historical
and structural endowments. They thus stand to benefit differently from
the various components of globalization. In some cases, they mainly
face hazards rather than prospective benefits. Indeed, the liberal system
toward which they are being encouraged to move is itself neither complete nor free of internal contradictions.

In view of this medley of characteristics, it is neither desirable nor
feasible to leave the dynamics of "globalization" entirely to the play of
the market forces. At least from the standpoint of most governments,
enterprises, and indeed citizens in peripheral countries, a degree of political cooperation and management would seem essential if the benefits
of globalization are not to be swamped by the dangers. At this point,
therefore, the liberalization of the international economy may need to

be accompanied by national processes of political liberalization in order to protect the interests of the broader societies that face the challenge
of restructuring. It may also need to go hand-in-hand with greater political cooperation, both regionally and internationally, in order to
manage the differential impact and potentially destabilizing consequences of globalization.

No doubt much more discussion is warranted concerning the consequences for emerging markets and peripheral democracies that arise from
the dynamics of contemporary globalization. For the purposes of this
volume, however, the foregoing broad sketch must suffice. Since our
focus is on East Asia–Latin America cross-regional comparisons, we
will now proceed to look more closely at the possible alternative domestic (and regional) responses to this global panorama.

Responses to Hazardous Liberalization

Faced by an international system that is still strongly geared toward
the promotion of further economic and political liberalization and convergence, but in which the hazards of incautious compliance have
become clear, three broad types of national responses can be discerned.

The first is to press ahead, extend economic liberalization, deepen
the commitment to democracy, and seek to implement longer-term structural reforms. The rationale for this is that the best defense against the
hazards of convergence is to accelerate the process, locking in support
from the leading liberal democracies, going the extra mile in attracting
direct foreign investment, and leaving domestic constituencies in no
doubt of their need to adapt. In economic policy terms this would involve making the rules of the game more predictable and impersonal.
For example, it would mean reinforcing fiscal discipline, increasing
central-bank autonomy, and observing some exchange-rate rule (possibly a clean float or a fixed rate, but not discretionary intervention). In
terms of state-business relations, every effort would have to be made to
outlaw "crony capitalism," while multinational investors would be given
guarantees with respect to property rights, the rule of law, and the neu-
trality of government policies. Domestic enterprises would need to meet
the transparent accounting standards required for a listing on a "first
world" stock exchange. Politically, electoral procedures would need to
be upgraded to international standards, press freedoms reinforced, human rights violations curbed, and the separation of powers respected,
with the judicial system arbitrating between the competing branches of
government.

Such a policy package would conform to the expectations of "convergence" theorists, even though in any particular country there would
inevitably be some tension and imbalance between the various components. The overall direction would be toward ever-increasing

liberalization and conformity with the "best practices" advocated by the leading democratic market economies. Probably the best example is provided by Mexico, where integration into NAFTA is apparently going hand-in-hand with cumulative institutional restructuring and greater democracy. Chile also belongs in this category, and likewise—at least until the crisis of 2001—Argentina. In East Asia, for reasons discussed more fully below, it is harder to identify clear-cut examples, but Taiwan has displayed a number of the features listed, and both South Korea and Thailand have made intermittent moves in the same direction, despite countercurrents. Even in the most favorable conditions, there will always be setbacks and these cannot be disregarded. In Mexico, for instance, despite NAFTA and the declared preferences of the Fox administration, there is already elite resistance to energy liberalization. A deeper economic downturn could further test the Mexican commitment to convergence, and the liberalizing consensus could also be challenged by interests linked to organized crime, although it is difficult to envisage any coherent alternative to the integration processes now so powerfully under way there.

The second broad response is to resist globalization, with many of the opposite reflexes to those just mentioned. Instead of pressing ahead with liberalization, movement toward political and economic opening would be abandoned or reversed. In response to heightened national vulnerability, the state's administrative capacity to defend national interests would be strengthened. Internally, this would involve tightening domestic discipline and reducing the scope for dissent. The reconcentration of state power, justified by the external threat, would limit the possibilities for electoral contestation and the ability of the courts to protect the rights of all parties, including those most associated with liberalization. In terms of state-business relations, this reflex would imply greater acceptance of what might be loosely characterized as "crony capitalism," since those enterprises willing to collaborate in such a response would seek government protection and guarantees. In this context, impersonal rules would become an impediment to policymaking rather than an asset, and insulated institutions (like central banks) would find their autonomy under attack. Discretionary methods of policymaking would thus stage a comeback.

Venezuela under President Chávez is perhaps the most obvious example of such a response in Latin America. Yet the potential also exists in other republics where public opinion is skeptical about the benefits of liberalization or there is despair at the prospect of the country falling ever further behind in the race toward liberalization. In East Asia, the nearest equivalent is probably Malaysia under Prime Minister Mahathir, although both the circumstances and the rationale are clearly very different from those in Venezuela. The official Malaysian response to the Asian currency crisis was to step up both the rhetorical and practical defiance of "Westernizing" ideology and demands. But in contrast to oil-dependent Venezuela, such resistance came on the back of longer-term economic success. Malaysia's strategy may also have been partially calculated to win concessions in return for a selective resumption of the liberal agenda. Countercurrents were also at work. Even in Venezuela the illiberalism of some of Chávez's policies was tempered by the recognition that the country's future was inextricably dependent on collaboration with neighbors committed to liberalization. Domestically, the Chávez administration may also come under mounting pressure to satisfy the expectations it has raised, and thus face up to the reality that durable policy success will require pragmatism. So, even when our second response is pressed to its limits, it is not easy to "opt out" of the liberalizing agenda.

The third option is more complex and difficult to characterize than the first two. It encompasses a variety of crosscutting reflexes and requires some disaggregation of the distinct components of what has so far been classified simply as a unified movement toward both economic and political liberalization. The national experiences are more numerous and diverse than in the first two cases, and they fall in between those polar opposites. Most countries in Latin America and East Asia can be located in this intermediate terrain. Here, we take the two largest economies—Brazil and South Korea—as exemplars of this option. In both Brazil and South Korea (and probably in most other cases as well), governing elites are not in much doubt that over the long run they must plan for further liberal international convergence. By contrast with those countries in the first category, however, there is no consensus about placing liberalization ahead of all other priorities and attempting to gain a competitive advantage over their neighbors. Rather, the consensus favors balancing liberalizing reforms with other offsetting measures.

In Brazil, external economic pressures are offset by the size of the internal market. The more internationally minded elites are not hegemonic in the sense that they would automatically succeed in overriding the countervailing arguments of the nationalists and anti-globalizers. Instead, some sort of compromise is required with a view to achieving incremental advances. Brazil thus contrasts with Mexico under President Salinas in its more pluralist make-up and the range of countervailing forces, including the influential Partido dos Trabalhadores (PT). Still, though Brazil could revert to the second option in view of the 2002 general elections, it seems unlikely that frontal resistance to globalization will gain ascendancy in the longer run.

In South Korea, the balance of responses is somewhat similar, albeit for different reasons: The principal national project that could conflict with liberalization concerns reunification with the North. The international pressures on South Korea are also different in strength and in kind from those constraining Brazil, even though the outcome may be similar. Wholehearted economic and political liberalization would be highly divisive since it would undermine unity in the South and detract from Seoul's ability to negotiate with its neighbors. Nevertheless, a directly anti-Western stance would be unthinkable for South Korea. So, while liberalizing reforms may be endorsed in principle, they will be implemented erratically and half-heartedly.

In both Brazil and South Korea, foreign investors and external partners may find such responses inadequate, but in neither will they be so unsatisfactory as to warrant withdrawal of support. Financial markets may be less critical at signs of vacillation, and even retreat, than the international financial institutions, which can ill afford to see such major players turn their backs on liberalization. Given the size and growth prospects of these large markets, multinational corporations will not be deterred by a little backsliding. Also, their strategic significance as bulwarks of democracy is such that outsiders will hesitate before seeking to set political conditions.

Thus far we have sketched three broad types of national response from Latin America and East Asia to the demands and hazards of internationalization. By contrast with this aggregate level of discussion, earlier chapters in this book look more closely at specific areas of response, bringing out the finer distinctions that separate cases (like South Korea and Taiwan) that are usually lumped together. Much can be learned from appropriately paired national comparisons, and comparisons that focus on specific variables or components of response. Both Brazil and South Korea, for example, have relatively autonomous labor movements that emerged from military rule with an appetite for protest and militancy. A paired comparison of the role played by such factors may help explain why neither of these two countries finds it easy, in a democratic context, to opt for wholehearted liberalization. By contrast, both Chile and Mexico made their commitment to economic liberalization while still under authoritarian rule. This made it easier to suppress labor opposition and to sweep aside other forms of resistance for long enough to make liberalization almost irreversible once democratization began. This helps to explain why they could remain at the forefront of market opening even after their belated transitions to democracy. A third paired comparison would be between Indonesia and Venezuela. Both belong to OPEC, and both rely heavily on oil revenues to finance public spending. While it is commonly assumed that this is why Venezuela resisted liberalization and backed away from multiparty electoral democracy, a paired comparison with Indonesia would indicate the incompleteness of this explanation. Fiscal dependence on a state oil company with its fluctuating surpluses may help explain certain shared characteristics, such as the incestuous nature of state-business relations. Nevertheless, just when a low oil price delivered the *coup de grace* to Venezuela's party-dominated electoral democracy, Indonesia reacted to an even more severe foreign-exchange problem by ousting the dictator, accepting the liberalizing demands of the IMF, and embracing competitive elections. Such a paired comparison should therefore serve as an antidote to reductionist ideas concerning the politics of "oil rent" states.

These and other possible examples of paired comparisons indicate the utility of in-depth research into alternative responses to the pressures for liberalization in these two regions. They help focus the analysis on key explanatory variables that may be significant in some countries, but absent (or of secondary importance) in others. They help fill in gaps between the three broad overall patterns of response outlined above. Such comparisons can be undertaken both within the two regions and between them. The selection of pairs depends on the precise issue that requires fuller research and needs to be based on a precisely specified hypothesis or theoretically grounded general proposition. A key feature of this type of comparison is that it should be based on "parity of esteem" between the two countries (or cases) paired, since each national experience merits an equally full explanation. The comparison between Brazil and South Korea should provide each with an external yardstick for evaluating what might otherwise be viewed as individual peculiarities, such as labor-movement militancy and its effects on liberalization. The South Korea–Taiwan comparison earlier in this volume shows how this can also be used to underscore the variations that exist between seemingly similar countries in a single large region. In principle, it would be useful to generate an inventory of such paired comparisons to survey the range of possible national trajectories among emerging market economies in our two regions. For our purposes here, however, the three broad alternative strategies outlined above will suffice, since we are primarily concerned with comparisons and contrasts between these two large and diverse geographical regions.

Comparing Two Large Regions

In the first place, we need to reflect on the scope and limitations of such comparisons between large regions of the world. As in the case of paired comparisons between nations, the utility and appropriateness of cross-regional comparisons depend upon the issues being researched. We can illustrate this by reference to the recent history of such cross-regional comparisons with regard to economic and political liberalization.

With regard to the former, Latin America during the 1970s and early 1980s was the principal source and focus of "dependency theory," a set of ideas that justified resistance to private foreign investment and a preference for import substitution over export promotion. Mexico's 1982 debt crisis seemed to confirm the worst fears of the dependency school and signaled to many that the best hope for the future lay with further state intervention and a "de-linking" from a hostile world economy. The

1982 bank nationalization, diametrically opposed to the prescriptions of economic liberalization, was symptomatic of this outlook. Yet the cyclical downturn of the world economy in 1982 precipitated debt crises not only in dependency-minded Latin America but also in the dynamic export-oriented economies of East Asia. South Korea, in particular, seemed to be on the brink of a sovereign debt crisis. In such circumstances, a cross-regional comparison would suggest to Latin America that other economies were responding with a different, but more successful, development strategy: embracing market disciplines and exporting their way out of the debt problem. While East Asia was not exactly an advertisement for "Washington consensus"–style economic liberalization, the high-performance export economies of East Asia provided an external reality check to the sweeping conclusions of the dependency school. Such comparisons helped to discredit dependency theory and pave the way toward the supremacy of neoliberal diagnosis and prescription in Latin America. After the East Asian financial crises of 1997, there was even a brief period in which Latin America's relatively complete embrace of economic and political liberalization was presented as something of an inspiration and indeed model for the troubled economies of East Asia. Quite soon, however, it became apparent that neither region had discovered the single formula that would address the economic development problems of both. Instead partial convergence (from different starting points) and mutual recognition of shared problems began to replace generalized lesson-teaching in either direction.

In the sphere of democratization, the history of cross-regional comparisons is equally instructive. Comparisons between the Southern European democratizations of the 1970s and subsequent South American experiences underpinned the debate over "transitions" in the 1980s. Then, with the fall of the Berlin Wall in 1989, big-region comparisons between Latin America and postcommunist Eastern Europe became fashionable. Subsequently, as East Asian states such as South Korea, Taiwan, Thailand, and eventually even Indonesia underwent democratic transitions, a further arena for cross-regional comparisons opened up. Each of these successive pairings raised separate issues and focused attention on different analytical issues. For example, the "parliamentarism" of the Southern European democratizations was used to contrast the "presidentialism" prevalent in Latin America. There was also the contrast between the new democracies in Europe which could hope to join the European Community, and those in Latin America that had to contend with Cold War fears about the consequences of legalizing the political left. After the fall of the Berlin Wall, the comparison was drawn between Latin America and postcommunist Eastern Europe. This directed attention to the fact that in the latter, but not the former, democratization was just one component of a triple transition: from communism to democracy, from state to market, and from East to West. Finally, the East Asia–Latin America comparison raises questions about the relationship between good economic performance and successful democratization, as well as about the role of culture (especially "Asian values") in differentiating the two regions. Since the crises of 1997, it also raises the question of whether there are other "contextual" factors that may influence the course and outcome of democratization.

Defining Large Regions

As this brief sketch indicates, cross-regional comparisons can be used for a variety of purposes and address a multiplicity of issues. Yet they also have their limitations and are subject to misuse. The approach may be legitimate, and indeed indispensable, but it must be undertaken with due methodological awareness. Particular care is needed to define the boundaries of the regions in question and the issues to be addressed.

The need for clarity on the boundaries of the large regions can be highlighted through reference to "Asian values." There has been lively discussion about the role of such values in blocking or filtering those Western liberal ideas and practices that purport to be universal. But what values are we talking about and where exactly in Asia are they to be found? Christianity is not distinctively Asian, yet there are many Christians all over Asia, and in the Philippines they are in the majority. Communism is not distinctively Asian either, yet it remains the official ideology of China, Vietnam, and North Korea. Islam also originates outside Asia, but is prevalent in Indonesia, Malaysia, Bangladesh, and Pakistan. So which parts of Asia can we identify as the large region that is inherently resistant to Western values? The "large region" argument, frequently invoked in the comparative democratization literature, lacks a clearly defined regional basis.

While the "Asian values" hypothesis does not lend itself to "large region" evaluation, there are other, more specific hypotheses that can be researched through cross-regional comparisons. For example, East Asia is home to the four "tigers" (Hong Kong, Singapore, South Korea, and Taiwan). It could be that these highly successful export economies— with well-educated and disciplined labor forces, guided by well-focused "developmental states"—can impart something of general significance about the relationship between economic success and durable democratic advance. The World Bank has in the past held them up, and the regional model, as worthy of study and even emulation. Not only have Washington-based advisers commended the economic performance of the "tigers," they have also suggested that their patterns of state-business relations, and more generally of "governance," may explain their success, thereby providing useful lessons for the reform-minded elsewhere.

Such analysis, however, may suffer from selection bias. The four "tigers" are a rather disparate and improbable grouping, on account of both the countries they include and those they omit. Why, for example, leave out Japan from what would otherwise be recognizable as the "Greater East Asia Co-prosperity Sphere" of pre-1945 vintage? Why include Singapore, but not Malaysia, with which it was federated until 1965, and which has a record of export-led industrialization? Hong Kong was not an independent state at all, but a British colony until 1997 and now a Special Autonomous Region of the People's Republic of China. Taiwan's legal status was, and remains, in dispute. It is certainly not a "normal" state, and the peculiarities of its status and security problems condition all aspects of its politics and economics. South Korea has yet to sign a peace agreement with North Korea, and must still devote manpower and resources to patrolling the so-called demilitarized zone. It, too, is a quite peculiar political entity, and may eventually merge into a reunited Korea. Even Singapore, perhaps the most "normal" of the four, is a city-state with no hinterland. Instead of classifying the four "tigers" as a "large region" for purposes of comparative analysis, they might more accurately be classed as a miscellany of deviant cases.

Even if "Asian values" and the four "tigers" lack clear regional foundations, there is a quite compelling case for comparing the eight "emerging market economies" of East Asia with those of Latin America. As we have seen, both groupings compete in the international capital markets for equity and bond finance of the same class. Both, therefore, have been under pressure to undertake economic liberalization in order to secure open markets for their industrial exports to the advanced economies. Both have discovered that this liberal and outward orientation brings with it new risks and external conditionalities, as well as benefits. The financial crises of 1997–98, which spread by contagion through the East Asian economies and then into Latin America, highlighted the interconnections. Most emerging market economies in the two regions have also undergone transitions to democracy in the same period that they have adopted liberalizing reforms. In both regions, therefore, there is debate about how closely, and through what linkages, economic and political liberalization may be connected.

Such links, then, provides a prima facie case for investigating the extent to which region-wide processes in Latin America parallel apparently similar processes in East Asia. This raises the question of how the two regions should be configured for the comparison. An outer boundary of geographical distinctiveness needs to be established in order to focus attention on those countries that best exemplify the processes under investigation. In the case of Latin America, this is fairly straightforward. The outer boundaries of Latin America are the Atlantic, the Pacific, and the U.S.-Mexican border. The central cases can also be identified quite easily. They are the larger economies with the clearest records of both economic and political liberalization. If one takes Argentina, Brazil, Chile, and Mexico as representative of Latin America, it simplifies the analysis without seriously falsifying the tendencies visible in the region as a whole.

In the case of East Asia, it is a little harder to apply the same procedure, although there is probably enough to the cross-regional comparison to justify the effort. The outer boundaries would be set by the Pacific to the east, Australia to the south, mainland China, Russia, and Japan to the north, and the Indian Ocean to the west. The most debatable part of this outer boundary is China, which is, of course, at the heart of East Asia and claims sovereignty over Hong Kong and Taiwan and exercises strong influence over Korea. While the coastal areas of the Chinese mainland may be subject to the same sort of liberalization evident elsewhere, at least for the time being communist-ruled China does not fully conform to an "emerging market democracy" paradigm. State-owned enterprises remain an important source of employment, many financial transactions are politically directed, and a single party with an anti-liberal ideology still monopolizes formal political power.

So, within the external boundaries of our East Asia region, we have eight emerging market economies, enough to constitute a "large area" that can be compared and contrasted to Latin America. Yet none of these eight are paradigms of the region as a whole. Indonesia has the largest population and is currently undergoing a chaotic process of both economic and political liberalization, but it is an oil-dependent economy, a latecomer, and subject to exceptionally severe problems of internal cohesion. At the other end of the scale, South Korea and Taiwan are both exemplary emerging market successes and remarkable instances of democratization, but—as we have seen—they are outliers in other respects. Hong Kong and Singapore are financial hubs, but they are city-states with little demographic weight and cannot be viewed as exemplary of East Asia as a whole. This leaves three middle-sized, average-ranking East Asian countries: Malaysia, the Philippines, and Thailand. These are closer than the rest to representing what we might regard as the regional norm concerning economic and political liberalization, but they do not dominate the region and differ substantially among themselves. Thus it will be seen that emerging East Asia is substantially less cohesive as a "large region" than Latin America. Comparison between the two will, therefore, require scanning a wider variety of cases and accepting a wider dispersion of experience in the former than in the latter.

Regional Influences on Liberalization

Having established the boundaries of our two regions, we need to consider the major themes or issues that can best be illuminated through such a cross-regional comparison. Three topics are considered here:

whether cultural traditions act as a filter for "liberalization," how geopolitical location can affect participation in a liberalized world system,
and the significance that should be given to other "contextual features"
that are sometimes thought to differentiate the two regions.

Culture and "Asian values." We have already touched on the question
of cultural traditions in our discussion of "Asian values." Who can deny
the striking contrasts in "culture" (broadly understood to include
language, religion, historical traditions, family structure, attitudes to
individualism, and so on) that characterize our two large regions? How
can it be doubted that such features shape and constrain responses to
liberal international convergence? Post–September 2001 tensions
between some currents of Islam and the West further dramatize the
significance of what has been provocatively labeled a "clash of
civilizations." The importance of these questions has spawned a growing
scholarly literature that attempts to specify more precisely how such
differences affect comparative development.

Yet cultural traditions can be construed narrowly or broadly. They
may refer to thousand-year continuities or to decade-long reinventions.
Moreover, the boundaries of culture zones are by no means fixed. Within
the liberal international system that has encompassed both regions for
half a century or more, culture zones also mix and interact. This is an
essential consequence of outward-looking policies and an inherent part
of "mutual recognition." A persuasive critique of the liberal international system advanced by proponents of "Asian values" should also be
persuasive to many non-Asians. A critique that lacks some universal
appeal is unlikely to be that convincing in Asia either.

Taking Japan as a distinctive type of civilization, recent history shows
that the preservation of its identity has been compatible with a sequence
of contrasting orientations toward the rest of the world, ranging from
isolation to competitive emulation, from aggressive expansion to loyal
participation in a liberal world system. If one strong "civilization" can
mutate so often and so radically, it leaves little basis for the idea that
such cultural traditions will determine the outcome of the current wave
of liberalization.

Beyond generalities, there seems to be no convincing reason to believe that the "culture bloc" approach can yield much explanatory insight.
Starting with our poorly demarcated region in East Asia, what are the
cultural traditions that can be identified as the explanatory variable? Is
it the syncretic Islam of Indonesia and Malaysia, or the Buddhism of
Thailand, or the Confucianism of Korea and Taiwan? Not only is there
no one dominant religion in the region; there are also multiple religions
and competing languages in each state. Chinese and English are both
region-wide languages. Perhaps there are historical traditions of resistance to Western imperialism that find resonance across the region but,

if so, Hong Kong and Singapore are striking outliers. Overall, it is virtually impossible to identify any one cultural tradition that could produce a single clear-cut orientation toward globalization. But if the idea of closed culture zones with clearly demarcated frontiers is not tenable (not for East Asia at any rate), then it seems questionable, to say the least, to frame an analysis of world politics in terms of necessary clashes between rigidly identified "civilizations."

Latin America, by contrast, may possess a more common cultural tradition, based on religion, language, and colonial heritage. Yet for our purposes the same objection arises. Consider the contrasting cultural traditions of the three largest republics. Brazilian culture is that of a former slave-based agricultural economy. Mexican culture is based on the conquest of a great pre-European civilization, on *mestizaje,* on mineral exports, and on reactions to the rising power of the United States. Argentina is a cattle and grain economy, a society largely composed of European immigrants, a culture that prides itself on being the "Paris of the southern hemisphere." Though gross simplifications, these comments suffice to show that Latin America is far from being a homogenous cultural bloc that will provide a uniform orientation toward a liberal world system.

In both our two large regions, cultural traditions are thus highly heterogeneous. They are also in considerable flux. Protestantism is displacing Catholicism in many parts of Latin America, and North American–based diasporas are transforming the relationships between the peripheral areas and the core of the liberal international order. Likewise in East Asia, rising technocratic elites, equipped with doctorates from U.S. universities, seem disengaged from traditional culture; their potential for sustained resistance to "Westernization" is doubtful. Those who look to cultural traditions either as an insuperable obstacle to economic and political liberalization or as a secure bedrock of support for it are likely to be disappointed. Indeed, perhaps the most reliable constant in the two regions is the fluidity and malleability of their cultural heritages.

So while it is certainly true that "culture matters," for our purposes in this volume it provides no more than a set of background constraints and potentialities. Even the strongest advocates of some form of cultural determinism concede that under current international conditions these constraints are variable. To quote Lawrence Harrison on Latin America:

> To be sure, Latin American values and attitudes are changing, as the transition to democratic politics and market economics of the past fifteen years suggests. Several forces are modifying the region's culture . . . [including] globalization of communications and economics, and the surge in evangelical/Pentecostal Protestantism.[2]

Geopolitical location. This provides a relatively precise and operational way of explaining contrasts between the two regions under consideration, at least more so than cultural heritage. At the simplest level, Latin America, like North America, enjoys a degree of insulation from balance-of-power conflicts, owing to the size of the Atlantic and Pacific oceans. Although the Monroe Doctrine was always contested and has been undermined by the ending of the Cold War, Washington still exercises a preponderant role in hemispheric security. Since the subcontinent is a zone of comparative geopolitical peace and tranquility, and since the United States provides it with a security umbrella, Latin America has little need for large defense spending or a powerful military establishment. This is clearly positive both for economic and political liberalization. It helps explain why Mexico occupies such a prominent place in the ranks of countries that are embracing liberalization with enthusiasm. The boundaries between the nations of the Americas are now almost all demarcated and internationally accepted, so governments need not be diverted by nationalist anxieties from alternative priorities, such as building democracies and strengthening market-based economic systems. Inevitably, there are some qualifications to be made—Colombia is perhaps the most obvious exception—and the regional drive for liberal convergence could still be thrown into reverse by a renewed global crisis, but for our purposes it is more important to highlight the geopolitical contrasts with our eight countries in East Asia.

Put simply, all the eight emerging market democracies of East Asia confront much more deeply rooted national security risks and boundary uncertainties of one kind or another. Although the United States still provides some security umbrella (with the exception of Hong Kong), the long-run status of this is less certain than in the Western hemisphere. The partial and potential scaling back of Washington's shield in the region is the mirror image of the incremental expansion of China's geopolitical reach. Japan, the third possible balance-of-power actor in the region, remains on the sidelines because of its ugly record during World War II and its current internal distractions. The general geopolitical context of East Asia's relations to a liberal world system is much less secure than that of the Western hemisphere. Two of our eight countries are not even universally recognized sovereign states, namely Hong Kong and Taiwan. Of the remaining six, South Korea is still technically in a state of war with the North and any eventual settlement seems likely to involve reunification. Security tensions between Malaysia and Singapore persist. Both the Philippines and Thailand still have politically influential military establishments that reflect ongoing security concerns. Finally, Indonesia has only just withdrawn its forces from East Timor and is vulnerable to risks of territorial secession and disintegration. East Asia's geopolitical setting is thus more adverse than Latin America's. This makes it more difficult to focus single-mindedly on the requirements of economic and political liberalization.

Given these conditions, it is necessary to explain why the emerging market democracies of East Asia have progressed so well, both in absolute terms and in comparison to much of Latin America. It may well be the case that this sense of national and regional insecurity, and uncertainty about the West's long-run commitment to defend these market democracies, has inspired ruling elites to press for fuller integration into a liberal world system. The evolution of Taiwanese policies since the early 1980s provides a good example of how this might be so, as does Kim Dae Jung's South Korea. Hong Kong has to be more circumspect, encouraging mainland China to draw closer to the West. The Malaysian case, however, suggests that insecurity does not necessarily produce a strategic choice to embrace the West. Likewise, Mexico demonstrates that the absence of any external threat does not necessarily preclude a strong drive toward liberalization.

It would seem, therefore, that although geopolitical contrasts are clear and materially relevant to the possibilities for sustained liberalization, they are not unilinear in their effects. Nor are they the only structural factors to be considered. Other contextual variables may be critical to the long-term future of these two regions.

Other contextual variables. Prior to the East Asian financial crisis, it was customary to argue that the region possessed effective "developmental states" capable of designing and implementing long-run and overarching strategies. By contrast, Latin American administrative structures were seen as rickety and as being further weakened by "anti-statist" reforms. This contrast was always exaggerated and one-sided. Indonesia, and even more the Philippines, was closer to Latin America than to the East Asian norm, while on the other side Brazil, Chile, and Mexico have demonstrated a much greater strategic capacity than their neighbors. Indeed, even the developmental choices taken in Argentina at the beginning of the 1990s were probably as long-run and transformative as those undertaken in East Asia, albeit of a different ideological hue. After 1997, it was much less clear that East Asia's developmental states were firmly in control or visionary in their judgments. Under the pressures of globalization, it seemed that governments in both regions were constrained in increasingly similar ways. Also, as democratization advanced, the demands of citizens tended to coincide. We do not wish to dismiss the insights of the developmental state literature or to assert that the eventual outcomes will be the same. It remains true that some East Asian societies have been characterized by a degree of discipline and long-term purpose that is not to be found in Latin America. One reason for this may be the geopolitical insecurities mentioned above. Nevertheless, as with the other contextual variables, the homogenizing pressures of international liberalization appear to be stronger than the forces pushing toward cross-regional differentiation. Also, and perhaps more importantly, such differentiating forces are seldom unambiguously aligned either for or against liberalization. As already mentioned when we considered the three alternative responses to pressures for liberalization, governments in both regions tended to face pressures that pushed them in different directions, and their responses were uneven and jerky. This applies even to developmental states, especially after 1997.

Prior to the financial crises of 1997, it was also common to celebrate the harmonious nature of state-business policy coordination in the most successful East Asian emerging markets. Subsequently, the analysis shifted to sweeping condemnation of the "crony capitalism" uncovered by the resulting cascade of corporate insolvencies. The chapters by Eduardo Silva and by T.J. Cheng and Yun-han Chu demonstrate that state-business relations were always more complex and differentiated. Yet emerging markets in both regions share some common vulnerabilities and face similar international challenges. The extent of financial "contagion" both within and between these two regions confirms that, at least from the perspective of world markets, they are mostly in the same league. Individual countries in either region may be untypical, either by establishing superior standards of corporate regulation and financial transparency (Singapore) or by demonstrating extreme laxity and disregard for business entities (Indonesia). Yet all are increasingly constrained by their competitive need for access to a single world capital market. While in both regions there may be alternative models of state-business coordination and more than one model may prove adaptable to the requirements of a liberal world system, in both East Asia and in Latin America the range of tolerable variation has narrowed. As convergence proceeds, the excesses of "crony capitalism" in either large region are likely to prove increasingly costly.

A final contextual variable that may shape cross-regional responses to liberalization is social inequality. The first chapter of this volume indicated that, by and large, Latin America has much worse indicators than East Asia for income inequality, primary education, and domestic savings rates. Such powerful, long-term structural characteristics can be expected to reduce the chances of achieving economic prosperity and democratic inclusiveness for future generations. So long as East Asia can maintain its advantage over Latin America in these areas, it should have better chances of success in integrating into a liberal world system. Since 1997, some indicators have suggested a worsening of income inequality and a deterioration in educational provision in East Asia. The scale of problems in the banking system also suggests that domestic savings may no longer be so efficiently collected or reliably assigned. East Asia may therefore be converging "downwards" toward Latin America in these respects. Competition from China, now inside the WTO, could accelerate this tendency. Indeed, the severity of the latest setback to East Asian manufactured exports has raised fears that many of these once super-competitive NICs may now find their market dynamism undercut by China, just as they previously undercut the market dynamism of Japan (and "hollowed out" its industrial base).

At the same time, the democratization of societies with few social safety nets may be creating pressures for convergence of a different kind. Some East Asian market democracies may now be raising their standards of social provision, thus reinforcing the legitimacy of their new democracies while reducing the scope for very rapid economic growth. These are but general possibilities, and given the strong cyclical forces at work it is too early to judge how East Asian social safety nets are likely to evolve under the pressures of global convergence. Indonesia and the Philippines have apparently begun to display some "Latin American" tendencies that will need careful monitoring. It is equally possible that current educational and social policy reforms in Latin America, accompanied by the easing of demographic pressures and by the scale of the remittances from growing Latino immigrant populations in North America, could also begin to narrow the inequality gap from the other side. Both outcomes would mean convergence, but types of convergence with contrasting implications for liberal internationalism. If these two regions both integrate into a world market system on the basis of a "leveling up" toward East Asian standards of equality, educational provision, and savings capacity, then the eventual outcomes should be favorable for democracy, for the market system, and for legitimate order. Convergence at current Latin American levels of social inequality would not be conducive to the stabilization of healthy emerging market democracies in either region.

The overall conclusion of this discussion of cross-regional comparisons is that, despite striking differences in terms of cultural traditions, geopolitical locations, developmental trajectories, and social inequalities, there is considerable potential for further convergence. Yet stress should be laid on the word "potential." There can be no guarantee that these internally diverse regions, each converging from very different starting points and bringing contrasting legacies and endowments to the liberal world system, will achieve satisfactory integration into it. The series of variables we have reviewed in this section are mostly quite malleable and ambiguous in sign. They may support and facilitate convergence around political democracy, an effective market economy, and a just and authoritative state. Equally, they could generate convergence at a lower standard of institutional performance, with both regions coming to resemble each other because they would contain a spectrum of liberal successes and illiberal failures.

Prospects for Convergence

During the 1990s, both the newly industrializing economies of East Asia and the Latin American republics (other than Cuba) became intensely involved with the sustained and cumulative processes of international economic opening and political liberalization. Despite diverse backgrounds and endowments, both large clusters responded to similar pressures to liberalize. Membership in the WTO encouraged the dismantling of trade barriers, alongside the adoption of common commercial standards and more neutral dispute-settlement procedures. The IMF and the World Bank were active in both regions, promoting a similar philosophy based on market opening and reduced state intervention. The financial markets also induced liberalization, and both regions were affected by the massive expansion of private capital flows to emerging markets. Such overlapping international incentives were backed up locally. As democratic regimes became stronger in both regions, new institutions and interests emerged, together with new international arenas for mutual recognition and collective support. This dynamic was particularly strong because East Asia and Latin America were the most convincing standard-bearers of liberalization. Neither Africa nor the former Soviet Union matched their progress, still less the Middle East.

We have also drawn attention to some of the countercurrents. One influential body of scholarship has stressed the contrasting cultural inheritances, another the contrast between the "success" of the East Asian development states and the weakness of public institutions in Latin America. By contrast, this chapter has stressed the heterogeneity of experiences within each region, and the scope for cross-regional, paired comparisons that disaggregate and test such large-region generalizations. Geopolitical differences may provide part of the explanation for the differences that do exist. Trends toward convergence were by no means steady or unilinear. The 1995 Mexican peso collapse transmitted an ominous signal of the potentially destabilizing consequences of financial liberalization, and the 1997 Asian financial crisis confirmed the exposure of both regions to such effects. Though disturbing at the time, both crises were contained by an active and coordinated international response. Seen in the longer run, they may be signs of resilience, not failures of convergence, since they served to demonstrate the need for further and better institutionalized liberalization. Thus Mexico, with U.S. support, emerged with its commitment unscathed. The election of Kim Dae Jung as president in South Korea suggested a similar sort of response in East Asia. So, despite the qualifications and the countercurrents in our two regions, the debate on convergence continues, as illustrated by the contributions to this volume from Francis Fukuyama and Gordon Redding.

This chapter has stressed that, even if global liberal convergence proves ultimately irresistible in the longer run, in the near term such processes are still incomplete and face new hazards. In their response to these hazards, government leaders and opinion makers find themselves caught between the absence of a solid consensus to press ahead and the near impossibility of mounting a sustained strategy of resistance. For this reason, we are witnessing a variety of confused and half-hearted responses that neither guarantee the triumph of convergence nor constitute the germ of any coherent alternative.

Yet the biggest imponderables may be located not so much at the periphery, but at the heart of the system. If constitutional government, open markets, and political democracy are to be integrated into a coherent and globally accepted liberal system, then they must be harmonized within and between the leading democratic market societies. North America, the European Union, and Japan constitute the indispensable core of this undertaking. As liberalization was being promoted in East Asia and Latin America in the 1990s, Japan was embarked on a different path, its capacity for global (or even regional) leadership diminished by economic weakness and an associated decline in national self-confidence. Undergoing protracted deflation, Japan proved unable to implement the structural reforms that might have reinvigorated its economy. It also failed to offer a model of constitutional rule and political democratization that could inspire its neighbors or satisfy the aspirations of its own voters. A critical OECD actor in the coalition for liberalization was therefore conspicuous by its absence. A second promoter might be the European Union, but its contribution has also lagged, its energies absorbed in the massive task of strengthening European integration. A top-down, bureaucratically led project with only a limited commitment to internal democracy or world market liberalization, the task of integration has reduced Europe's global presence and its influence over reform in both East Asia and Latin America. Agricultural protectionism remains a major component of European integration, and inward-looking priorities have taken precedence over international strategy considerations. Thus the EU's role in the design and promotion of a liberal world system has been a relatively minor one, and it seems unlikely that its stance will change—at least until enlargement is completed.

The Impetus from Washington

Most of the impetus for liberalization has therefore come from Washington, often acting on its own. This was particularly clear for Latin America, for which the 1989 Brady Plan (named after the first President Bush's Treasury Secretary Nicholas Brady) offered a way out of the debt crisis through partial debt reduction in return for liberalizing reforms, negotiated country by country. Shortly thereafter the United States began promoting a longer-term framework for hemispheric trade liberalization. In 1994 Mexico entered NAFTA and also initiated a series of negotiations geared toward hemispheric free trade. Cuba alone was excluded on the grounds that only democracies were eligible for membership. More recently Washington has backed changes at the Organization of American States (OAS) designed to strengthen the commitment of this grouping (from which Cuba was suspended in 1963) to political democracy. The United States thus has a clear record of backing and directing the economic and political liberalization that made such headway in Latin America in the 1990s. This is not to deny the extent of the support for liberalization and initiatives taken from within Latin America over the same period, or to suggest that without such strong leadership from Washington nothing of the sort would have happened. Yet at crucial points when the process might have veered off course (notably the 1995 Mexican peso crisis and the 1999 Brazilian devaluation), Washington's decided support helped to keep it on track.

The same pattern is also evident in a weaker form in the newly industrializing economies of East Asia, but without the clear regional framework provided by the Brady Plan, the Free Trade Area of the Americas (FTAA), or the OAS. U.S. leadership in promoting economic liberalization was less evident, since most East Asian countries (except the Philippines) had been relatively untouched by the 1980s debt crisis. U.S. influence over political liberalization was likewise weaker and more uneven, especially once the effect of the Tiananmen Square crisis had faded and Washington had decided to cultivate good relations with Beijing. Arguably, Asia-Pacific Economic Cooperation (APEC) is a counterpart to the FTAA, but the former is a much more diffuse grouping. APEC commits the eight newly industrializing economies of East Asia (Hong Kong, Indonesia, Malaysia, the Philippines, Singapore, South Korea, Taiwan, and Thailand) to the removal of trade barriers by 2010. APEC is not confined to East Asia—it has 21 members that include Canada, Chile, Mexico, Peru, and the United States, as well as such diverse major powers as China, Russia, and Japan. It is therefore not a process driven by the United States. Nor does it pretend to promote democracy. In its support of democracy in East Asia, Washington has given bilateral support at various times—the Philippines is a case in point—when democratization seemed at risk. The U.S. government, together with the Washington-based international financial institutions, also responded to the 1997 Asian financial crisis in a manner reminiscent of its earlier responses in Latin America. So, though the extent and duration of Washington's commitment to steering liberalization in East Asia was certainly less consistent than in the Western hemisphere, its influence was unmistakable. No other source of external support was comparable. It may have been the case that pressures within each country would have been sufficient in the absence of this external support, but Washington clearly played its part.

Looking ahead, there are grounds for uncertainty about the strength of North American commitment to further global liberalization. The Clinton administration failed to secure congressional "fast track" authority to enlarge NAFTA or to press ahead with the FTAA.

Anti-globalization protesters succeeded in disrupting the 1999 Seattle WTO summit, and subsequent protests confirm that an activist minority in leading OECD countries is set on obstructing further steps toward "globalization." The new Bush administration has reiterated U.S. support for negotiations—global and regional—to further economic opening and democratization and is hopeful of securing a "fast track" negotiating mandate from the U.S. Congress. With the U.S. economy facing uncertain prospects, however, the American public may have lost its appetite for dismantling protective barriers or for taxpayer-backed "bailouts" of troubled emerging markets.

Although Washington can be expected to continue a selective policy of support for democratization in our two regions, the devastating terrorist assaults of September 2001 are sure to bring other foreign and security policy objectives to the fore. These may weaken U.S. resolve to pursue further political and economic liberalization. So, despite U.S. leadership in this direction during the past decade, there are grounds for doubting whether the momentum will be sustained. This obviously remains an open question, but governments and leaders in both East Asia and Latin America are bound to adjust their expectations of external assistance in light of such considerations. The hazards of liberalization may seem larger than before if international support is less robust. In the aftermath of September 11, there are two obvious manifestations of the convergence between East Asian and Latin American "emerging markets." The first, a shared negative effect, is that they have all received the same abrupt downgrading of international market confidence, while the distraction of U.S. concerns elsewhere implied that Washington might be less willing to take steps to mitigate the effects. The second, potentially more positive, is that both large regions are able to differentiate themselves from the Middle East and pose as constructive allies and partners, although in this respect the cultural and geopolitical endowments of East Asia are substantially less favorable than those of Latin America. It may be that the climate of vulnerability will cause liberal democratic market economies to renew their commitments to cooperation and convergence, but this is only one of a number of possible responses, and arguably not the easiest one to engineer. There are numerous crosscurrents and countertrends, and the outcome is unlikely to be uniform in either of these two large regions.

Future Hazards

Looking further ahead, just as there are doubts as to how long the leading market democracies will sustain the drive behind further economic and political liberalization, there are signs that the governing elites of the emerging market democracies are increasingly aware of the associated hazards. This chapter has touched on a considerable range of doubts and uncertainties in countries in both regions, but for the purposes of this conclusion the various hazards can be grouped under two headings: external risks and uncertainties and problems of internal cohesion.

Externally, the underlying worry is that after the efforts expended overcoming local resistance to liberal restructuring, full membership in the international liberal order may turn out to be a mirage. As they liberalize, emerging market democracies expose themselves to intrusive and overlapping forms of external discipline: The market, the law, the media, and NGOs all impose conditions intended to underpin internationalization and to prevent backsliding. These disciplines, however, are asymmetrical. The advanced market democracies do not work under the same constraints, and other major players—such as China and the Arab oil states—are also partially exempt. The disciplines therefore fall disproportionately on the newly industrializing economies and the new democracies. East Asia and Latin America are both particularly exposed to the surveillance and conditionality of the IMF, the WTO, the ratings agencies, and the monitors of both democracy and human rights. However helpful and beneficial this external supervision may be, it carries a political price: National authorities appear not to be masters in their own house. A major argument in accepting such conditionality is that it is transitory and is the route to full membership of a liberal world system. Their worry, then, is that the asymmetrical disciplines may persist indefinitely while the membership of the liberal system is but a mirage.

Domestically, a similar source of concern can be identified. A criticism of liberalization has always been that it would destroy domestic harmony and internal social cohesion. The standard approach of those in favor has been to think in terms of a coalition-building model: Assuming that an illiberal system is either inferior or unviable, the transition to a liberal market democracy will involve dismantling or overriding the interests associated with the previous model. It then involves creating and then strengthening new interests that benefit from a more open and pluralist system. This envisages the development of objective interests that will form part of a supportive coalition as liberalization proceeds, and that eventually will become sufficiently powerful to replace external conditionalities and block any return to the past. Although this framework has considerable explanatory power, there is mounting evidence that it is insufficient on its own to overcome all the problems of cohesion that endanger nascent liberal market democracies. In particular, the postulated dichotomy between old clusters of interests that must be dissolved and newly emerging supportive interests is clearly too crude. If major interests from the old order are likely to persist, adapt, and perhaps even attempt to "capture" key positions in the "new" system, then a somewhat different analysis is required. It could be that liberal market democracy is but a façade behind which all the old practices are reproduced. To counter this, it would be necessary for the process of coalition building to include an additional ingredient beyond the objective interests of the power blocs. Thus some sort of unifying vision, or convergence, around liberal ideals and values may also be required, and without it legitimacy and social cohesion may prove unattainable.

If persuasive ideas are required as well as organized interests, then the second area of concern would be that alternatives to the liberal vision could capture the popular imagination or distract the attention of governing elites. Religious fundamentalism, for example, could obstruct the proselytism of a liberalizing coalition, or national-security fears might induce elites to retreat from outward-looking policies. Although in neither of our two large regions are such alternatives as much in evidence as in, say, the Middle East, South Asia, or North Africa, doubts about liberal orthodoxies are gaining ground. In Latin America, these arise more from the disappointing results of the measures taken so far than from any fundamental repudiation of their underlying tenets. In East Asia, some anti-Western fundamentalism has become apparent in critical locations. For the region as a whole there is an additional problem: So much depends upon the future course adopted by China. If Beijing follows an "emerging market democracy" path then the liberal vision would become much more difficult to contest. Yet many East Asians know that it was Russia, not China, that most wholeheartedly adopted Western prescriptions on economic and political liberalization. The lesson drawn is that there may be some central flaw in the market democracy prescription, at least when applied to their region. So long as such doctrinal doubts persist, pro-liberalization coalitions are liable to suffer internal weakness and uncertainty of purpose.

One response to such concerns is to complete the various transformations that have already advanced so far. This would mean further strengthening the market economy and raising it to best-practice international standards, while perfecting the new systems of democratic governance and habituating all power contenders to that logic. It would also involve further state reform to establish the neutral and efficient institutions needed to coordinate market economics and democratic politics. Above all, this response would involve knitting together the separate components—state, market, and democracy—into an integrated whole. If this could be achieved, the unifying appeal of the liberal vision might be restored. The countries we have been discussing are all quite advanced along this road already. They have more effective markets, more convincing democracies, and a better record of state reform than most other new democracies, with the possible exception of those on the brink of joining the European Union.

In troubled times the availability of a coherent solution can be a source of reassurance and guidance, even when the "solution" in question seems beyond reach. For most countries in East Asia and Latin America, this requires something of a leap of faith; it involves transformations well beyond those already undertaken and at odds with much immediate experience. The self-confidence and stability of mature market democracies may provide some encouragement that this is where the future lies, a view supported by an influential corpus of social theory and liberal ideology. Yet, as governing elites confront the immediate hazards, their attention may be deflected. Within both our two large regions, it may be possible to find well-organized groups, or even nations, resolved to persist regardless. Nevertheless, what we have seen is that this is far from the consensus view.

Given the apparent hazards, it is hardly surprising that governing elites may choose to proceed more cautiously and incrementally. Whatever the long-term attractions may be, there are substantial risks of dislocation in the interim. Economic liberalization risks exposing important social sectors to new external vulnerabilities. Democratization provides political access to inexperienced, and possibly immature, new power contenders. External opening weakens the traditional sources of state authority and the tools of state control over national affairs. At the very least, such transformations need to be managed with great care to minimize the risk of dislocation. Furthermore, the decentralized market, the democratized polity, and the reformed state would have to be coordinated according to a new and perhaps unfamiliar liberal logic. Even at the best of times, attempting all this would be unsettling, but for many of our emerging market democracies these seem far from the best of times. In a context of fast world growth, strong international support, and strong momentum toward liberalization, cumulative processes of economic and political opening can perhaps be triggered and sustained across large and diverse regions. If what is in prospect is slow growth, intense and perhaps deflationary competition, and a lack of commitment on the part of advanced market democracies, then the dynamic could well go into reverse. The authorities in most emerging markets would need to face up to domestic fears that economic liberalization may be leading to a convergence of weak, low-growth, peripheral market democracies. They would also face external concerns that incomplete economic liberalization and partial democratization would effectively entrench unreformed elites and parasitic forms of governance. The recent impeachment of President Joseph Estrada in the Philippines, the Thai Supreme Court's 8-to-7 vote not to pursue anti-corruption charges against Prime Minister Thaksin Shinawatra, and the scandals associated with ousted Peruvian president Alberto Fujimori and former Argentine President Carlos Menem all underscore the risks of a perverse kind of convergence taking place.

In conclusion, then, in East Asia and Latin America the long-term logic of economic and political liberalization may remain compelling, but the obstacles and hazards are evident and widespread. This volume has drawn attention to the scope for mutual recognition and convergence between the emerging market democracies of these two large regions, but it has also underlined the countervailing forces that may now be stronger than before. Convergence could involve the progressive adoption of international best practices or, alternatively, descent toward a lowest common denominator. This chapter has argued that both regions, despite their internal diversity and contrasting initial endowments, are relatively well positioned to pursue the higher standards of liberal convergence. Yet we have also rehearsed the reasons for expecting that, if it happens at all, the strengthening of liberal democratic market economies in East Asia and Latin America may proceed in fits and starts, with uneven geographical coverage and on the basis of patchy and incremental reforms.

NOTES

1. In the early 1990s, the World Bank used the term "East Asia" as shorthand for the so-called High Performing East Asian economies, excluding China, Japan, and Indonesia. Here we include Indonesia. Here most references to "Latin America" exclude Cuba and the less developed minor states.

2. Lawrence E. Harrison and Samuel P. Huntington, eds., *Culture Matters: How Values Shape Human Progress* (New York: Basic Books, 2000), 298.

INDEX